SCHOLASTIC

100 MATHS FRAMEWORK LESSONS

D0588928

TERMS AND CONDITIONS

IMPORTANT – PERMITTED USE AND WARNINGS – READ CAREFULLY BEFORE USING

YEAR 6

Scottish Primary 7

Minimum specification:
- PC with a CD-ROM drive and 512 Mb RAM (recommended)
- Windows 98SE or above/Mac OSX.1 or above
- Recommended minimum processor speed: 1 GHz

John Davis, Julie Dyer and Sonia Tibbatts

CREDITS

Authors
John Davis, Julie Dyer and
Sonia Tibbatts

Series Consultant
Ann Montague-Smith

Development Editor
Niamh O'Carroll

Editor
Helen Kelly

Assistant Editors
Mairi Sutherland, Jennifer Regan
and Margaret Eaton

Series Designers
Micky Pledge and Joy Monkhouse

Designers
Melissa Leeke, Micky Pledge, Geraldine Reidy and Shelley Best

Illustrations
Phil Garner and Mike Phillips
(Beehive Illustration)

CD-ROM development
CD-ROM developed in association with Vivid Interactive

Published by Scholastic Ltd
Villiers House
Clarendon Avenue
Leamington Spa
Warwickshire CV32 5PR

www.scholastic.co.uk

Designed using Adobe InDesign.

Printed by Bell and Bain Ltd, Glasgow

1 2 3 4 5 6 7 8 9   7 8 9 0 1 2 3 4 5 6

Text (Blocks A, C and D) © 2007 John Davis
Text (Block B) © 2007 Julie Dyer
Text (Block E) © 2007 Sonia Tibbatts

© 2007 Scholastic Ltd

British Library Cataloguing-in-Publication Data
A catalogue record for this book is
available from the British Library.

ISBN 978-0439-94551-6

ACKNOWLEDGEMENTS

Extracts from the *National Numeracy Strategy* (1999) and the Primary National
Strategy's *Primary Framework for Mathematics* (2006)
www.standards.dfes.gov.uk/primaryframework
and the Interactive Teaching Programs originally developed for the National
Numeracy Strategy © Crown copyright. Reproduced under the terms
of the Click Use Licence.

Every effort has been made to trace copyright holders for the works reproduced in this
book, and the publishers apologise for any inadvertent omissions.

Contents

100 Maths Framework Lessons

About the series
100 Maths Framework Lessons is designed to support you with the implementation of the renewed *Primary Framework for Mathematics*. Each title in the series provides clear teaching and appropriate learning challenges for all children within the structure of the renewed Framework. By using the titles in this series, a teacher or school can be sure that they are following the structure and, crucially, embedding the principles and practice identified by the Framework.

About the renewed Framework
The renewed *Primary Framework for Mathematics* has reduced the number of objectives from the original 1999 Framework. Mathematics is divided into seven strands:
- Using and applying mathematics
- Counting and understanding number
- Knowing and using number facts
- Calculating
- Understanding shape
- Measuring
- Handling data.

The focus for teaching is using and applying mathematics, and these objectives are seen as central to success for the children's learning. While the number of objectives is reduced, the teaching programme retains the range of learning contained in the 1999 Framework. There are, though, significant changes in both the structure and content of the objectives in the new Framework and this series of books is designed to help teachers to manage these changes of emphasis in their teaching.

About this book
This book is set out in the five blocks that form the renewed *Primary Framework for Mathematics*. Each block consists of three units. Each unit within a block contains:
- a guide to the objective focus for each lesson within the unit
- links with the objectives from the 1999 objectives
- the 'speaking and listening' objective for the unit
- a list of key aspects of learning, such as problem solving, communication, etc.
- the vocabulary relevant to a group of lessons.

Within each unit the 'using and applying' objectives are clearly stated. They are incorporated within the individual lessons through the teaching and learning approach taken. Sometimes they may be the only focus for a lesson.

Lessons
Each lesson contains:
- A guide to the type of teaching and learning within the lesson, such as Review, Teach, Practise or Apply.
- A starter activity, with a guide to its type, such as Rehearse, Reason, Recall, Read, Refine, Refine and rehearse, or Revisit.
- A main activity, which concentrates on the teaching of the objective(s) for this lesson.
- Group, paired or individual work, which may include the use of an activity sheet from the CD-ROM.
- Clear differentiation, to help you to decide how to help the less confident learners in your group, or how to extend the learning for the more confident. This may also include reference to the differentiated activity sheets found on the CD-ROM.
- Review of the lesson, with guidance for asking questions to assess the children's understanding.

You can choose individual lessons as part of your planning, or whole units as you require.

What's on the CD-ROM?

Each CD-ROM contains a range of printable sheets as follows:

● **Core activity sheets** with answers, where appropriate, that can be toggled by clicking on the 'show' or 'hide' buttons at the bottom of the screen.

● **Differentiated activity sheets** for more or less confident learners where appropriate.

● Blank core activity sheets or **templates** to allow you to make your own differentiated sheets by printing and annotating.

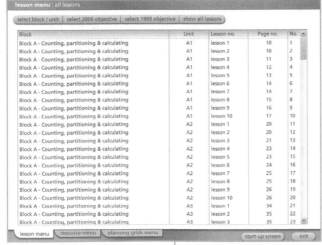

● **General resource sheets** (such as number grids) designed to support a number of lessons.

● **Editable curriculum grids** (in Word format) to enable you to integrate the lessons into your planning. In addition, the CD-ROM contains:

● **Interactive whiteboard resources** – a set of supporting resources to be used with the whole class on any interactive whiteboard or on a PC for small group work. These include number grids, money, clocks and so on.

● **Interactive Teaching Programs** – specific ITPs, originally developed for the National Numeracy Strategy, have been included on each CD-ROM.

● **Whiteboard tools** – a set of tools including a 'Pen', 'Highlighter' and 'Eraser', have been included to help you to annotate activity sheets for whole-class lessons. These tools will work on any interactive whiteboard.

● **Diagrams** – copies of all the diagrams included on the lesson pages.

How to use the CD-ROM
System requirements

Minimum specification:

● PC with a CD-ROM drive and 512 Mb RAM (recommended)
● Windows 98SE or above/Mac OSX.1 or above
● Recommended minimum processor speed: 1 GHz

Getting started

The *100 Maths Framework Lessons* CD-ROM should auto run when you insert the CD-ROM into your CD drive. If it does not, use **My Computer** to browse the contents of the CD-ROM and click on the '100 Maths Framework Lessons' icon.

From the start-up screen there are four options: click on **Credits & acknowledgements** to view a list of acknowledgements. You should also view the **Terms and conditions** of use and register the product to receive product updates and special offers. Finally, you can access extensive **How to use this CD-ROM** support notes and (if you agree to the 'Terms and conditions') click on **Start** to move to the main menu.

Each CD-ROM allows you to search for resources by block, unit or lesson. You can also search by Framework objective (both 2006 and 1999 versions) or by resource type (for example, activity sheet, interactive resource or ITP).

Planning

The renewed Framework planning guidance sets out the learning objectives in blocks, and then subdivides these into units. The blocks are entitled:

● **Block A:** Counting, partitioning and calculating
● **Block B:** Securing number facts, understanding shape
● **Block C:** Handling data and measures
● **Block D:** Calculating, measuring and understanding shape
● **Block E:** Securing number facts, relationships and calculating.

Within each block there are three progressive units, which set out the learning objectives for a two- or three-week teaching period. Because of the interrelated nature of learning in mathematics, some of the same learning objectives appear in different blocks so that the children have the opportunity to practise and apply their mathematics.

It is recommended that planning for the year takes the blocks and units in the following order:

	Block A: Counting, partitioning and calculating (6 weeks)	**Block B:** Securing number facts, understanding shape (9 weeks)	**Block C:** Handling data and measures (6 weeks)	**Block D:** Calculating, measuring and understanding shape (6 weeks)	**Block E:** Securing number facts, relationships and calculating (9 weeks)
Autumn	Unit A1	Unit B1	Unit C1	Unit D1	Unit E1
Spring	Unit A2	Unit B2	Unit C2	Unit D2	Unit E2
Summer	Unit A3	Unit B3	Unit C3	Unit D3	Unit E3

However, the book has been structured in block order (Block A1, A2, A3 and so on), so that teachers can plan progression across units more effectively, and plan other configurations of lessons where required. You can use the different menus on the CD-ROM to find suitable teaching and learning material to match your planning needs.

In each unit in this book, the 1999 Framework objectives are listed, so that it is possible to use materials from previous planning alongside these lessons. The CD-ROM has a facility that allows for searching by 2006 and 1999 learning objectives in order to find suitable lessons.

The blocks and units, taught in the order above, make a comprehensive teaching package which will effectively cover the teaching and learning for this year group.

Differentiation

Each lesson contains three levels of differentiation in order to meet the wide variety of needs within a group of children. There are differentiated activity sheets for many lessons that can be accessed on the CD-ROM (see 'What's on the CD-ROM', above). The units within a block are placed together within this book. This is in order to enable you to make choices about what to teach, when and to which children, in order to encourage more personalised learning.

Assessment

Within this book the guidelines for 'Assessment for learning' from the Framework are followed:
• Assessment questions are provided within each lesson in order to identify children's learning and to provide the children with effective feedback.
• The questions encourage children to be actively involved in their own learning.
• Many activities are undertaken in groups or pairs so that children have the opportunity to plan together and assess the effectiveness of what they have undertaken.
• The assessment outcomes give the teacher the opportunity to adjust teaching to take account of the results of assessment.
• The crucial importance of assessment is recognised, and the profound influence it has on the motivation and self-esteem of children, both of which are essential for learning.
• The assessment questions offer children the opportunity to understand what they know, use and understand and also to understand how to improve.

Counting, partitioning and calculating

Key aspects of learning
- Social skills
- Problem solving
- Communication
- Self-awareness

Expected prior learning

Check that children can already:
- explain reasoning using text, diagrams and symbols
- solve one- and two-step problems involving whole numbers and decimals and all four operations, choosing and using appropriate calculation strategies
- order positive and negative numbers in context
- explain what each digit represents in whole numbers and decimals with up to two places, and partition, round and order these numbers
- multiply and divide whole numbers and decimals by 10, 100 or 1000; multiply pairs of multiples of 10 and 100 and derive corresponding division facts
- use mental methods to find sums, differences, doubles and halves of decimals (eg 6.5 ± 2.7, halve 5.6, double 0.34), to multiply a two-digit by a one-digit number, to multiply by 25 and to subtract one near multiple of 1000 from another (eg 6070 - 4097)
- use efficient written methods to add and subtract whole numbers and decimals with up to two places, to multiply HTU × U, TU × TU and U.t × U, and to divide HTU ÷ U
- use a calculator to solve problems, interpreting the display correctly
- use rounding and inverse operations to estimate and check calculations.

Objectives overview

The text in this diagram identifies the focus of mathematics learning within the block.

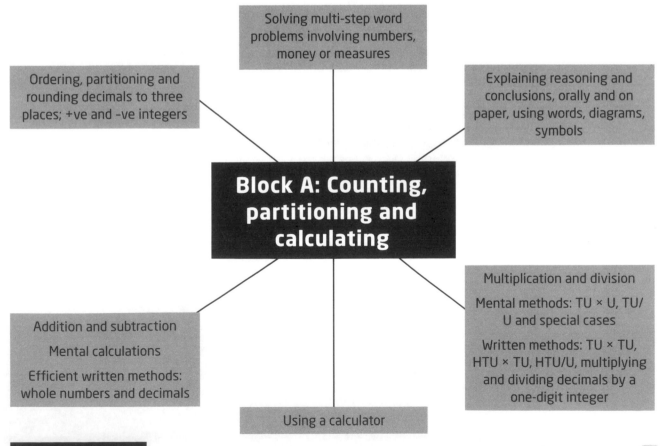

Solving multi-step word problems involving numbers, money or measures

Ordering, partitioning and rounding decimals to three places; +ve and -ve integers

Explaining reasoning and conclusions, orally and on paper, using words, diagrams, symbols

Block A: Counting, partitioning and calculating

Multiplication and division

Mental methods: TU × U, TU/U and special cases

Written methods: TU × TU, HTU × TU, HTU/U, multiplying and dividing decimals by a one-digit integer

Addition and subtraction

Mental calculations

Efficient written methods: whole numbers and decimals

Using a calculator

Unit 1 ▪ 2 weeks

Counting, partitioning and calculating

Speaking and listening objectives
- Use a range of oral techniques to present persuasive arguments.

Introduction
There are ten lessons in this block. Using and applying mathematics is more specifically dealt with in the first two lessons, where children work with number sequences. They are encouraged to explain how sequences are formed and predict how they will progress. Children investigate positive and negative numbers in practical settings, like reading temperature, and strengthen their understanding of decimal notation both in written form and mentally. There are also activities in which they use their knowledge of place value and multiplication facts to solve multiplication and division problems including decimals.

Use and apply mathematics
- Explain reasoning and conclusions, using words, symbols or diagrams as appropriate.

Lesson	Strands	Starter	Main teaching activities
1. Teach	Use/apply	• Explain reasoning and conclusions using words, symbols or diagrams as appropriate. • **Use knowledge of place value and multiplication facts to 10 × 10 to derive related multiplication and division facts involving decimals.**	Explain reasoning and conclusions using words, symbols or diagrams as appropriate.
2. Review	Use/apply Knowledge	**Use knowledge of place value and multiplication facts to 10 × 10 to derive related multiplication and division facts involving decimals.**	• Explain reasoning and conclusions using words, symbols or diagrams as appropriate. • Use approximations, inverse operations and tests of divisibility to estimate and check results.
3. Teach	Counting	Explain reasoning and conclusions using words, symbols or diagrams as appropriate.	Find the difference between a positive and a negative integer, or two negative integers, in context.
4. Apply	Counting	Find the difference between a positive and a negative integer, or two negative integers, in context.	As for Lesson 3
5. Teach and apply	Counting	As for Lesson 4	Use decimal notation for tenths, hundredths and thousandths; partition, round and order decimals with up to three places, and position them on the number line.
6. Teach	Counting	Use decimal notation for tenths, hundredths and thousandths; partition, round and order decimals with up to three places, and position them on the number line.	As for Lesson 5
7. Teach	Counting	As for Lesson 6	As for Lesson 5
8. Practise and apply	Counting	As for Lesson 6	As for Lesson 5
9. Review	Calculate	Calculate mentally with integers and decimals: U.t ± U.t, TU × U, TU ÷ U, U.t × U, U.t ÷ U.	Use a calculator to solve problems involving multi-step calculations.
10. Teach and evaluate	Calculate	• **Use knowledge of place value and multiplication facts to 10 × 10 to derive related multiplication and division facts involving decimals.** • Calculate mentally with integers and decimals: U.t ± U.t, TU × U, TU ÷ U, U.t × U, U.t ÷ U.	As for Lesson 9

Lessons 1-2

Preparation
Lesson 1: Prepare the whiteboard before the start of the lesson to put up number sequences.

You will need
Photocopiable pages
'All square' (page 17), one per child.
CD resources
Extension version of 'All square'. Interactive resource: 'Multiplication square'.
Equipment
Calculators.

Learning objectives

Starter
- Explain reasoning and conclusions using words, symbols or diagrams as appropriate.
- Use knowledge of place value and multiplication facts to 10×10 to derive related multiplication and division facts involving decimals.

Main teaching activities
2006
- Explain reasoning and conclusions using words, symbols or diagrams as appropriate.
- Use approximations, inverse operations and tests of divisibility to estimate and check results.
1999
- Explain methods and reasoning, orally and in writing.
- Check results of calculations.

Vocabulary
problem, solution, calculate, calculation, operation, answer, method, strategy, explain, reason, predict, relationship, rule, formula, sequence, term, consecutive, place value, digit, numeral, partition, integer, decimal point, decimal place, thousandths, positive, negative, order, ascending, descending, round, estimate, approximate, approximately, add, subtract, multiply, divide, square number, pair, calculator, display, key, enter, clear, constant, memory

Lesson 1 (Teach)

Starter
Recall: Ask the children to chant the 8-times table. Tell them they are going to continue to count in multiples of 8 from 8×10. Continue until children stumble over the multiples. Discuss the strategy they could use quickly (for example, add 10 and subtract 2). Try again. Does this strategy help children to continue the sequence more quickly? Repeat for multiples of 80 or 0.8. Try counting in multiples of 0.8 from a given starting point that is not a multiple of 0.8, such as 1.8 or 2.5.

Main teaching activities
Whole class: Write the following number sequence on the board: 15, 30, 45. Explain that each number is a term in a sequence. Ask the children to identify the pattern. Ask: *If the sequence continued, what would be the seventh term? What would be the tenth term?* Model another sequence (say, 2.5, 4, 5.5, ?, 8.5, ?, ?). Ask children to fill in the missing terms. *What are the steps in the sequence?* Show how, if steps are equal, a calculator can be used to continue a sequence. On the calculator pad, press 1.5 + =. Explain that each time the = key is pressed 1.5 is added to the sequence. Show that the steps in a sequence are not always equal, for example: 2, 5, 9, 14, 20. Ask: *What is happening in this sequence?* The pattern increases by 1 each time: + 3, + 4, + 5, and so on.
Paired work: Ask the children to work in pairs to make up number sequences for their partner to solve.

Differentiation
Less confident learners: Suggest that this group works through some of the sequences in the times-tables (eg 4×, 6×, 8×) before branching out.
More confident learners: Move this group quickly on to sequences where the gap between the numbers consists of two different steps, for example, 2, 5, 11, 14, 20, and so on (+3, +6).

Review
Choose some of the children's number sequences for the class to solve. Then challenge them with the following sequence: 2, 5, 11, 23, 47. Ask: *Who can work out the next term? How does the sequence increase?* (Each term is double the previous number and +1.)

Unit 1 ▢ 2 weeks

▶

Lesson 2 (Review)

Starter
Refine: Present the children with a division statement (say, 56 ÷ 7 = 8). Ask them what other division and multiplication facts can be derived from this: for example, 7 × 8 = 56, 8 × 7 = 56 and 56 ÷ 8 = 7. Ask them to consider what would happen if 7 was multiplied by 0.8. (5.6) Also consider 5.6 ÷ 7 (0.8) and 5.6 ÷ 8 (0.7). Try this with other multiplication and division statements like 5 × 9 = 45 and 60 ÷ 6 = 10. Introduce other related questions. For example: *What number multiplied by 8 = 3.2?* (0.4) *What number divided by 6 = 0.7?* (4.2)

Main teaching activities
Whole class: Recap on square numbers from Year 5. Ask: *What are square numbers?* List all the square numbers to 100. Ask: *How can larger square numbers be calculated? What, for example, is 20²?* Responses should include partitioning (10 × 20 = 200, 2 × 200 = 400) and using 2² as a starting point. (2² = 4 so 20² = 400.)

Remind the children that it pays to estimate before doing calculations, to help check the reasonableness of the answer. Ask them to estimate 16² then check with a calculator. How close were they? Extend more confident children by asking them to estimate 2.5².
Group work: Provide the children with the 'All square' activity sheet.

Review
Recap on square numbers to 100. Given this information, ask children to list square numbers to 10,000. What do they notice? *Can anyone work out 200²?*

Differentiation
Less confident learners: Work with this group during the lesson to provide extra support. Use the 'Multiplication square' interactive resource to aid their recognition of the square numbers.
More confident learners: This group should be provided with the extension version of 'All square', which involves finding the squares of decimal numbers.

Lessons 3-8

Preparation
Lesson 3: Prepare the cards from the 'Digit (+ and -) and decimal point cards' resource sheet. Draw a sequence involving shapes and numbers on the board.
Lesson 4: Prepare the 'Golfing score card' resource sheet for display.
Lesson 5: Draw the decimal place value chart on the board.
Lesson 6: Draw the number lines on the board or OHT.

You will need
Photocopiable pages
'Goals galore' (page 18) and 'Number games' (page 19), one per child.
CD resources
Core, support and extension versions of 'Golfing score card' and 'Mini Olympics'; support and extension versions of 'Number games'; support, extension and template versions of 'Goals galore'. General resource sheets: 'Digit (+ and -) and decimal point cards' and 'Positive and negative number line'. ITP 'Thermometer'.
Equipment
Washing line and pegs; tape measures and metre sticks.

Learning objectives

Starter
● Explain reasoning and conclusions using words, symbols or diagrams as appropriate.
● Find the difference between a positive and a negative integer, or two negative integers, in context.
● Use decimal notation for tenths, hundredths and thousandths; partition, round and order decimals with up to three places, and position them on the number line.

Main teaching activities
2006
● Find the difference between a positive and a negative integer, or two negative integers, in context.
● Use decimal notation for tenths, hundredths and thousandths; partition, round and order decimals with up to three places, and position them on the number line.
1999
● Find the difference between a positive and a negative integer, or two negative integers, in a context such as temperature or the number line.
● Know what each digit represents in a number with up to three decimal places.
● Order numbers or measurements with up to three decimal places.
● Consolidate rounding an integer to the nearest 10, 100 or 1000.
● Round a number with two decimal places to the nearest tenth or to the nearest whole number.

Vocabulary
place value, digit, numeral, partition, integer, decimal point, decimal place,

▶ thousandths, positive, negative, order, ascending, descending, round, estimate, approximate, approximately

Lesson 3 (Teach)

Starter
Reason: Put up a sequence on the whiteboard involving symbols/diagrams as well as numbers. For example, use multiples of 3 starting at zero and alternate shapes, say squares, triangles and circles (see below). Ask children to predict which numbers will come up on certain shapes as the sequences progress. Use questions such as: *Which number will come in the next circle? Which number will come in the next square? What shape will the number 42 come on? What shape will the number 60 come on? What will the 20th shape be? What will the 36th shape be?*

Main teaching activities
Whole class: Tell the children they are going to work with positive and negative numbers, but keep the positive/negative number line covered to start with. The children should put the –10 to 10 digit cards (from the 'Digit (+ and –) and decimal point cards' general resource sheet) in front of them and shuffle them. Say: *Put the numbers in order, with zero in the middle, the negative numbers on the left and the positive numbers on the right.* Display the number line. Choose children to come out and find the differences between numbers by pointing to the moves they are making on the number line, reminding them that negative numbers go left and positive numbers go right. For example: 4 to –6 (10), –3 to –5 (2), –2 to +8 (10) and 3 to –7 (10).

Illustrate a practical use of this sort of calculation by giving an example involving temperatures, using the 'Thermometer' ITP. For example: *The temperature rises from –2 degrees Celsius to 7 degrees Celsius. How many degrees has it risen? What is the temperature difference if it fell from 3°C to –4°C?* Introduce other examples.

Individual/paired work: Explain to the class the meaning of the term 'goal difference' as applied to football league tables (the difference between the number of goals scored and the number conceded). Then, working individually or in pairs, the children should complete the 'Goals galore' activity sheet.

Review
Go through the various 'Goals galore' activity sheets and check solutions with the children. Make sure they have understood the fact that, in this particular instance, goal difference can be in negative numbers if teams have conceded more goals than they have scored.

Differentiation
Less confident learners: Give these children a copy of the support version of 'Goals galore', with only four teams. Provide a –10 to 10 number line so that they can physically count the steps as they move from one number to another.
More confident learners: Working in pairs, these children should progress to work though the extension version of the activity sheet, which has ten teams.

Lesson 4 (Apply)

Starter
Recall: Revise counting up and back using positive and negative numbers. For example, count in threes in a negative direction from 10 (10, 7, 4, 1, –2, –5, and so on). Or count in fives in a positive direction from –20 (–20, –15, –10, –5, 0, 5, and so on).

Main teaching activities
Whole class: Display the 'Golfing score card' resource sheet and ask the children a series of questions about it. Discuss the meaning of 'par for the course' (the standard number of shots it should take to go round the whole

course). For example, if a course is par 60 and the scores are Smith 63, Brown 58, Jones 65, Davis 55 and Evans 59, you could ask the following questions: *How far over par is Smith?* (3) *How far under par is Davis?* (5) *What is the difference between the scores of Evans and Jones?* (From 59 (-1) to 65 (5) is six shots.) Devise other questions like these. Note that hole distances in golf are still measured in yards.

Review
Check through the questions the children have answered. Ask them to devise their own score cards based on the same format and set some questions of their own.

Lesson 5 (Teach and apply)

Starter
Revisit: Revise finding the difference between positive and negative numbers using the ITP 'Thermometer'. Use questions such as: *By how many degrees does the temperature rise between -3°C and 5°C?* (8 degrees.) *By how many degrees does the temperature fall between 7°C and -4°C?* (11 degrees.) Choose some children to make up similar questions for the rest of the class.

Main teaching activities
Whole class: Draw a decimal place value chart on the board: T U . t h th. Place digits on the chart and discuss values, for example: $0.02 = {}^2/_{100}$; $0.007 = {}^7/_{1000}$; $0.46 = {}^{46}/_{100}$. Begin to relate this to measurements. Tell the children a class is running in a charity race. They have to run for one kilometre. Ask: *How many metres in one kilometre?* Say: After 0.735km, two of the class stop for a rest. Discuss the value of each digit: ${}^7/_{10}$km, ${}^3/_{100}$km and ${}^5/_{1000}$km. Establish that this equals 700m, 30m and 5m. Ask the children: *So how far is left to run?*

Repeat for other distances, ensuring the children understand the value of each digit and its value in relation to distance. In particular, ensure that they know that $^1/_{1000}$km = 1m.

Independent/paired work: Ask the children to measure various items around the classroom, such as an exercise book, the height of a table, and so on. Results should be written both in centimetres and as a decimal fraction of a metre, for example 38cm = 0.38m.

Review
Write 67.5cm on the board. Ask for ideas on how this could be written in metres. Elicit that there are 0 metres, 6 tenths, 7 hundredths and 5 thousandths = 0.675m.

Differentiation
Less confident learners: These children may need to be supported in the writing of measurements as decimal fractions.
More confident learners: Encourage these children to measure larger distances around the school (eg length of rooms, corridors, playground etc).

Lesson 6 (Teach)

Starter
Read: Put a series of decimal numbers on the whiteboard. Put rings around one of the digits in each of the numbers and ask the children to give you the value of that digit. For example: 6.**5**2 (${}^5/_{10}$), 12.7**6** (${}^6/_{100}$), **5**.793 (5), **1**4.627 (10) and 5.29**1** (${}^1/_{1000}$). Ask for volunteers to come to the whiteboard to put up some of their own questions.

Main teaching activities
Whole class: Display the following number line:

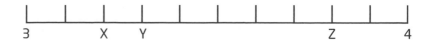

▷ Ask the children for the values of X, Y and Z (3.2, 3.3 and 3.8). Focus on 3.2 and 3.3 and draw another number line as below:

3.2   3.3

Ask: *How can we find the values of the numbers in between?* Elicit that we can mark the divisions in hundredths. Mark on each of the divisions, 3.21, 3.22, 3.23, etc.

Tell the children they are going to focus on 3.22 to 3.23. Ask them to draw a number line for 3.22 to 3.23, drawing the divisions in between and labelling each division. Discuss findings, establishing that the new divisions are thousandths (3.221, 3.222, 3.223, and so on).

Use the number lines on the board, plus the one on the children's whiteboards, to round decimals with two decimal places to the nearest tenth, and decimals with three places to the nearest hundredth. For example, on the number line 3.2 to 3.3, point to 3.23 and ask: *Is 3.23 nearer to 3.2 or 3.3?* Choose various numbers on each of the number lines and ask children to round to the nearest tenth or hundredth.

Independent work: Provide the children with the 'Number games' activity sheet. Ask them to find the values of points on the number lines and round them to the nearest tenth.

Review

Remove any number lines from the whiteboard and ask the children to cover up their resource sheets. Without these visual aids, invite the children to round the following numbers to one decimal place (in other words, to the nearest tenth): 5.39, 4.41, 8.356, 2.75. Focus on 8.356 and 2.75. Ask for an explanation of the procedure that was needed to round 8.356 to the nearest tenth. Ask questions such as: *What about 2.75 – what happens when the last digit is a 5?*

Tell the children they are now going to round to two decimal places. Ask: *What decimal position will this be?* (Hundredths.) Ask them to round the following numbers to two decimal places: 23.592, 4.335, 19.044.

Differentiation

Less confident learners:
Provide this group with the support version of 'Number games', with rounding to the nearest whole number only.

More confident learners:
Provide this group with the extension version of the activity sheet, which challenges children to work on rounding to the nearest hundredth.

Lesson 7 (Teach)

Starter

Recall: Give the children decimal numbers and instruction about how they should be rounded. Round to whole numbers first – for example, 6.7 (7), 12.4 (12), 9.8 (10) and 15.3 (15). Then round to one decimal place, such as 5.63 (5.6), 9.17 (9.2), 17.49 (17.5).

Finally, move on to round to two decimal places, such as 4.753 (4.75), 11.859 (11.86), 52.347 (52.35).

Main teaching activities

Whole class: Tell the children that in this lesson, they will learn about ordering a set of decimal numbers. Have a set of digit cards and a decimal point card (from the 'Digit (+ and –) and decimal point cards' general resource sheet), plus a washing line and pegs, ready at the front of the room. Ask a child to select three digits (say, 7, 3 and 2). Ask the children, using the cards and the point card, to make a series of four decimal numbers, such as 73.2, 0.372, 3.27 and 237. Put each of the numbers on the washing line in turn and ask the children to say them out loud and in full, avoiding the word 'point'. For example: seventy-three and two tenths, three hundred and seventy-two thousandths, three and twenty-seven hundredths, two hundred and thirty-seven. Write all the selected numbers on the whiteboard and ask the children to arrange them in order of size smallest to largest (0.372, 3.27, 73.2 and 237). Reinforce place value by asking the value of individual digits in these numbers. For example, ask: *What is the value of the 3?* Repeat the process with another set of cards.

Differentiation

Less confident learners: Provide this group with numbers to order that only have one digit on the left of the decimal point. Say: *Order the following: 5.84, 4.58, 4.85 and 8.45.*
More confident learners: Ask these children to suggest a decimal fraction that lies between two others (eg 5.26 and 5.27). Invite them to make a decimal number with their cards, such as 8.6, and attach it to the washing line. Ask: *If a 1 card is fastened onto the line, where must it be placed to make the largest possible number?* (81.6) *And the smallest possible number?* (8.16)

Paired work: Working in pairs, children use digit cards and the decimal point card to make their own sets of four decimal numbers. Make sure they can say the numbers in full to each other and then order them smallest to largest. Answers should be recorded in maths books.

Review

Revise solutions children have produced during paired work. Discuss the methods they used to order the numbers. Write a series of decimal numbers on the whiteboard to three decimal places. Ring certain digits within these numbers and ask children to give you the value. For example: *In 53.742, what is the value of the 2?* (Two thousandths.) *In 7.645, what is the value of the 6?* (Six tenths.)

Lesson 8 (Practise and apply)

Starter

Refine: Ensure that the children have correct strategies to add simple decimal numbers mentally. Give them examples to work with, such as 6.3 + 7.5 (13.8), 5.9 + 4.3 (10.2) and 2.7 + 9.8 (12.5). Remind them to add the tenths column first and carry any whole numbers over into the units column. Then work on subtracting the same kind of decimal numbers, for example 7.6 - 4.3 (3.3), 9.5 - 4.7 (4.8) and 7.6 - 2.9 (4.7). Discuss methods, including adding on from the lower number to the higher number.

Main teaching activities

Whole class: Remind the children of previous work on rounding numbers to the nearest tenth. Draw a number line with 1.6 at one end and 1.7 at the other. Mark ten divisions and write in 1.64 on the line. Explain that you need to round 1.64 to the nearest tenth. The class must decide whether to round down or round up. (They should round down.) Repeat with 1.65. (Round up.) Continue with further examples and extend by asking the children to round to the nearest whole number (again model this using number lines on the board).

Tell the children there are a number of practical situations when it is necessary to round decimal numbers to the nearest tenth and the nearest whole number. Point out that a lot of these are to do with measurements of distance. Use the example of some children in school throwing a beanbag as part of a mini Olympics athletics event. Write some distances they might have thrown on the whiteboard and ask the children to round them to the nearest tenth and the nearest whole number so they are easier to record on a graph. Some examples might be 7.52 metres (7.5 metres and 8 metres), 10.65 metres (10.7 metres and 11 metres) and 12.71 metres (12.7 metres and 13 metres).
Group work: Provide the children with a copy of the 'Mini Olympics' activity sheet, where measurements have to be rounded off to the nearest whole number and the nearest tenth. It may be possible to take measurements from the class's own efforts during a PE or games lesson and to use these as well.

Differentiation

Less confident learners: Work with this group on the support version of the 'Mini Olympics' activity sheet to reinforce their knowledge of rounding a decimal measurement to its nearest whole number. Stress that they round down if the number of tenths is less than 5 and round up if it is 5 or more.
More confident learners: These children should move on to the extension version of the activity sheet where they have to round more measurements with a greater degree of accuracy.

Review

Mark a number line on the whiteboard from 1 to 2, divided into tenths and hundredths. Point to different positions on the line and ask children to round each to the nearest tenth and the nearest whole number. For example, 1.45 would be 1.5 and 1, while 1.87 would be 1.9 and 2.

Lessons 9-10

You will need
CD resources
Core, support, extension and template versions of 'Planet Zogtroon'; core, support and extension versions of 'Brackets first'.
Equipment
OHP/interactive whiteboard calculator; calculators.

Learning objectives

Starter
● Use knowledge of place value and multiplication facts to 10 × 10 to derive related multiplication and division facts involving decimals.
● Calculate mentally with integers and decimals: U.t ± U.t, TU × U, TU ÷ U, U.t × U, U.t ÷ U.

Main teaching activities
2006
● Use a calculator to solve problems involving multi-step calculations.
1999
● Develop calculator skills and use a calculator effectively.

Vocabulary
problem, solution, calculate, calculation, operation, answer, method, strategy, explain, reason, predict, relationship, rule, formula, sequence, term, consecutive, place value, digit, numeral, partition, integer, decimal point, decimal place, thousandths, positive, negative, order, ascending, descending, round, estimate, approximate, approximately, add, subtract, multiply, divide, square number, pair, calculator, display, key, enter, clear, constant, memory

Lesson 9 (Review)

Starter
Refine: Work on quick mental methods of multiplying and dividing two-digit numbers by a single-digit number. When multiplying, suggest the children round numbers to get an approximate idea of the answer. For example, 57 × 3 (approximate answer 60 × 3 = 180, actual answer 171) or 62 × 7 (approximate answer 60 × 7 = 420, actual answer 434). Then switch to division, such as 85 ÷ 5 and 72 ÷ 6. Encourage the children to use and/or extend their knowledge of table facts up to 10 × 10.

Main teaching activities
Whole class: Review work on percentages from previous lessons. Demonstrate on the OHP calculator two methods that can be used to find percentages of numbers and amounts when the problem is more difficult and a calculator needs to be used. Set the problem: Find 16% of 50. Using the first method, change the 16% to 16/100 and multiply by 50: 0.16 × 50 = 8. Using the second method, use the percentage facility found on most calculators: enter 5 0 × 1 6 % to get the answer 8.
Group work: Provide the children with the 'Planet Zogtroon' activity sheet.

Differentiation
Less confident learners: Provide this group with the support version of the activity sheet, with simpler data (or use the template to prepare your own versions of the sheet if desired).
More confident learners: Provide this group with the extension version of the activity sheet.

Review
Check the children's responses to the activity sheet and go through any common misunderstandings. Also, discuss mental methods of finding some percentages (for example 50%, 25% or 10%) and the use of calculator methods when questions become more difficult. Review how to use the percentage key facility on the calculator.

Lesson 10 (Teach and evaluate)

Starter
Refine: Focus this time on quick mental methods of finding solutions to U.t × U and U.t ÷ U. The children should rely heavily on their knowledge of multiplication tables up to 10 × 10. Point out that if they know that 8 × 3 = 24 they should be able to calculate the answer to 0.8 × 3 quickly (2.4)

and that if 12 × 6 = 72 then 1.2 × 6 would be 7.2. Try other examples. Then switch to consider division. Use the following examples. *If 21 ÷ 7 = 3 then 2.1 ÷ 7 = 0.3. If 48 ÷ 6 = 8 then 4.8 ÷ 6 = 0.8.*

Main teaching activities

Whole class: Tell the children they are going to use a calculator to solve problems involving multi-step calculations. Ask them to calculate 5 + 7 × 3 and discuss the two possible answers (36 and 26). Discuss the use of brackets in calculations and try examples where they come in different places, for example 5 × (9 – 3) and (5 × 9) – 3. Discuss the usual order of operations in calculations (BODMAS ie brackets, of (^{2}), ÷, ×, +, –) but stress that brackets avoid any misunderstanding. Try other problems involving brackets, such as (5 × 3) – 9, 8 + (5 × 2) and (5 × 20) – (8 × 9). Using an OHP/interactive whiteboard calculator, demonstrate how to use the MC key to clear the memory, the M+ and M– keys to store and amend stored calculations and the MR Button to retrieve stored calculations.

Group work: Give out calculators for children to use when working through the 'Brackets first' activity sheet.

Review

Go through the activity sheets, marking them with the children. Check that they understand the use of BODMAS in multi-step operations and check on their calculator skills. When would they use the memory on a calculator? How would they enter a calculation in the memory?

Ask the children to discuss with their partner what they have learned during this unit and to list the areas where they feel confident. Ask them to write down any areas where they feel that they need more help. Collect in what they have written and use it to help you with forward planning.

Differentiation

Less confident learners: This group should work on the support version of the activity sheet, with only one set of questions. Provide table squares, if necessary, so multiplication and division problems can be solved more quickly.

More confident learners: Provide this group with the extension version of the activity sheet. In the second section, the children, working in pairs, can devise their own problems involving brackets.

Name _____   Date _____

All square

Calculate the squares of these numbers.

Remember to estimate first and then show your working out. If you need more space for your working out, use the back of this sheet.

26^2	Estimate		Working out	Answer
	Calculator check		I was correct ☐ wrong ☐	

73^2	Estimate		Working out	Answer
	Calculator check		I was correct ☐ wrong ☐	

87^2	Estimate		Working out	Answer
	Calculator check		I was correct ☐ wrong ☐	

17^2	Estimate		Working out	Answer
	Calculator check		I was correct ☐ wrong ☐	

54^2	Estimate		Working out	Answer
	Calculator check		I was correct ☐ wrong ☐	

69^2	Estimate		Working out	Answer
	Calculator check		I was correct ☐ wrong ☐	

BLOCK A

Counting, partitioning and calculating

Name _____   Date _____

Goals galore

Work out the goal difference for these six football teams, who have completed their league programme.

In each case, take the 'goals against' away from the 'goals for'.

	Goals for	Goals against	Goal difference
Ayr Albion	84	69	
Rigby Rangers	53	64	
Topham Town	54	62	
Clark City	65	41	
Ulwell United	82	89	
Sutton Swifts	72	63	

Now answer these questions.

1. Which teams have scored more goals than they let in?

_____

2. Which teams have let in more goals than they have scored?

_____

3. Which team has the best goal difference?

_____

4. Which team has the worst goal difference?

_____

5. Put the teams in order, going from best goal difference to worst goal difference.

_____

6. What is the difference between the results of:

Rigby Rangers and Topham Town? _____

Ayr Albion and Sutton Swifts? _____

Clark City and Ulwell United? _____

Name _____   Date _____

Number games

1. Write the position of each arrow.

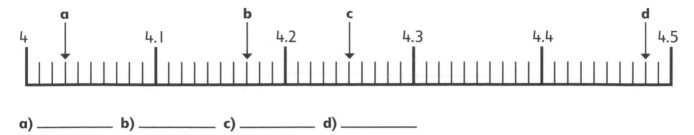

a) _____ b) _____ c) _____ d) _____

2. Write the position of each arrow, then round each answer to the nearest tenth.

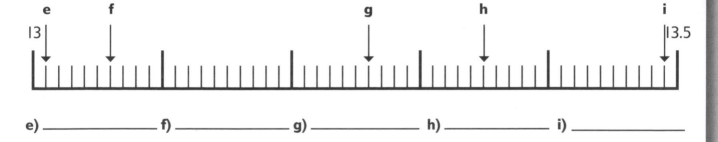

a) _____ b) _____ c) _____ d) _____

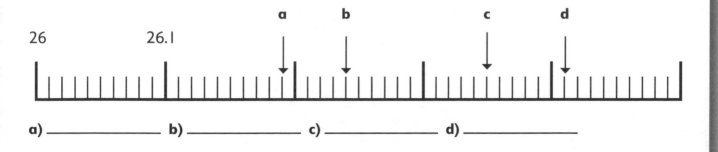

e) _____ f) _____ g) _____ h) _____ i) _____

3. Look carefully at this number line. Write the position of each arrow.

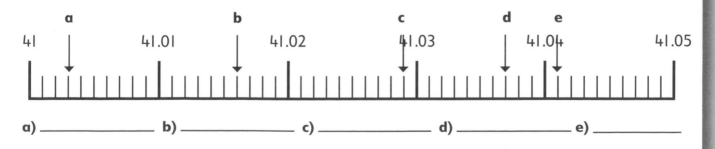

a) _____ b) _____ c) _____ d) _____ e) _____

4. Round these numbers to the nearest tenth:

37.07   12.62   48.05   19.36

_____ _____ _____ _____

5. A challenge! Round this number to the nearest hundredth: 76.076 _____

Unit 2 ▭ 2 weeks

Counting, partitioning and calculating

Speaking and listening objectives
• Participate in whole-class debate using the conventions and language of debate, including Standard English.

Introduction
This ten-lesson block opens with more using and applying mathematics work on finding missing numbers, including decimals. Here children will be required to explain orally how they reached solutions. This is followed by a group of lessons on solving 'real life' word problems. The focus switches in the second week to written methods for the addition and subtraction of integers, multiplying a three-digit number by a two-digit number and dividing three-digit numbers by a single digit. The unit concludes with using approximation to estimate and check answers. Oral/mental starters concentrate on using number facts and place value to consolidate mental calculations.

Use and apply mathematics
• Explain reasoning and calculations, using words, symbols or diagrams as appropriate.
• Solve multi-step problems, and problems involving fractions, decimals and percentages; choose and use appropriate calculation strategies at each stage, including calculator use.

Lesson	Strands	Starter	Main teaching activities
1. Teach and practise	Use/apply	Calculate mentally with integers and decimals: U.t ± U.t, TU × U, TU ÷ U, U.t × U, U.t ÷ U.	Explain reasoning and conclusions, using words, symbols or diagrams as appropriate.
2. Review and teach	Use/apply	As for Lesson 1	**Use knowledge of place value and multiplication facts to 10 × 10 to derive related multiplication and division facts involving decimals (eg 0.8 × 7, 4.8 ÷ 6).**
3. Teach	Use/apply	Use decimal notation for tenths, hundredths and thousandths; partition, round and order decimals with up to three places, and position them on the number line.	Solve multi-step problems, and problems involving fractions, decimals and percentages; choose and use appropriate calculation strategies at each stage, including calculator use.
4. Practise	Use/apply	Calculate mentally with integers and decimals: U.t ± U.t, TU × U, TU ÷ U, U.t × U, U.t ÷ U.	As for Lesson 3
5. Practise	Use/apply Calculate	As for Lesson 4	• Solve multi-step problems, and problems involving fractions, decimals and percentages; choose and use appropriate calculation strategies at each stage, including calculator use. • Use a calculator to solve problems involving multi-step calculations.
6. Teach	Calculate	As for Lesson 4	• Solve multi-step problems, and problems involving fractions, decimals and percentages; choose and use appropriate calculation strategies at each stage, including calculator use. • Use a calculator to solve problems involving multi-step calculations. • **Use efficient written methods to add and subtract integers and decimals, to multiply and divide integers and decimals by a one-digit integer, and to multiply two-digit and three-digit integers by a two-digit integer.**
7. Teach	Calculate	As for Lesson 4	As for Lesson 6
8. Teach	Calculate	As for Lesson 4	As for Lesson 6
9. Review and teach	Calculate Knowledge	As for Lesson 4	• **Use efficient written methods to add and subtract integers and decimals, to multiply and divide integers and decimals by a one-digit integer, and to multiply two-digit and three-digit integers by a two-digit integer.** • Use approximations, inverse operations and tests of divisibility to estimate and check results.
10. Practise and evaluate	Knowledge	Use a calculator to solve problems involving multi-step calculations.	Use approximations, inverse operations and tests of divisibility to estimate and check results.

Lessons 1-5

Preparation

Lesson 2: Prepare 'Random times and share machines' for display.
Lesson 3: Write a set of number statements on the board for pairs of more confident children.
Lesson 5: Write up questions on the whiteboard for group work and check the exchange rate for £ sterling to euros and vice versa.

You will need

Photocopiable pages
'In the swim' (pages 30-31), one per child.
CD resources
'Random times and Share machines' and 'Quick thinker'. General resource sheet: digit cards previously made up from 'Digit (+ and -) and decimal point cards'. Interactive resource: 'Number sentence builder'.
Equipment
Number fans; OHP/interactive whiteboard calculator; calculators for children.

Learning objectives

Starter

● Calculate mentally with integers and decimals: U.t ± U.t, TU × U, TU ÷ U, U.t × U, U.t ÷ U.
● Use decimal notation for tenths, hundredths and thousandths; partition, round and order decimals with up to three places, and position them on the number line.

Main teaching activities

2006
● Explain reasoning and conclusions, using words, symbols or diagrams as appropriate.
● Use knowledge of place value and multiplication facts to 10 × 10 to derive related multiplication and division facts involving decimals.
● Solve multi-step problems, and problems involving fractions, decimals and percentages; choose and use appropriate calculation strategies at each stage, including calculator use.
● Use a calculator to solve problems involving multi-step calculations.
1999
● Develop calculator skills and use a calculator effectively.
● Explain methods and reasoning, orally and in writing.
● Identify and use appropriate operations (including combinations of operations) to solve word problems involving numbers and quantities based on 'real life', money or measures (including time), using one or more steps; explain methods and reasoning.

Vocabulary

problem, solution, calculate, calculation, equation, operation, answer, method, strategy, jotting, explain, reason, predict, relationship, place value, digit, numeral, partition, integer, decimal point, decimal place, thousandths, round, estimate, approximate, approximately, double, halve, half, average, range, how much more?, highest, lowest, quickest, add, subtract, multiply, divide, sum, total, difference, plus, minus, product, quotient, dividend, divisor, remainder, calculator, display, key, enter, clear, constant, currency, convert, pound (£), penny/pence (p), percentage

Lesson 1 (Teach and practise)

Starter

Revisit: Revise the work on using related facts to halve and double numbers mentally. For example, use the partition method. Double 189 = 200 + 160 + 18 = 378 and double 257 = 400 + 100 + 14 = 514. Apply a similar method to halving. Half of 156 = 50 + 25 + 3 = 78 and half of 548 = 250 + 20 + 4 = 274.

Main teaching activities

Whole class: Tell the children that they are going to play 'What am I?' games, in which they think of a number, provide clues to its identity and then get their partner to say what it is and explain how they found the solution. Work through some examples using the 'Number sentence builder' interactive resource. For example: *I am thinking of a number.* (Use the ? symbol to denote the unknown.) *I add 3 to the number and then multiply the result by 4. The answer is 36. What is the number?* Working in reverse the solution would be 36 ÷ 4 = 9 and 9 - 3 = 6. Try other examples. *I am thinking of a number. I divide it by 5 and then add 3 to the result. The answer is 7. What is the number?* The solution this time would be 7 - 3 = 4 and 4 × 5 = 20.

Differentiation

Less confident learners: Work with this group to ensure they understand the procedures being used. Let them work with small numbers initially.

More confident learners: Encourage these children to make their problems more complicated: *I am thinking of a number. I add ¼ of 12 to the number and then multiply by 5. The answer is 70. What is the number?* (70 ÷ 5 = 14 and 14 – 3 = 11.)

Paired work: Get the children to work in ability pairs. Ask them to take it in turns to make up 'What am I?' problems. Stress that when they have found a solution they must be able to explain verbally how they reached the answer.

Review

Check through some of the number puzzles produced by the children, but emphasise they must explain how the solution was reached. Encourage clear explanations. Also examine more general puzzles with the children. Here is an example: *If you add a two-digit number to a two-digit number you cannot get a four-digit answer. Is this correct? Why?*

Lesson 2 (Review and teach)

Starter

Recall: Display the grids for the games 'Random times' and 'Share machines'. Revise the children's knowledge of multiplication and division facts up to 10×10, especially with the 6- and 8-times tables. The children either give the answers verbally as the spaces are indicated, show the answers using number fans, or come out to fill in the answers on the whiteboard. Alternate between multiplication and division games to sharpen up thinking and response.

Main teaching activities

Whole class: Tell the children they are going to play a game called 'Keep it in the family' using decimal numbers. Explain that this activity will revise the close relationship between multiplication and division. Revise the meaning of the word 'inverse'. Use the 'Number sentence builder' interactive resource to show some simple examples, such as: If $12 \times 9 = 108$ and $9 \times 12 = 108$, the inverse is also true that $108 \div 9 = 12$ and $108 \div 12 = 9$. Then write the calculation $3.56 \times 4 = 14.24$ on the whiteboard. Remind the children that the same rules apply to decimal numbers and that if one member of the 'family' is known, we know the other three as well: $4 \times 3.56 = 14.24$, $14.24 \div 4 = 3.56$ and $14.24 \div 3.56 = 4$. Repeat the process with other examples, such as 4.12×6 and 8.74×3.

Paired work: Let the children work in pairs. Shuffled digit cards drawn at random and a decimal point card can be used to generate numbers. The children should devise questions with missing numbers for a partner to complete. Boxes should be used to indicate missing numbers. For example, $6.45 \times 3 = \square$, $\square \times 6.45 = 19.35$, $19.35 \div \square = 6.45$ and $\square \div 6.45 = 3$. Calculators can be used to check calculations. Remind the children to put the answer back into the question to check that it works.

Review

Check through examples produced during the group work activities. Once the first family member was known, how quickly could the children complete the others? Can the children start with a division fact and provide the other family members from there? Can they use a calculator to find missing numbers in statements such as $453.25 \div \square = 9.8$ and use the inverse operation to check their answers?

Differentiation

Less confident learners: Focus first on statements given to one decimal place, for example 7.3×4 and 4.8×5. Reinforce with these children that decimal numbers can be multiplied in any order.

More confident learners: These children should progress quickly on to using a decimal point in both numbers, for example 3.2×7.4. They should estimate the answer first and then work out the first family member using a calculator. The other numbers are then written without the aid of a calculator.

Lesson 3 (Teach)

Starter

Read: Ask children to enter 4.764 into their calculators. Check they have entered the correct number by demonstrating on the OHP/interactive whiteboard calculator. Then ask the following: *What is a tenth more than the number on your display? What will the display show?* (4.864) *What is one hundredth less than the number now in the display?* (4.854) *What is one thousandth more than the number now in the display?* (4.855) Try other decimal numbers like 5.231 and 9.504 and ask similar questions. Make sure children know that to add one tenth they key in + 0.1, to add one hundredth they key in + 0.01 and to add one thousandth they key in + 0.001.

Differentiation

Less confident learners: Ask this group to write down all working out in order to analyse the strategies they are using.
More confident learners: This group should be able to provide their own one-step problems from the information contained on the factsheet. You could also provide them with a set of number statements (eg 108, 15, 32; £50, 1/2, 10%) and then ask them to make up their own 'real life' problems from them. For example: *108 runners enter a long-distance race. If 15 fail to start and 32 drop out during the race, how many complete the course? Paul is given £50 for his birthday. If he puts half of it into a Building Society account and spends 10%, how much money will he have left?* (Saves £25, spends £5, £20 left.)

Main teaching activities

Whole class: Explain to the children that in this lesson they are going to choose and use suitable operations to solve word problems involving numbers and quantities. Discuss with them key words and phrases that might come up, such as total, altogether, difference, average, range, how much more?, highest, lowest, quickest. Also consider strategies to be used. Ask: *Can you calculate answers mentally? Do you need the help of jottings? Are formal written calculations like adding and subtracting in columns necessary?* Stress that, where possible, answers should be approximated first and checked at the end, but that calculators should not be used for these activities.

Paired work: Let the children work in mixed-ability pairs so that they can discuss operations and strategies. Provide each pair with a copy of the activity sheets 'In the swim (factsheet)' and 'In the swim (problems)'. In this lesson, focus on the single-step operations on the problem sheet.

Review

At the end of the session, check through solutions with the children. Discuss the strategies they have used. *What alternative approaches were there? Did working out estimated answers first prove to be helpful?*

Lesson 4 (Practise)

Starter

Refine: Look at using factors to assist with multiplication and division problems. For example, 29 × 18 can be found like this: 29 × 6 = 174; 174 × 3 = 522. Or: 378 ÷ 21 is 378 ÷ 7 = 54; 54 ÷ 3 = 18.

Main teaching activities

Whole class: Concentrate this time on the multi-step problems on 'In the swim', with the children working in mixed-ability pairs. When the problems have been completed, some children may be able to make up their own questions from the information provided.

Review

Check the solutions of the problems tackled and the types of methods used for checking answers, such as reverse order, equivalent calculations and inverse operations.

Lesson 5 (Practise)

Starter

Revisit: Give the children a 20-question timed test featuring addition and subtraction of decimals, so that they get used to listening to questions carefully, interpreting key mathematical words and phrases and calculating solutions quickly within a given time span. Twenty possible questions are provided on the activity sheet 'Quick thinker'. Number prompts could be given for some questions if they are thought to be necessary.

Main teaching activities

Whole class: Inform the children that the purpose of this lesson is twofold. It will provide the opportunity to continue with the work on solving problems involving numbers in 'real life' situations, and to practise calculator skills. Remind the children about previous work on converting pounds to euros and vice versa. Show examples using £1 = 1.6 euros and a euro = £0.62. (Again, check current exchange rates.) So, £5 can be converted by 5 × 1.6 = 8 euros and 5 euros would be 5 × 0.62 = £3.10.

Also revise with the children how the calculator can be used to work out percentage problems including VAT. Start by revising some easy examples on the OHP calculator, such as 10% of £12 (0.10 × 12 = £1.20) and 15% of £50 (0.15 × 50 = £7.50). Remind the children that when the calculator shows 1.2 as an answer, a zero needs to be placed on the end of the number to make sense in money terms.

Then look at more difficult percentage questions like how much VAT (17½%) would be paid on an item costing £19.99. The calculation would be 0.175 × 19.99 = £3.49825. Show the children how in money terms and to two decimal places this would become £3.50.

Group work: Write the following questions on the whiteboard or the OHP for children to work through using a calculator. They are graded so that they gradually become more difficult.

1. Converting £ to €: £2, £4, £8, £10, £15, £35, £58, £175, £250, £625.

2. Converting € to £: €4, €10, €18, €24, €40, €96, €120, €195, €270, €550.

3. Work out the following percentages: 10% of £15, 15% of £24, 5% of £30, 25% of £75, 70% of £120, 12% of £12.50, 34% of £25.75, 17½% of £20, 17½% of £49.99 and 17½% of £107.98.

Review

Mark the three types of questions featured in the lesson. Invite children out to the OHP calculator to demonstrate how solutions were calculated. Revise converting calculator read-outs into money amounts, for example: *What does 1.4 represent?* (£1.40) *What does 16.7 represent?* (£16.70) Also revise rounding money answers to two decimal places: *What would £5.72964 become?* (£5.73) *What would £12.04327 become?* (£12.04)

Differentiation

Less confident learners: Work with this group, focusing on the earlier questions in each section. Check that the correct method is being used on the calculator and that children can convert readings into money amounts and round numbers to two decimal places where necessary.

More confident learners: This group can go on to make up their own questions if time allows. Also encourage them to develop a formula for use with the conversion questions, for example: If P represents pounds and € stands for euros, then changing pounds to euros would be € = 1.6 × P and changing euros into pounds would be P = € ÷ 1.6 rounded to the nearest penny.

Lessons 6–10

Preparation

Prepare the calculations for display on the board, OHP or interactive whiteboard as necessary.

Lesson 9: If necessary, prepare your own version of the 'Division time' activity sheet from the template.

You will need

CD resources
Core, support, extension and template versions of 'Down the column', 'Starting grid' and 'Division time'; core and support versions of 'Opposites attract'.

Equipment
Calculators.

Learning objectives

Starter

● Calculate mentally with integers and decimals: U.t ± U.t, TU × U, TU ÷ U, U.t × U, U.t ÷ U.

● Use a calculator to solve problems involving multi-step calculations.

Main teaching activities

2006

● Solve multi-step problems, and problems involving fractions, decimals and percentages; choose and use appropriate calculation strategies at each stage, including calculator use.

● Use a calculator to solve problems involving multi-step calculations.

● Use efficient written methods to add and subtract integers and decimals, to multiply and divide integers and decimals by a one-digit integer, and to multiply two and three-digit integers by a two-digit integer.

● Use approximations, inverse operations and test of divisibility to estimate and check results.

1999

● Identify and use appropriate operations (including combinations of operations) to solve word problems involving numbers and quantities based on 'real life', money or measures (including time), using one or more steps; explain methods and reasoning.

● Choose and use appropriate number operations to solve problems, and appropriate ways of calculating: mental, mental with jottings, written methods, calculator.

● Round up or down after division, depending on the context.

● Extend written methods to column addition and subtraction of numbers involving decimals.

● Extend written methods to short multiplication of numbers involving decimals; short division of numbers involving decimals.

● Check results of calculations.

● Know and apply simple tests of divisibility.

Vocabulary

problem, solution, calculate, calculation, equation, operation, answer, method, strategy, jotting, explain, reason, predict, relationship, place value, digit, numeral, partition, integer, decimal point, decimal place, thousandths, round, estimate, approximate, double, halve, half, average, range, how much more?, highest, lowest, quickest, add, subtract, multiply, divide, sum, total, difference, plus, minus, product, quotient, dividend, divisor, remainder, calculator, display, key, enter, clear, constant, currency, convert, pound (£), penny/pence (p), percentage, inverse, adjust, decomposition

Lesson 6 (Teach)

Starter

Reason: Write the following on the board: 2.7 + 3.9 + 4.3. Ask the children what strategy they would use to work it out. (Adding units, adding tenths and then adding both numbers; looking for pairs that make whole numbers; starting with the largest number.) Then try 6.3 + 6.9 + 6.2 + 6.6. Ask: *What method could be used here?* ((6.0 × 4) + (0.3 + 0.9 + 0.2 + 0.6))

Write the following on the board, telling the children to add them mentally using the most efficient strategy each time:

4.2 + 4.3 + 4.4 + 4.5
3.6 + 4.2 + 1.8 + 2.4
1.7 + ? + 5.3 = 9.2
4.0 + 9.0 + 6.0 + 5.0
3.3 + 2.8 + ? = 8.9

Collect answers and discuss the methods used.

Main teaching activities

Whole class: Explain to the children that they are going to learn the standard column methods of addition and subtraction. Write the questions shown below on the board. Show the children how to add each column, carrying the tens into the next column and so on. Remind them that digits should be placed correctly, with units, tens, hundreds and so on lining up underneath each other. Provide a few examples for the children to try.

```
   493        599
 + 106      - 495
   599        104
```

Now write on the board: 3265 - 1746. Explain the decomposition method to the children, working it through on the board with them.

```
  2 1 5 1
  3 2 6 5
- 1 7 4 6
  1 5 1 9
```

Ensure the children understand that the bottom row is taken from the top row and not vice versa. Tell them that 6 cannot be taken away from 5, so take 10 from the 6 tens, and so on. Work through another example with the children, asking them to explain each step in the process.

Independent/paired work: Provide the children with the 'Down the column' activity sheet.

Differentiation

Less confident learners: Provide this group with the support version of 'Down the column'.

More confident learners: This group should work through the core version of the activity sheet as quickly as possible, and then concentrate on the extension version.

Review

Write the following numbers on the board: 1274, 39, 864, 19 and 2021. Ask children to find the total using the column addition method. Check that they all understand the importance of writing digits in the correct place. Discuss the various methods: mental, mental with jottings, and written. Ask: *Which do you find the quickest and most efficient? When would you use these methods? When would it be quicker to use mental methods? Which of these calculations would you do mentally and for which would you use a written method: 126 - 34, 472 + 320, 1276 - 904, 18,932 + 7641, 9062 - 4387?*

Lesson 7 (Teach)

Starter

Refine: Tell children that you are going to call out a number. They must double it, showing the answers on their whiteboards. Encourage a quick response. All the answers should be worked out mentally. Numbers to be doubled could include: 2.6, 0.47, 3½, 0.37, 9.4.

Main teaching activities

Whole class: Write calculation (a) below on the board. Ask the children for suggestions as to how they could find the missing numbers in the calculation. Elicit that they could subtract 426 from 1413. Explain that addition and subtraction are inverse operations. Carry out the calculation and then check (see (b)).

Ask the children to try another one on their whiteboards. Check calculations and discuss strategies.

a
```
    4 2 6
+   □□□
  1 4 1 3
```

b
```
  13 10 1
  1̶4̶1̶3̶    check    426
-  426           + 987
   987            1413
                   1 1
```

c
```
  □□□
- 4 9 3
  1 0 6
```

d
```
  493    check    599
+ 106           - 493
  599             106
```

e
```
  9 8 2           9 8 2
- □□□           - 3 2 7
  3 2 7           _____
```

Now try calculation (c) above. Ask the children how the numbers already given can be used to find the numbers that are missing. Remind them that addition and subtraction are inverse operations. Elicit that 493 + 106 should equal the missing number. Tell the children to work through the calculation on their whiteboards (see (d)).

Ask the children to try the calculations in (e) on their whiteboards. Check the results and discuss strategies. What did they have to do to solve the second calculation? Establish that in this example the calculation was 982 – 327 to find the missing number: the inverse operation was not used this time. Remind the children again that addition and subtraction are inverse operations and can be used to check the results of calculations.

Group work: The children should work from the 'Opposites attract' activity sheet.

Review

Write the following on the board: 3689 – 1642 = 2047; 847 – 350 = 497; 8724 + 917 = 9641. Ask: *What method would you use to check each answer is correct?* Make sure the children offer correct use of the inverse operation. Choose one of the examples and work it out as a class.

Differentiation

Less confident learners: Provide this group with the support version of 'Opposites attract'.

More confident learners: Once the activity has been completed, challenge this group to devise some addition and subtraction calculations in which random missing numbers have to be found.

Lesson 8 (Teach)

Starter

Reason: Ask: *How many 25s are there in 100?* Explain to the children that to multiply by 25 they can multiply by 100 and divide by 4. Ask questions such as: *What is 40 multiplied by 25? 30 × 25? So what would 31 multiplied by 25 be? How could you work that out?* Repeat for other multiples of 25, using multiples of 10 or near multiples of 10.

Main teaching activities

Whole class: Tell the children you are going to show them how to multiply a three-digit number by a two-digit integer using the grid method (as shown). Use 248 × 53 as an example. Estimate first: 250 × 50 = 12,500.

×	200	40	8	Totals
50	10,000	2000	400	= 12,400
3	600	120	24	= 744
				13,144

Then write the following on the board. Explain the steps being taken and how they link to the grid method.

```
   248
 × 53
10000    200  × 50
 2000     40  × 50
  400      8  × 50
+ 600    200  ×  3
  120     40  ×  3
   24      8  ×  3
13144
   1
```

```
   248
 × 53
12400    248 × 50
+ 744    248 ×  3
13144
   1
```

Finally, demonstrate the compact method (above right) to show how 248 × 50 and 248 × 3 can be calculated using the least number of steps.
Group work: Provide groups of children with the 'Starting grid' activity sheet. Emphasise that they should estimate answers first, that they must use the methods outlined in the lesson and that they should show all their working out.

Review

Work through selected examples on the board to ensure the methods used by children are secure. Ask volunteers to come out to the front of the class and show others on the whiteboard each stage in the working out process. Which part of the processes did they find most difficult? Can they come up with a set of instructions or rules to help them follow the various procedures? If time is available, look at the word problems set by the more confident group. Pick out the key vocabulary used in the questions. Ask: *Which calculation methods would you use to solve these problems?*

Differentiation

Less confident learners: Provide this group with the support version of the activity sheet. Make sure children are comfortable with multiplying a three-digit number by a single digit using the grid method before progressing to the type of calculations shown here.
More confident learners: This group should work on the extension version of the activity sheet, in which multiplication problems are given as word problems. There is also scope for them to make up similar problems of their own for friends to work out.

Lesson 9 (Review and teach)

Starter

Reason: Repeat the Starter for Lesson 8. Include examples such as 42 × 25 and 19 × 25.

Main teaching activities

Whole class: Revise dividing HTU by U by setting the children the following practical problem: *Toy trains are packed in boxes of six. If 158 toy trains have been made during the day, how many boxes are needed?* Approximate

Unit 2   2 weeks

first: 150 ÷ 5 = 30. Then calculate the answer using the 'chunking' method (see the worked example). Remind the children to set out digits in the correct columns – units under units, tens under tens, and so on.

```
6)158
 -  60   10 × 6
    98
 -  60   10 × 6
    38
 -  36    6 × 6
    02   26
Answer: 26   r2
```

Show that the answer can also be written like this:

```
      26 r2
6 )158
```

The answer is 26 r2. Compare this with the estimate. Remind the children that as a mixed number this would be $26^2/_6$ or $26^1/_3$. Also stress that the answer would need to be rounded up, and that 27 boxes would be needed.

Independent work: Invite the children to practise examples using the 'Division time' activity sheet. Ask them to show their working out and to write their answers as mixed numbers, for example $26^1/_3$ flowers.

Review

Review the 'Division time' answers. Discuss whether all the examples are 'sensible'. For example, the balloon seller would not be given $^2/_7$ of a balloon because it would burst! Ask the children to decide whether to round up or round down these answers, based on the context. Invite them to model examples on the board using the short division method. Collect answers and correct any misconceptions.

Provide some additional examples if necessary. For example, say: *There are 374 children divided equally in 13 classes. How many children are in each class? What fraction of a class would be left?* (28 children in each of 13 classes with 10 children ($^{10}/_{13}$) left.)

Differentiation

Less confident learners:
Provide these children with the support version of 'Division time', which includes some less demanding examples. You might also wish to limit the children to using integer remainders (such as 26 r2), or adapt the template provided as desired.

More confident learners:
Provide these children with the extension version of the sheet, which includes some more demanding examples (including HTU ÷ TU). You might also require the children to show evidence in their calculations that they have checked answers by using the inverse operation (multiplication in this case).

Lesson 10 (Practise and evaluate)

Starter

Read: Give out calculators, either to individuals or to pairs, depending upon groupings required. Ask the children to enter 10 ÷ 6 on their calculators and respond with the answer (1.666). Ask them what the answer is to the nearest whole number (2).

Provide the children with more calculations to round to the nearest whole number, including questions in context, such as: *Four children spend £35.60 on birthday presents. How much does each child spend to the nearest pound?*

Main teaching activities

Whole class: Ask children to approximate the answer to 768 ÷ 30. To help, check the reasonableness of their calculation. Write two or three of the approximations on the board to refer to later.

Remind the children of work in Year 5, when they used multiples of the divisor for division. Work through the calculation together (as shown on the following page). Discuss how it is more efficient to subtract multiples of the divisor than single amounts of the divisor.

▷
```
    768
 -  300  (10 × 30)
    468
 -  300  (10 × 30)
    168
 -  150  (5 × 30)
     18
    Answer = 25 r18
```

Refer to the approximations on the board. *Were any of them close to the correct answer?* If so, discuss how the approximation was made. Give the children another calculation to do, such as 652 ÷ 23. Ask them to use the 'chunking' method to complete the calculation. Collect answers and check understanding of the method. If necessary, work through another example with the class.

Independent work: Write a selection of division sentences on the board for the children to solve, for example:

$$37\overline{)839} \qquad 42\overline{)916}$$

Review

Refer back to the first calculation in the main teaching activities: 768 ÷ 30. Remind the children that you subtracted 10 multiples of 30, then 10 more multiples of 30. Ask: *Was there a more efficient way of doing this sum?* Elicit that they could have subtracted 20 multiples of 30. Discuss that the larger the 'chunks' they subtract, the more efficient the method.

Try the following together: 845 ÷ 24. Work through the children's suggestions for the size of the 'chunks' to subtract.

Ask the children to discuss with their partner what they have learned from this unit of work and what they still need to practise. Take feedback from those children that you are targetting for assessment.

Differentiation

Less confident learners: Give this group sentences with smaller divisors. In addition, the first two or three should contain only TU to be divided to ensure the children understand the method. For example:

$$6\overline{)85} \qquad 7\overline{)83} \qquad 19\overline{)237}$$

More confident learners: This group can work with larger divisors, and with Th H T U, for example:

$$42\overline{)3285} \qquad 112\overline{)5482}$$

○

BLOCK A

Counting, partitioning and calculating

Name _____   Date _____

In the swim (factsheet)

- Some of the Year 6 children at Copthorne Primary School hold a swimming day. They take part in a sponsored swim first to raise money for the school's computer suite, and then some of them compete in races.

- The results of the sponsored swim and the races are given in the charts below.

Sponsored event:

Name	Height (m)	Lengths completed (max 20)	Sponsorship for each length	Total money raised
Anya Allen	1.24	18	50p	
Ben Bridge	1.16	12	£1.00	
Carla Chase	1.15	4	£2.00	
Daniel Dunn	1.23	7	£2.50	
Eva Evans	1.25	6	£0.40	
Fiona French	1.19	10	£1.25	
Gary Green	1.17	14	£3.00	
Helen Harris	1.31	20	£1.60	
Ian Inch	1.29	9	60p	
Jamil Jones	1.18	20	£2.30	
Kumar Khan	1.26	16	£1.30	
Leroy Lovell	1.29	12	40p	

Race results: All times are given in seconds.

Scoring system: 1st = 10 points, 2nd = 7 points, 3rd = 5 points, 4th = 2 points

Name	Race 1	Race 2	Race 3	Race 4	Race 5	Points
Anya	32.3	19.0	20.2	18.32	54.36	
Daniel	29.7	21.3	20.1	22.08	58.20	
Gary	33.4	22.1	21.6	20.27	49.74	
Fiona	28.4	17.8	24.6	19.91	45.78	
Helen	31.2	20.2	17.9	19.56	50.06	
Jamil	40.6	16.5	18.0	18.27	47.29	
Leroy	39.2	23.7	22.1	18.57	55.72	
Carla	30.7	18.7	23.2	20.45	52.45	

☞

Name _____   Date _____

In the swim (problems)

You will need a copy of 'In the swim (factsheet)' to answer these word problems.

One-step problems

1. Calculate the money raised by each child in the sponsored swim.

2. Find the total number of lengths swum in the sponsored swim.   _____

3. How much taller is Helen than Jamil?   _____

4. What is the difference in height between Anya and Fiona?   _____

5. What is the average number of lengths swum by each child?
    Give your answer to the nearest whole number.   _____

6. How much more does Helen raise than Ian?   _____

7. Find the difference between the shortest and the tallest child.   _____

8. In Race 1, how much quicker is Fiona than Gary?   _____

9. Work out the total time taken by Daniel, Helen and Carla in Race 4.   _____

10. If a third of Year 6 took part in the sponsored swim, how many
    children are there in Year 6 altogether?   _____

Multi-step problems

1. Work out the positions taken by each child in the five races and then calculate the number
    of points they have scored.

2. Which child scored the highest points total?   _____

3. What margin did he win by?   _____

4. The school requires £1000 for improvements to the computer suite.
    How much more money do they need to raise after the sponsored swim?   _____

5. Find the average height of the children who took part in the races.   _____

6. The rest of the school, 235 pupils and 11 staff, travel to the baths to watch.
    How many 38-seater coaches are needed to transport them?   _____

7. If 152 adults paying £3.00 each, and 48 children paying £1.50 were
    spectators, how much money did the baths collect?   _____

8. If 15 rows of chairs are put out with 12 chairs in each row,
    how many spectators have to stand?   _____

9. In the car park, 36 cars can fit into each of the 15 bays.
    How many car parking spaces are provided?   _____

10. What was the total time taken by Leroy in all his five races?   _____

Unit 3 ☐ **2 weeks**

Counting, partitioning and calculating

Speaking and listening objectives
- Analyse and evaluate how speakers present points effectively through use of language and gesture and models/images.

Introduction
During this ten-lesson unit there is more practice of using decimal numbers, as well as adding and subtracting numbers mentally. Using and applying mathematics activities again feature number sequences, this time utilising suitable apparatus. Children work on word problems involving money, mass and capacity, and also develop strategies for finding percentages of amounts. Formal written methods of addition, subtraction and multiplication are examined in detail. Children are also shown how to estimate answers and check results using approximation, inverse operations and knowing and applying simple tests of divisibility.

Use and apply mathematics
- Explain reasoning and calculations, using words, symbols or diagrams as appropriate.
- Solve multi-step problems, and problems involving fractions, decimals and percentages; choose and use appropriate calculation strategies at each stage, including calculator use.

Lesson	Strands	Starter	Main teaching activities
1. Practise	Use/apply	Use decimal notation for tenths, hundredths and thousandths; partition, round and order decimals with up to three places, and position them on the number line.	Explain reasoning and calculations, using words, symbols or diagrams as appropriate.
2. Teach	Counting	Calculate mentally with integers and decimals: U.t ± U.t, TU × U, TU ÷ U, U.t × U, U.t ÷ U.	Use decimal notation for tenths, hundredths and thousandths; partition, round and order decimals with up to three places, and position them on the number line.
3. Teach and apply	Use/apply Calculate	Use decimal notation for tenths, hundredths and thousandths; partition, round and order decimals with up to three places, and position them on the number line.	• Solve multi-step problems, and problems involving fractions, decimals and percentages; choose and use appropriate calculation strategies at each stage, including calculator use. • **Use efficient written methods to add and subtract integers and decimals, to multiply and divide integers and decimals by a one-digit integer, and to multiply two-digit and three-digit integers by a two-digit integer.**
4. Practise and apply	Use/apply Calculate	Use approximations, inverse operations and tests of divisibility to estimate and check results.	Solve multi-step problems, and problems involving fractions, decimals and percentages; choose and use appropriate calculation strategies at each stage, including calculator use.
5. Practise and apply	Use/apply Calculate	As for Lesson 4	As for Lesson 3
6. Teach	Calculate	Calculate mentally with integers and decimals: U.t ± U.t, TU × U, TU ÷ U, U.t × U, U.t ÷ U.	**Use efficient written methods to add and subtract integers and decimals, to multiply and divide integers and decimals by a one-digit integer, and to multiply two-digit and three-digit integers by a two-digit integer.**
7. Teach	Calculate	As for Lesson 6	As for Lesson 6
8. Teach	Calculate	As for Lesson 6	As for Lesson 6
9. Teach	Calculate	Use decimal notation for tenths, hundredths and thousandths; partition, round and order decimals with up to three places, and position them on the number line.	As for Lesson 6
10. Teach and evaluate	Knowledge	As for Lesson 9	Use approximations, inverse operations and tests of divisibility to estimate and check results.

Lessons 1-5

Preparation

Lessons 1: Display the number lines for the Starter.
Lesson 2: Display the list of numbers for the Starter.
Lesson 4: Write the percentage questions on the board or on OHT.
Lesson 5: Ask children to bring in an old till receipt for the final activity on the extension version of 'Weekly shop'.

You will need

Photocopiable pages
'Dominoes' (page 42), one per group.

CD resources
Core, support, extension and template versions of 'Word problems'; core, support and extension versions of 'Weekly shop'. General resource sheet: 'Blank 100 square'. Interactive resource: 'Number grid'.

Equipment
Counters, squared paper or interlocking cubes; coloured pencils.

Learning objectives

Starter

● Use decimal notation for tenths, hundredths and thousandths; partition, round and order decimals with up to three places, and position them on the number line.
● Calculate mentally with integers and decimals: U.t ± U.t, TU × U, TU ÷ U, U.t × U, U.t ÷ U.
● Use approximations, inverse operations and tests of divisibility to estimate and check results.

Main teaching activities
2006
● Explain reasoning and calculations, using words, symbols or diagrams as appropriate.
● Use decimal notation for tenths, hundredths and thousandths; partition, round and order decimals with up to three places, and position them on the number line.
● Solve multi-step problems, and problems involving fractions, decimals and percentages; choose and use appropriate calculation strategies at each stage, including calculator use.
● Use efficient written methods to add and subtract integers and decimals, to multiply and divide integers and decimals by a one-digit integer, and to multiply two-digit and three-digit integers by a two-digit integer.
1999
● Explain methods and reasoning, orally or in writing as appropriate.
● Know what each digit represents in a number with up to three decimal places.
● Order numbers or measurements with up to three decimal places.
● Consolidate rounding an integer to the nearest 10, 100 or 1000.
● Round a number with two decimal places to the nearest tenth or to the nearest whole number.
● Identify and use appropriate operations (including combinations of operations) to solve word problems involving numbers and quantities based on ' real life' money and measures (including time) using one or more steps; explain methods and reasoning.
● Choose and use appropriate number operations to solve problems, and appropriate ways of calculating: mental, mental with jottings, written methods, calculator.
● Round up or down after division, depending on the context.
● Extend written methods to column addition and subtraction of numbers involving decimals.
● Extend written methods to short multiplication of numbers involving decimals; short division of numbers involving decimals.
● Express a quotient as a fraction or as a decimal rounded to one decimal place.

Vocabulary
problem, solution, calculate, calculation, equation, operation, answer, method, strategy, explain, reason, predict, relationship, rule, formula, pattern, sequence, term, consecutive, represent, place value, digit, numeral, partition, integer, decimal point, decimal place, round, estimate, approximate, approximately, add, subtract, multiply, divide, convert, sum, total, difference, plus, minus, product, quotient, dividend, divisor, remainder, pound (£), penny/pence (p), note, coin, units of measurement and their abbreviations (mass and capacity)

Unit 3 ▯ **2 weeks**

Lesson 1 (Practise)

Starter

Read: Draw three number lines on the board, marked in divisions of 10, and label them as follows:

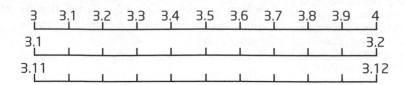

Indicate various points on the number line and ask the children to give the values. Then, without giving any visual clues, ask them to write down decimal numbers lying between the numbers given. For example: *Give me a decimal number between 6.12 and 6.13.*

Main teaching activities

Whole class: Provide the children with counters, squared paper or other suitable apparatus, such as interlocking cubes. Ask them to make the pattern shown here, either using the equipment or drawing on the paper. Ask them to add the next row. *How many counters/ squares are needed? What about the next row?* Continue until ten rows have been created. Ask the children to list how many counters/squares they have used row by row to create the following sequence: 1, 3, 6, 10, 15, 21, 28, 36, 45, 55. Explain that these are triangular numbers. Ask: *Can you spot how the pattern increases?* (Add 2, add 3, add 4, add 5...) *Can you predict the next two numbers in the sequence?*

Paired work: Ask the children, working in pairs, to write the first 20 triangular numbers. Ask them to choose any two consecutive numbers and add them together. They should try this at least four times. Ask: *What do you notice about your answers? Have you seen these numbers before?*

Review

Ask the children to explain what they have discovered when adding pairs of adjacent numbers. Elicit that two adjacent triangular numbers add up to a square number. Check some of the pairs to prove the statement. Tell the children they need to know square numbers to 100 and at least the first ten triangular numbers.

Differentiation

Less confident learners:
Suggest to this group that they focus on some of the lower pairs of consecutive numbers when adding.

More confident learners:
Challenge this group to continue with the pattern of triangular numbers so that they are dealing with three-digit numbers.

Lesson 2 (Teach)

Starter

Recall: Write the following numbers on the board: 10, 15, 45, 3, 5, 17, 150, 1, 225, 96, 30, 12, 4, 75, 83. Ask the children to draw a 4 × 2 grid on their whiteboards, choosing a different number from the list above to go in each box. Play 'Percentage Bingo' by asking questions that have answers from the list above, for example: *What is 10% of 150? What is 20% of 20?* The first child to cross out all eight answers on his/her board is the winner.

Main teaching activities

Whole class: Remind the children that $^1/_{10}$ can be written as 0.1 and $^1/_{100}$ as 0.01. If necessary, show this pictorially (as shown below).

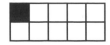

Give out the general resource sheet 'Blank 100 square' and ask the children to colour in one square. Ensure that they understand that this is equivalent to $^1/_{100}$ or 0.01 or 1%. Ask them to colour in the following numbers of squares, in a different colour each time, writing each set as a decimal, a fraction and a percentage: 10 squares; 20 squares; 25 squares and 40 squares. You could do this with them using the 'Number grid' interactive resource. Discuss the relationships between decimals, fractions and percentages.

Group work: Give out the 'Dominoes' activity sheet. Ask the children to cut out the dominoes. Working in mixed-ability groups of four, invite them to arrange the dominoes to form a continuous loop by matching equivalent percentages, decimals and fractions.

Review

Choose three dominoes from the set that do not go together. Draw them on the board and ask the children to explain why they do not match. Ask for volunteers to bring out the correct dominoes.

Lesson 3 (Teach and apply)

Starter

Read: Explain that you will write four decimal numbers on the board. Ask the children to order the numbers from smallest to largest on their whiteboards. Ask them to hold up their answers when you say *Show me*. Write sets of numbers such as: 6.21, 1.26, 6.61, 1.62; 54.3, 54.5, 66.6, 65.6; examples of negative decimals such as: 1.5, –2.5, 3.1, –2.3; and money and measures such as: £2.40, £1.50, £3.20, £2.20; and 4.7cm, 17.4cm, 7.4cm, 3.2cm.

Main teaching activities

Whole class: Pose the following problem: *The 32 children in Class 6 go on a visit to a safari park. The trip costs £450 altogether. If the coach costs £250, how much did each child pay for their safari park ticket?*

Establish the procedure for solving the problem. Read it carefully, then decide upon the appropriate operations to use. In this case, the children should realise that first they have to subtract the cost of the coach. Once this has been done, they will need to use a division method. Discuss whether this can be done mentally or whether a pencil and paper method should be used. Work through the problem together (as shown). Each ticket cost £6.25.

$$£450 - £250 = £200$$

$$32\overline{)200.00}^{\ 6.25}$$

Write the next problem on the board: *A chocolate bar costs 32p. A pack of six of the same bar costs £1.86. Which is the cheaper way to buy the bar?* Ask the children to work in pairs to solve it. Remind them that if there is a remainder, they must decide whether or not it needs to be rounded up or down. Collect answers. Discuss the method used. Ask: *Could this be done mentally or did you need to use a written method?* Establish that it is cheaper to buy a six-pack (the bars cost 31p each).

Write the final problem on the board: *A school magazine contains 21 pages. The photocopier produces 2949 pages and then breaks down. How many magazines can be made?* Ask the children to work in pairs to solve the problem. Collect answers. Establish that the calculation gives the answer 140 r9. Discuss what to do with the remainder – in this case, round down, as the question asks 'how many magazines can be made'.

Independent work: Give the children the activity sheet 'Word problems'.

Review

Remind the children about solving real-life and multi-step problems. Ask them, with a partner, to produce a set of rules or guidelines to show how to solve written problems. These can be displayed in the maths area as a reminder for use in other units.

Differentiation

Establish a group to work with adult support, made up of those children who are finding it particularly difficult to understand the links between fractions, decimals and percentages.

Differentiation

Less confident learners: Give this group the support version of the activity sheet.
More confident learners: Provide these children with the extension version of the activity sheet, with multi-step problems.

Lesson 4 (Practise and apply)

Starter

Revisit: Look again at using approximations to estimate answers and check results, this time featuring adding and subtracting decimal numbers. For example, 19.6 + 14.3 = (20 + 14 = approximate answer of 34), 58.9 + 72.1 = (60 + 72 = approximate answer of 132). Switch to subtraction: 20.2 – 9.8 = (20 –10 = approximate answer of 10) and 137.8 – 97.9 = (140 – 100 = approximate answer of 40).

Main teaching activities

Whole class: Discuss with the children the best way of finding these percentages without using a calculator.
11% of 200 (find 10% and then 1%)
52% of 1500 (find 50% and then 1%)
89% of 2700 (find 100%, 10% and 1%)
14% of 4500 (find 10%, 5% and 1%)
44% of 1800 (find 50%, 5% and 1%)
    Work through the examples. Suggestions are given in brackets, although children should be encouraged to come up with their own alternatives. Examine their solutions. Which strategies did they find most useful?

Paired work: Ask the children to use appropriate strategies to work out the total number of votes received by each party in the following elections: **Downtown:** Red Party 43%, Blue Party 31%, Green Party 26%. Total votes 15,000. **Upstate:** Red Party 63%, Blue Party 19%, Green Party 18%. Total votes 24,000. **Knoxville:** Red Party 72%. Blue Party 19%, Green Party 9%. Total votes 18,000. **Marston:** Red Party 32%, Blue Party 22%, Green Party 46%. Total votes 32,000. At the end of the task, provide the children with calculators so they can check their answers.

Review

Go through the problems the children were asked to solve. Ask questions such as: *Which of the percentages were more straightforward to find? Which were more difficult?* Discuss the methods used to check the answers on the calculator. Which method did they find easier to use – changing the percentage to a decimal and multiplying, or changing the percentage to a fraction and multiplying?

Differentiation

Less confident learners: Work with this group and help them break down the percentage total into small, more manageable amounts eg 26% is 10% × 2 + 5% + 1%.

More confident learners: Ask this group to calculate the total votes cast for each party in all four of the elections.

Lesson 5 (Practise and apply)

Starter

Reason: Use the inverse operation to check results. Write on the whiteboard calculations such as the following 45 + 72 = 117, 327 + 109 = 436, 98 – 29 = 69 and 302 – 157 = 145. Ask the children to explain how they would check the results of these calculations using the inverse operation. For example, 117 – 45 = 72 and 145 + 157 = 302. Select children to come up and give their own examples.

Main teaching activities

Whole class: Tell the children that in this final problem-solving session the focus is on mass, capacity and money in the context of shopping at the supermarket. Some revision of adding amounts of money may be needed, and also of changing mass and capacity amounts into either larger or smaller units.

Paired work: Ask the children to continue to work in pairs as before, this time on the 'Weekly shop' activity sheet.

Review

Provide the children with number statements involving mass, capacity and money amounts and ask them to make up their own questions from them. For example, provide the statements: A 400g tin of baked beans costs 64p.

Differentiation

Less confident learners: Provide this group with the support version of 'Weekly shop'. Give support with fractions of amounts (eg ¼ kilogram, ¹/₅ litre) and key words and phrases in questions (eg total weight, least, most, what is the difference?).

More confident learners: Provide this group with the extension version of the sheet. Encourage them to move on as quickly as possible to the extension task where they need to bring in an old till receipt from home to make up their own questions for friends to answer.

A two-litre bottle of lemonade costs £1.05. Questions might include: *How much would three tins of beans cost?* (£1.92) *What change would there be from a £2 coin after buying both items?* (31p)

Lessons 6-10

Preparation
Lesson 9: Display the grid required for the Starter. Prepare sets of questions for the independent work.
Lesson 10: Display a chart showing the rules of divisibility.

You will need

CD resources
'Make your choice'; core, support, extension and template versions of 'Multiplication problems' and 'Quick check'. General resource sheet: 'Digit (+ and –) and decimal point cards'.
Equipment
Calculators.

Learning objectives

Starter
● Calculate mentally with integers and decimals: U.t ± U.t, TU × U, TU ÷ U, U.t × U, U.t ÷ U.
● Use decimal notation for tenths, hundredths and thousandths; partition, round and order decimals with up to three places, and position them on the number line.

Main teaching activities
2006
● Use efficient written methods to add and subtract integers and decimals, to multiply and divide integers and decimals by a one-digit integer, and to multiply two-digit and three-digit integers by a two-digit integer.
● Use approximations, inverse operations and tests of divisibility to estimate and check results.
1999
● Extend written methods to column addition and subtraction of numbers involving decimals.
● Extend written methods to short multiplication of numbers involving decimals; short division of numbers involving decimals.
● Express a quotient as a fraction or as a decimal rounded to one decimal place.
● Check results of calculations; know and apply simple tests of divisibility.

Vocabulary
problem, solution, calculation, operation, answer, method, strategy, explain, reason, place value, partition, decimal point/place, round, add, subtract, multiply, divide, decomposition, convert, sum, total, difference, plus, minus, product, quotient, dividend, divisor, remainder, pound (£), penny/pence (p)

Lesson 6 (Teach)

Starter
Recall: Practise quick-fire questions where children total three and then four decimals, for example, 4.3 + 2.5 + 5.8 and 5.8 + 7.5 + 3.1 + 1.6. Then work on groups of three or four numbers, where children create whole numbers first to make the calculation more straightforward, for example: 1.2 + 1.9 + 2.8 = 1.2 + 2.8 + 1.9 = 5.9; 2.7 + 3.8 + 1.3 = 2.7 + 1.3 + 3.8 = 7.8 and 2.4 + 1.5 + 1.7 + 3.5 = 1.5 + 3.5 (5.0) + 2.4 + 1.7 = 9.1.

Main teaching activities
Whole class: Tell the children they are going to focus on formal written methods of column addition, including using decimal numbers. Revise briefly informal methods (like adding the most significant digits first), before concentrating on the use of 'carrying'. Demonstrate on an OHP or whiteboard how to add numbers by transferring them from a horizontal position into vertical columns, ensuring digits are correctly positioned. See the first example on the following page. Show how digits being carried are written underneath the lower line of the answer box. Then try a further calculation, like example 2, again stressing that each digit must come in the correct column. Extend to consider decimal numbers, pointing out that decimal points should line up under each other (see examples 3 and 4). Also include examples of what happens when adding mixed amounts (see example 5).

Unit 3 ▢ 2 weeks

Example 1
236 + 198 + 6409
becomes

```
      236
 +    198
     6409
     6843
      1 2
```

Example 2
945 + 19 + 6 + 3492
becomes

```
      945
 +     19
        6
     3492
     4462
     1 1 2
```

Example 3
513.6 + 17.9
becomes

```
    513.6
 +   17.9
    531.5
      1 1
```

Example 4
74.27 + 3.94 + 105.6
becomes

```
     74.27
 +    3.94
    105.60
    183.81
      1 1 1
```

Example 5
1.275kg + 845g
becomes

```
    1.275
 +  0.845
    2.120  kg
    1 1 1
```

Differentiation

Less confident learners: Work with this group and restrict questions to three-digit whole numbers and numbers to one decimal place.

More confident learners: Encourage this group to move on as quickly as possible to examples in which numbers have a different number of digits, including decimal numbers, and where a range of mixed amounts have to be added, such as 4.275kg + 84g + 1kg 257g.

Group work: Encourage the children to practise adding numbers using the column methods shown during the lesson. They could generate their own numbers to work with, using digit cards and a decimal point card, or use the quantities provided in the first section of 'Make your choice'. Remind the children to show their working out in full.

Review

Mark and check the children's work with them, covering a range of different examples. Ask the children to compare written methods of addition and express their preferences. Encourage them to give reasons.

Lesson 7 (Teach)

Starter

Recall: Concentrate this time on decimal numbers. Ask: *What do you need to add to 2.63 to make 2.7?* (0.07) *What do you need to add to 5.27 to make 5.3?* (0.03) *What do you need to add to 7.49 to make 7.5?* (0.01)

Extend the activity to considering numbers with two decimal places. Ask: *What do you need to add to 8.37 to make 9?* (0.63) *What do you need to add to 12.94 to make 13?* (0.06) *What is the difference between 6.6 and 3.7?* (2.9)

Main teaching activities

Whole class: Tell the children that the focus of this lesson will be written methods of subtraction. Briefly revise other methods they should be familiar with, like counting up and compensation, but put the emphasis on revising the 'decomposition' method. Look at four-digit numbers first, such as: find the difference between 9576 and 4092 (see example 6 below), again transferring from the horizontal position to vertical columns, and demonstrate the method using the OHP or whiteboard. Show examples with different numbers of digits (see example 7) and decimal numbers with a different number of digits (see examples 8 and 9). As before, include examples of subtraction involving mixed amounts (see example 10). Remind the children that decimal points should always line up under each other.

Example 6
9576 - 4092
becomes

```
    ⁴1
    9⁵76
 -  4092
    5484
```

Example 7
45,264 - 3107
becomes

```
      ⁵1
    452⁶4
 -   3107
    42157
```

Example 8
34.72 - 9.6
becomes

```
    ²1
    ͹4.72
 -   9.60
    25.12
```

Example 9
427.3 - 19.7
becomes

```
    1 ¹⁶ 1
    42͹.30
 -   19.70
    407.60
```

Example 10
1.412l - 98ml
becomes

```
    ³ ¹⁰1
    1.4͹2
 -  0.098
    1.314
```

Group work: The children now practise subtracting numbers using the column methods shown during the lesson. Again, they could generate their

Unit 3 ▮ 2 weeks

own numbers or use the subtraction questions provided on 'Make your choice'. Working out should always be shown in full.

Review
Check a selection of the questions the children worked through. Ask for volunteers to explain the stages of the 'decomposition' method to the others. Which parts of the process caused the most difficulty? Revise these parts if necessary.

Lesson 8 (Teach)

Starter
Revisit: Count together from zero in increments of 0.2 up to 1.8 using fingers during the counting. For 0.2 show one finger, 0.4 two fingers, 0.6 three fingers and so on. Ask the children how many steps there were to reach 1.8. (9) They should make the link with the number of fingers they have displayed. Try other examples, such as from zero in increments of 0.3 to 2.4, from zero in increments of 0.5 to 3.5, and from zero in increments of 0.6 to 4.8. Stop at stages along the way and ask the children to make up a number sentence (such as $0.3 \times 5 = 1.5$, $0.5 \times 6 = 3.0$ and $0.6 \times 3 = 1.8$).

Main teaching activities
Whole class: Show the class how to multiply 278×3, first by using the partitioning method and then by using the grid method. Estimate first by working out that $300 \times 3 = 900$.

```
Partition 278 × 3     200 × 3  = 600
                       70 × 3  = 210
                        8 × 3  =  24
                                 834
```

Then draw the grid method:

	200	70	8	
3	600	210	24	= 834

Practise some examples (eg 4294×4) using both methods, encouraging the children to estimate the answer first. Repeat the activity for U.t h, linking to money. For example: *A box of chocolates costs £4.76. How much will six boxes cost?*

```
4.00 × 6 =  24.00
0.70 × 6 =   4.20
0.06 × 6 =   0.36
            28.56
```

Ensure that the children understand that the decimal points must line up under each other. Encourage them to practise examples using the partitioning and grid methods.
Independent work: Give each child a copy of the 'Multiplication problems' activity sheet, which has a range of written problems to be solved using either the grid or the partitioning methods.

Review
Ask the following questions and discuss with the class: *What different ways of multiplying have we learned this week? What important fact must we remember when we multiply numbers involving decimals? What method could we use to multiply 42 × 30?*

Lesson 9 (Teach)

Starter

Revisit: Draw the following grid on the whiteboard:

0.86	4.02	1.08
3.75	8.63	6.19
1.51	2.74	1.18

Ask the children to copy a blank version of the grid onto their whiteboards. Ask them to round each number to the nearest whole number and write the answer in the corresponding space on their blank grid. Repeat, rounding to the nearest tenth. Answers: (l to r, top to bottom) 1, 4, 1, 4, 9, 6, 2, 3, 1; 0.9, 4.0, 1.1, 3.8, 8.6, 6.2, 1.5, 2.7, 1.2.

Main teaching activities

Whole class: Extend the children's work on partitioning and grid methods of multiplying to recording in columns. Try 3782 × 5. Ask the children to estimate first: 4000 × 5 = 20,000.

$$
\begin{array}{rr}
\text{Work out with the children} & 3782 \\
& \times\ 5 \\
\hline
\end{array}
$$

3000 × 5	15000
700 × 5	3500
80 × 5	400
2 × 5	10
	18910

Ensure the children understand that when calculations are set out in columns ThHTU they must line up under each other. Try a few examples together or in pairs. Explain to the children that this method can be made more efficient by writing the result of each step of the calculation in the answer box, rather than setting out in columns, for example:

$$
\begin{array}{r}
3782 \\
\times\quad 5 \\
\hline
18910 \\
\underline{\scriptstyle 3\ 4\ 1}
\end{array}
$$

Make sure that the children understand that the units go directly into the answer box, directly under the number that has just been multiplied. The tens are 'carried' to be added to the answer to the next stage in the multiplication. Again, try a few together on the board.

Independent work: Write ten questions for each ability group on the whiteboard in order to practise this method. Once the children feel comfortable with the partitioning method and recording in columns, encourage them to use the standard format for short multiplication. The majority of the class could work on HTU × U.

Review

Display the following grids. Ask: *Can you work out the missing numbers?* Ensure that the children draw on their recent work on inverses and division. (Answers: 60 and 3076; 6, 5000, 600, 20 and 33,762)

Differentiation

Less confident learners: Give this group problems that work on TU × U.
More confident learners: Give this group problems that work on ThHTU × U.

	700	?	9	
4	2800	240	36	?

	?	?	?	7	
?	30 000	3600	120	42	?

Lesson 10 (Teach and evaluate)

Starter
Revisit: Write some numbers with two places of decimals on the board, such as 3.76, 9.03, 8.07. Ask the children to round these firstly to the nearest tenth, and then to the nearest whole number. Repeat for the decimal numbers.

Main teaching activities
Whole class: Tell the children that the purpose of this session is to learn about simple tests of divisibility that can be applied to most of the times-tables up to 10. First, go quickly over the rules for dividing by 2 (it must be an even number, eg 158 or 3294), 5 (the last digit will be a 5 or 0, eg 95 and 2730) and 10 (the last digit will be 0, eg 790 and 32,570). Then look at divisibility by 3 and 6. Explain these in more detail. Say: *A number is divisible by 3 if the sum of its digits is divisible by 3. For example, 87 will divide by 3 since 8 + 7 = 15, and 15 is divisible by 3.* Try 345 ÷ 3. 3 + 4 + 5 = 12 and since 12 is in the three times-table, 345 is divisible by 3. A number is divisible by 6 if it is even and also divisible by 3. For example, try 462 ÷ 6. 462 is an even number and 4 + 6 + 2 = 12. Since 12 is divisible by 3, then 462 is divisible by 6. Also try 3744. It is even, and as 3 + 7 + 4 + 4 = 18, which is a multiple of 3, then 3744 is divisible by 6.

Move on to consider divisibility by 4 and 8. A number is divisible by 4 if 4 will divide exactly into the last two digits. Look at 196. 96 is divisible by 4, so the whole number will work. Try 2512. As 12 is a multiple of 4, the whole number will be divisible by 4. A number is divisible by 8 if half the number is divisible by 4 or the last three digits are divisible by 8. For example, 448 halved would be 224, and 224 ÷ 4 = 56. 35,576 would also work since 576 ÷ 8 = 72. Lastly, a number is divisible by 9 if the sum of its digits is divisible by 9. So, since 153 makes 1 + 5 + 3 = 9 and 4734 makes 4 + 7 + 3 + 4 = 18, both these numbers are divisible by 9.

Independent/paired work: Set the children to work individually or in pairs on the 'Quick check' activity sheet. Calculators should not be used during the main part of the lesson but could be used for quickly checking answers in the Review session.

Review
Display each of the rules of divisibility prominently in the classroom so the children can refer to them when carrying out calculations in the future. Check through the activity sheets to sort out any problems that have occurred.

Ask those children that you are targetting for assessment purposes to say what aspects they feel confident with, and what they still need to practise further.

Name _____   Date _____

Dominoes

Cut out each domino.

Share them out between your group. Take it in turns to place a domino to form a loop. Who will place all of theirs first?

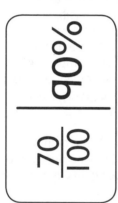
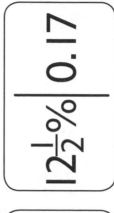

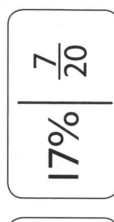
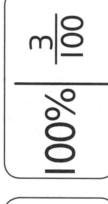
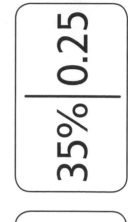

80%	$\frac{65}{100}$
65%	$\frac{1}{8}$
$12\frac{1}{2}\%$	0.17
17%	$\frac{7}{20}$
35%	0.25
90%	$\frac{70}{100}$
$\frac{4}{10}$	$\frac{9}{10}$
40%	1
$\frac{3}{100}$	100%
$\frac{4}{5}$	0.03
$\frac{3}{10}$	$\frac{1}{10}$
30%	0.5
5%	$\frac{3}{6}$
15%	0.05
70%	0.15
20%	$\frac{1}{4}$
0.75	$\frac{2}{10}$
60%	$\frac{3}{4}$
1%	$\frac{3}{5}$
10%	0.01

100 MATHS FRAMEWORK LESSONS · YEAR 6

Securing number facts, understanding shape

Key aspects of learning
- Information processing
- Communication
- Reasoning
- Creative thinking

Expected prior learning
Check that children can already:
- propose a general statement involving numbers or shapes
- organise information in a table
- use knowledge of place value, addition and subtraction of two-digit numbers to derive sums, differences, doubles and halves of decimals (eg 6.5 ± 2.7, halve 5.6, double 0.34)
- identify pairs of factors of two-digit whole numbers and find common multiples
- recognise parallel and perpendicular lines
- identify, visualise and describe properties of rectangles, regular polygons and 3D solids.

Objectives overview
The text in this diagram identifies the focus of mathematics learning within the block.

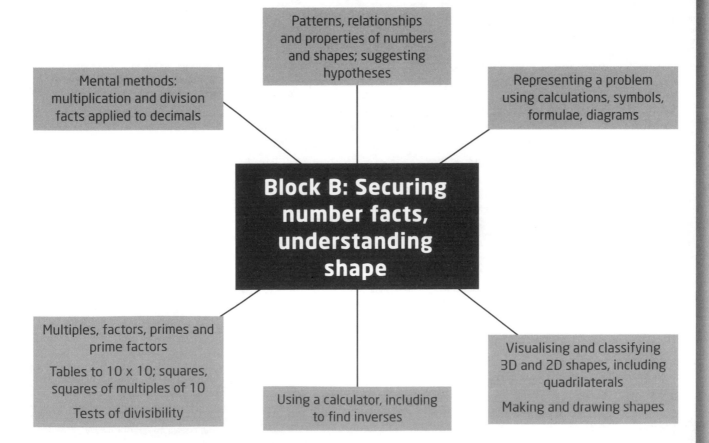

Patterns, relationships and properties of numbers and shapes; suggesting hypotheses

Mental methods: multiplication and division facts applied to decimals

Representing a problem using calculations, symbols, formulae, diagrams

Block B: Securing number facts, understanding shape

Multiples, factors, primes and prime factors

Tables to 10 x 10; squares, squares of multiples of 10

Tests of divisibility

Using a calculator, including to find inverses

Visualising and classifying 3D and 2D shapes, including quadrilaterals

Making and drawing shapes

Securing number facts, understanding shape

Speaking and listening objectives

- Use a range of techniques to present persuasive argument.

Introduction

There are a total of 15 lessons in this block. Using and applying is dealt more specifically in the first three lessons where children describe and explain number sequences, patterns and relationships. Children use their knowledge of multiplication facts to find square numbers and to derive related multiplication and division facts for decimal numbers. They investigate prime numbers and use inverse operations and tests of divisibility.

The latter part of the unit focuses on shape; children use properties to classify 2D shapes and 3D solids. They make and draw shapes and apply knowledge of their properties.

Lesson	Strands	Starter	Main teaching activities
1. Teach	Use/apply	**Use knowledge of place value and multiplication facts to 10 × 10 to derive related multiplication and division facts involving decimals (eg 0.8 × 7, 4.8 ÷ 6).**	Represent and interpret sequences, patterns and relationships involving numbers and shapes; suggest and test hypotheses; construct and use simple expressions and formulae in words then symbols (eg the cost of *c* pens at 15 pence each is 15*c* pence).
2. Apply	Use/apply	As for Lesson 1	As for Lesson 1
3. Teach and practise	Use/apply	As for Lesson 1	As for Lesson 1
4. Review	Knowledge	As for Lesson 1	Use knowledge of multiplication facts to derive quickly squares of numbers to 12 × 12 and the corresponding squares of multiples of 10.
5. Teach	Knowledge	As for Lesson 1	As for Lesson 4
6. Practise	Knowledge	As for Lesson 1	**Use knowledge of place value and multiplication facts to 10 × 10 to derive related multiplication and division facts involving decimals (eg 0.8 × 7, 4.8 ÷ 6).**
7. Review and apply	Knowledge	Calculate mentally with integers and decimals: U.t ± U.t, TU × U, TU ÷ U, U.t × U, U.t ÷ U. (Revision of Block A)	Recognise that prime numbers have only two factors and identify prime numbers less than 100; find the prime factors of two-digit numbers.
8. Review and teach	Knowledge	As for Lesson 7	As for Lesson 7
9. Teach	Knowledge	Use decimal notation for tenths, hundredths and thousandths; partition, round and order decimals with up to three places, and position them on the number line. (Revision of Block A)	Use approximations, inverse operations and tests of divisibility to estimate and check results.
10. Apply	Knowledge	As for Lesson 9	As for Lesson 9
11. Apply	Shape	Solve multi-step problems, and problems involving fractions, decimals and percentages; choose and use appropriate calculation strategies at each stage, including calculator use. (Revision of Block A)	Describe, identify and visualise parallel and perpendicular edges or faces; use these properties to classify 2D shapes and 3D solids.
12. Review and apply	Shape	As for Lesson 9	As for Lesson 11
13. Apply	Shape	Make and draw shapes with increasing accuracy and apply knowledge of their properties.	As for Lesson 11
14. Teach and apply	Shape	Calculate mentally with integers and decimals: U.t ± U.t, TU × U, TU ÷ U, U.t × U, U.t ÷ U. (Revision of Block A)	Make and draw shapes with increasing accuracy and apply knowledge of their properties.
15. Apply and evaluate	Shape	As for Lesson 14	As for Lesson 14

Unit 1 ◻ 3 weeks

Use and apply mathematics
- Represent and interpret sequences, patterns and relationships involving numbers and shapes; suggest and test hypotheses; construct and use simple expressions and formulae in words then symbols (eg the cost of c pens at 15 pence each is $15c$ pence).

Lessons 1-3

Preparation
Lesson 2: Draw the patterns on the board.
Lesson 3: Write the algebra problems on the board.

You will need
Photocopiable pages
'What's it worth?' (page 57), one per child.
Equipment
1cm squared paper; isometric paper or pegboards and pegs.

Learning objectives

Starter
- Use knowledge of place value and multiplication facts to 10 × 10 to derive related multiplication and division facts involving decimals (eg 0.8 × 7, 4.8 ÷ 6).

Main teaching activities
2006
- Represent and interpret sequences, patterns and relationships involving numbers and shapes; suggest and test hypotheses; construct and use simple expressions and formulae in words then symbols (eg the cost of c pens at 15 pence each is $15c$ pence).

1999
- Solve mathematical problems or puzzles, recognise and explain patterns and relationships, generalise and predict. Suggest extensions asking 'What if...?'
- Recognise and extend number sequences.
- Make and investigate a general statement about familiar numbers or shapes by finding examples that satisfy it; develop from explaining a generalised relationship in words to expressing it in a formula using letters as symbols (eg the cost of n articles at 15p each).

Vocabulary
problem, solution, calculate, calculation, equation, reasoning, predict, rule, formula, relationship, sequence, pattern, multiple, factor, algebra, represent, decimal

Lesson 1 (Teach)

Starter
Recall: Chant together the 7-times table. Tell the children that, in pairs, they are going to use their knowledge of this table to find the answers to other tables. Ask less confident children to work on the ×70 table (1 × 70, 2 × 70 and so on), more confident children to work on the ×0.7 table and the rest of the class on the ×700 table. Ask for a volunteer from each group to feed back their results. Focus on the ×0.7 table. Ask the children questions such as 0.7 × 8 or 4.9 ÷ 0.7.

Main teaching activities
Whole class: Write this sequence of numbers on the board: 3, 5, 9, 17, 33. Working in pairs, ask children to write the next two terms in the sequence (double then subtract 1). Collect answers and ask for explanations of the relationship between each term.
   Write the following sequence and repeat: 1, 8, 27, 64 (cubic numbers).
Paired work: Working in pairs, ask the children to generate a number sequence of their own. Collect examples and try them with the class. Ensure that, as well as finding the next two terms in each sequence, the children are able to explain how each sequence is generated.

Review
Write 1.3, 1.5, 2.8 on the board. Make the statement: *To continue the*

Differentiation

Less confident learners: Encourage these children to use a multiplication table they are confident with as a starting point.

More confident learners: Ask these children to generate sequences that decrease as well as increase, and which may go into negative numbers.

sequence, add the two previous numbers. Show how 1.3 and 1.5 = 2.8. Ask: *Which are the next two numbers which need to be added?* Ask the children to work individually to find the next four numbers in the sequence. Check answers.

Lesson 2 (Apply)

Starter

Recall: Draw a Venn diagram on the board, with one circle labelled 'Can be divided by 0.4' and the other labelled 'Can be divided by 0.3'. Write the following numbers on the board: 1.5, 2.4, 7.2, 3.6, 2.7, 1.2, 4.5, 5.6, 8.1, 6.3, 2.1, 3.2. Ask the children to use their knowledge of multiplication facts to insert the numbers into the correct part of the Venn diagram. Collect answers and check accuracy. Repeat for other times-tables if required

Main teaching activities

Whole class: Draw the following pattern on the board and fill in the chart shown.

No. of ✓	No. of ×
3	2
4	4
5	6

Ask: *What would the next two sequences be?* (6–8 and 7–10.) Draw another pattern, again asking the children to work out the next two terms in the sequence.

Term	✓	×
1	1	1
2	2	3
3	3	5
4	?	?
5	?	?

Ask: *What is the pattern?* Elicit the fact that it is necessary to double the number of ticks and then subtract one to find the number for ×. Ask: *How can you use this information to find the twentieth term… the fortieth term… the one-hundredth term without having to draw pictures to fill in the chart?* (The twentieth term would be 20 ticks and 39 crosses – double 20 and then subtract 1.) Repeat for the fortieth and one-hundredth terms.

Independent/paired work: Give out squared or isometric paper, or apparatus like coloured pegs and peg boards. Tell the children they are going to create a pattern up to the fifth term and then give it to a partner to work out the eighth, tenth and twelfth terms. Emphasise that there must be a relationship between the two aspects of their pattern; the pattern cannot just occur randomly.

Review

Invite children to show their patterns. Discuss the relationship between the two aspects of the sequence. Ask: *Is it possible to work out any term in the sequence by using a formula?* As a teaching point, try to include sequences

Differentiation

Less confident learners: This group may benefit from using apparatus rather than paper. Suggest that they start with very simple patterns.

More confident learners: Encourage these children to extend the sequence even further. Can they find out what the twentieth, fiftieth and one-hundredth term might be?

that do not work. (Note: You may wish to make these up yourself to avoid drawing attention to any children who have not been able to grasp the concept behind the pattern relationship.)

Lesson 3 (Teach and practise)

Starter
Refine: Write the following facts on the board: $1 \times 3.6 = 3.6$, $2 \times 3.6 = 7.2$, $4 \times 3.6 = 14.4$, $8 \times 3.6 = 28.8$, $16 \times 3.6 = ?$. Discuss how each answer has been arrived at. *What is the missing answer?* Ask the children questions such as: *What is 5×3.6? What is 12×3.6?* How can they use the given information to help them find the answers? Discuss answers, recapping on strategies used.

Main teaching activities
Whole class: Explain that in mathematics, letters sometimes represent numbers. This is called algebra. Write up the following example: *If $x = 4$, what is 2 times x?* Show the children that this can be written as $2x$ and that the multiplication sign is not needed. Try these examples: *If $x = 4$, what is $8x$? $12x$? $9x$?* How can the children combine this technique of using letters to write formulae? Remind them of formulae they know already, for example: area = length × width ($a = l \times w$) and perimeter = (length + width) × 2 ($p = (l + w) \times 2$).

Show the children how to devise simple formulae. Give an example: *If sweets cost 7p, how much will it cost for any number of sweets?* Work through the process with the children, asking the following questions: *What do we want to find out? The cost, so call this c. What do we know? Sweets are 7p each, so c = 7. How many do we want? We don't know, so call the missing number n. So, the cost = 7p × the number of sweets or c = 7n.* Try it out together. Ask: *I want 6 sweets, how much will this cost?* ($c = 7n$ so $c = 7p \times 6 = 42p$.)

Ask the children to write the formula or equation for the cost of sweets at 4p each. Elicit that $c = 4n$. Then, as a class, work on the following:
● *What is the number of months in y years?* ($m = 12y$)
● *What is the formula for finding the nth term of this sequence: 4, 8, 12, 16, 20?* ($n = 4n$)
● *There are x carrots in a field. How many carrots will each rabbit get if there are 6 rabbits?* ($x/6$)

Before the children work on their own, show and explain these additional algebra statements: $n \div 5 = n/5$; $n \times n = n^2$; $a \times b = ab$; $3 \times n = 3n$.
Independent work: Give out copies of the 'What's it worth?' activity sheet. This will provide the children with practice in basic algebra.

Review
Write the following on the board and ask the children to explain what they mean: d/n; xy; $12n$; p^2. Invite individuals to make up a question to go with each statement. Then ask the rest of the class to work it through to see if they are correct.

Differentiation
Less confident learners: This group should focus only on Section 1 of the activity sheet and some will need adult support.
More confident learners: Encourage this group to move on to Section 2 of the activity sheet as soon as possible. Once this is complete, challenge them to write their own word problems and then make up simple formulae for solving them.

Lessons 4-10

Preparation
Lesson 10: Display the calculations for the main teaching activities on the board.

You will need
Photocopiable pages
'Five square' (page 58), 'Jake's clever thoughts' (page 59) and 'Division bingo' (page 60).
CD resources
Support version of 'Square search'; support and extension versions of 'Jake's clever thoughts'; support, extension and template versions of 'Division bingo'. General resource sheets: 'Hundred square' and 'Digit (+ and –) and decimal point cards'. Interactive resources: 'Number sentence builder' and 'Number grid'.
Equipment
Individual whiteboards and pens; calculators.

Learning objectives

Starter
● Use knowledge of place value and multiplication facts to 10×10 to derive related multiplication and division facts involving decimals (eg 0.8×7, $4.8 \div 6$).
● Calculate mentally with integers and decimals: U.t ± U.t, TU × U, TU ÷ U, U.t × U, U.t ÷ U. (Revision of Block A)
● Use decimal notation for tenths, hundredths and thousandths; partition, round and order decimals with up to three places, and position them on the number line. (Revision of Block A)

Main teaching activities
2006
● Use knowledge of multiplication facts to derive quickly squares of numbers to 12×12 and the corresponding squares of multiples of 10.
● Use knowledge of place value and multiplication facts to 10×10 to derive related multiplication and division facts involving decimals (eg 0.8×7, $4.8 \div 6$).
● Recognise that prime numbers have only two factors and identify prime numbers less than 100; find the prime factors of two-digit numbers.
● Use approximations, inverse operations and tests of divisibility to estimate and check results.
1999
● Recognise squares of numbers to at least 12×12.
● Derive quickly squares of multiples of 10 (eg 60×60).
● Use factors; use known number facts and place value to consolidate mental multiplication and division.
● Recognise prime numbers; factorise numbers to 100 into prime factors.
● Check results of calculations; know and apply simple tests of divisibility.

Vocabulary
integer, decimal, square number, multiple, factor, divisor, divisible, prime, inverse, operation, product, complement

Lesson 4 (Review)

Starter
Revisit: Ask children: *If 63 ÷ 9 = 7, what is 6.3 ÷ 9?* Elicit 0.7. Ask similar questions such as 4.8 ÷ 6, 2.5 ÷ 5, 2.8 ÷ 2. Ask the children to show answers on their whiteboards.

Main teaching activities
Whole class: Recap square numbers from Year 5. Scribe the numbers on the board, finding the squares up to 12×12. Discuss how to find squares of multiples of 10 up to 100, using the information written on the board (for example, $20 \times 20 = 400$). Working in pairs, ask the children to find the squares of all the multiples of 10 up to 100. Share outcomes and ask for explanations as to how they worked out the answers.
Paired work: Ask the children to work in pairs. Explain that they are going to investigate the squares of multiples of 5. Provide each pair with a copy of the 'Five square' activity sheet. Tell the children that there is a set pattern to finding the squares of the odd multiples of 5. (Firstly all numbers end in 25; to find the preceding digits, multiply the first digit by one more than itself, for example 65^2 will have 25 on the end. To find the first digits, multiply 6 by one more than itself, $6 \times 7 = 42$. So the answer is 4225.) Most children will be able to recognise that each answer ends in 25 as $5 \times 5 = 25$. Encourage them to look carefully at the relationship between the first digit of the

BLOCK B

Securing number facts, understanding shape

Differentiation

Less confident learners: Provide this group with the 'Square search' support sheet, which asks the children to identify square numbers.

More confident learners: You may wish the children to extend this investigation to see if there are similar patterns for other square numbers (eg squares of numbers ending in 6).

number to be squared and the digits before the 25 in the answer. If they use table facts, they should see the pattern.

Review

Ask children for the answers and write them on the board. Invite children to explain how they found the pattern.

Ask: *Would the pattern continue for odd multiples of 5 over 100?* Invite the children to make a prediction, then get them to check this with a calculator.

Lesson 5 (Teach)

Starter

Refine: Write the number 84 on the board. Ask the children to write down as many multiplication and division facts that they can, using what they know about the factors of 84, such as 14 × 6, 84 ÷ 7 = 12. Repeat for 8.4. What do the children notice about the factors of 8.4?

Main teaching activity

Whole class: Use the 'Number sentence builder' interactive resource to display the calculations in this lesson. With the class, work out 8 × 40. Ask the children what other number facts they know using these figures. Try to elicit: 320 ÷ 40 = 8; 320 ÷ 8 = 40; 40 × 8 = 320. Tell them to write the answer to 9 × 30 on their whiteboards, plus the associated number facts. If any children find this difficult, remind them to use the known fact 9 × 3 as a starting point. Discuss the relationship between × and ÷. Establish that they are 'inverse operations'. Check the children's understanding by drawing the following diagram on the board:

Establish that 7 × 60 = 420. In turn, cover each number and ask children to give a fact using the numbers left. Repeat until all four facts are established. Extend the task using decimals, for example, 3.6 ÷ 4. Explain to the children that they can use their understanding of the process above to help: 3.6 ÷ 4 can be found by 4 × ? = 3.6. Establish that 4 × 9 = 36, so 4 × 0.9 = 3.6. List associated number facts.

Give the children a few problems to practise on their whiteboards, differentiated for each ability group. For example, use 3.75 × 3 for more confident children and use whole numbers only for the less confident group if they are not secure with decimals.

Independent work: Distribute 'Jake's clever thoughts' activity sheet and explain that the children must use the given number facts to solve the related problems on the sheet.

Differentiation

Less confident learners: Give these children the support version of the activity sheet, which uses mostly whole numbers.

More confident learners: Give these children the extension version of the sheet, which uses a mixture of decimals and simple fractions.

Review

What can the class tell you about multiplication and division? Ensure that children know the term 'inverse'. Ask them to complete the following: For every multiplication or division fact there are ? others that can be found.

Write the following on the board: 75 × 4 = 300. Ask the children to use this information to work out the answers to questions such as:

● *Four children share £3. How much does each get?*
● *What is ¹/₄ of 300?*
● *How many 75s in 300?*

▶ ## Lesson 6 (Practise)

Starter
Reason: Pose the following question: *The answer to a calculation is 0.48. What could the calculation be?* Give a time limit (say, two minutes) for the children to write down on their whiteboards as many calculations as possible, for example 0.6 × 0.8. Repeat for other decimals, such as 0.72, 3.6.

Main teaching activities
Whole class: Use the 'Number sentence builder' interactive resource to display the calculation 72 ÷ 9 = ?. Ask the children how they will work this out. Elicit that they will need to use multiplication facts for the 9-times table. Remind them that multiplication is the inverse of division. Ask for the answer (8). Next, show 480 ÷ 60. Remind the children to use known multiplication facts to help them with the calculation. Elicit that 8 × 6 = 48 so 8 × 60 = 480. Give the children a few examples to practise on their whiteboards.

Tell the children they are going to continue their work on division by dividing by 10, 100 and 1000. Write 670 ÷ 100 on the board. If necessary, write the number under a place value chart: TH H T U . t h. Remind them that when multiplying or dividing by 10, 100 or 1000, the numbers must move along the place value chart - the decimal point does not move. Solve the calculation together, talking the process through with the children. Write 23.6 on the board and ask the children to divide it by 10 and also by 100. Collect answers and correct any misunderstandings. Practise as necessary.
Paired work: The children work in pairs on the 'Division bingo' activity sheet, which has a division game based on dividing integers by 10, 100 and 1000 and decimals by 10 and 100.

Review
Write a selection of calculations on the board, some of which are correct and some not, for example 5.2 × 100 = 52. Ask the children to check which ones are correct and which not, and explain why.

Differentiation
Less confident learners:
Provide this group with the support version of the activity sheet, which requires the children to divide integers by 10 and 100 only, and decimals by 10.
More confident learners:
Provide this group with the extension version of the activity sheet, which requires children to divide both integers and decimals by 10, 100 and 1000.

Lesson 7 (Review and apply)

Starter
Reason: Pose the question: *Multiplication always makes a number bigger – true or false?* Ask children to investigate in pairs. Remind them to use decimals as well as whole numbers. Collect responses. Establish that when decimals are multiplied, the number becomes smaller, for example 0.8 × 0.2 = 0.16.

Repeat for division. *Does it always make a number smaller?* Establish that dividing by decimals less than 1 makes the number bigger, such as 0.8 ÷ 0.2 = 4. Ask the children to discuss in their groups why this happens. Invite explanations.

Main teaching activities
Whole class: Remind the children that factors are whole numbers that divide exactly into another number without a remainder. For example, the factors of 20 are 1, 2, 4, 5 and 20. Ask the children to find the factors of 12, 17, 19 and 25. What do they notice about 17 and 19? Elicit that there are only two factors for each: 1 and the number itself. Explain that these are prime numbers. Ask the children to work in pairs to find two more prime numbers less than 20. Collect results.
Paired work: Give a copy of 'Hundred square' to each pair. Pose the question for investigation: *There are 26 prime numbers between 0 and 100. True or false?* Encourage the children to cross out numbers on the hundred square that they know are not prime numbers, such as table facts.

Review
Display the 'Number grid' interactive resource (or display the 'Hundred

Differentiation

Less confident learners: These children may need table squares to help with this activity.
More confident learners: This group should be able to calculate prime numbers to 200.

square' on an OHP) and highlight the prime numbers. *Was the statement correct?* (No – there are 25 as 1 is not a prime number.) Ask why there will never be a prime number in the 4th, 6th, 8th and 10th columns. (They are all even numbers, so have 2 as a factor.)

Lesson 8 (Review and teach)

Starter

Recall: Remind the children of the term 'complement'. Explain that the complement of 0.6 to make 1 is 0.4. Give the children a selection of whole numbers and decimals and ask them to find the complement to 1, 10, 100 or 1000. Examples could be: find the complement to 10 for 0.3; 3.65. Find the complement to 1 for 0.12; 0. 375. Find the complement to 1000 for 145, etc.

Main teaching activities

Whole class: Recap on the prime numbers between 0 and 100. Then, writing an example on the whiteboard, demonstrate how to express a number in prime factors. Explain that every whole number can be factored into a product of prime factors – that is, it can be expressed using prime numbers only. Write 33 and 36 on the board. *What are the factors of 33?* (33 and 1, or 3 and 11.) 3 and 11 are the lowest factors and they are both prime numbers, so they are the prime factors of 33. For 36, choose two factors (such as 9 and 4). Break 9 and 4 down into their factors ($3 × 3$ and $2 × 2$). These are the lowest factors and they are both prime numbers. Both can be written using indices as a shorthand method. Therefore, $3^2 × 2^2$ are the prime factors of 36. Show the children that, whichever factors are used, they will break down to the same prime factors. For 36, instead of $9 × 4$, choose $3 × 12$. 3 is a prime already. 12 can be factorised to $2 × 6$; 6 is then factorised to $2 × 3$. Therefore, the prime factors are $2 × 2 × 3 × 3$. The diagram below can be used to show children how to break down each numbers into prime factors.

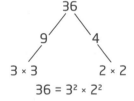

$$36 = 3^2 × 2^2$$

Differentiation

Less confident learners: This group should focus on the first five numbers in the list. Support may need to be given.
More confident learners: This group could go on to demonstrate that the final roots of any factor tree will be the same whichever factors they use. For example, 18 $= 2 × 9 = 2 × 3 × 3 = 2 × 3^2$, while 18 $= 3 × 6 = 3 × 2 × 3$ which also produces $2 × 3^2$.

Group/paired work: Write the following numbers on the board: 8, 10, 16, 20, 28, 32, 40, 48. Ask the children, working in small groups/pairs, to write each number as a product of its prime factors. Stress that all stages in the process should be shown and indices should be used to show the answer in its most concise form.

Review

Put a selection of numbers (such as 33, 36 , 49, 16) on the board, and some prime factors ($3^2 × 2^2$, 3 and 11, and so on). Ask the children to work in pairs to match the prime factors to the prime numbers. Correct any mistakes and misunderstandings.

Lesson 9 (Teach)

Starter

Recall: Write on the board a list of numbers such as 3.75, 9.4, 6, 7.123. Invite the children to order the numbers from smallest to largest. Repeat with a set such as 9.27, 5.437, 9.227. Repeat, extending the number range to include some numbers with three places of decimals.

Main teaching activities

Whole class: Tell the children they are going to establish which rules apply when odd and even numbers are multiplied. Remind them that the word

Differentiation

Less confident learners: Work with these children to check that multiplication calculations are correct, otherwise they may gather confusing results at the investigation stage. Table squares may be needed by some.

More confident learners: Encourage this group to check rules using two-digit numbers. They could go on to check the rules that apply when odd and even numbers are divided, but this should only be done with numbers that will divide equally without leaving remainders.

'product' means the answer to a multiplication calculation. For example, the product of 6 and 3 is 18. Work through several examples of each on the whiteboard or OHP. For example: even × even, $8 \times 6 = 48$ and $4 \times 10 = 40$; odd × odd, $7 \times 5 = 35$ and $9 \times 11 = 99$; even × odd, $6 \times 9 = 54$ and $10 \times 7 = 70$; odd × even, $5 \times 14 = 70$ and $13 \times 6 = 78$.

Paired work: Ask pairs to divide a set of 1–9 digit cards into odd and even numbers and shuffle them. Choosing cards at random from both or either piles of cards, they should test out the rules that apply to the products of odd and even numbers by trying out as many examples as they can (even × even, odd × odd, even × odd and odd × even). Towards the end of the session they should be able to suggest some general rules.

Review

Compare the rules about the products of odd and even numbers with those to do with adding and subtracting odd and even numbers.

Lesson 10 (Apply)

Starter

Revisit: Play 'Decimal swap' in pairs. Give the children calculations to do on calculators, which give answers to two decimal places (such as $26.2 \div 3$). The first child does the calculation and the other child in the pair rounds the answer to the nearest tenth, then the nearest whole number. Swap and repeat for different numbers.

Main teaching activities

Whole class: Give out calculators to each child and write the following on the board:

$6.9 \div 3 = 2.3$
$2.4 \div 4 = 0.7$
$\frac{1}{6}$ of $1.5 = 0.25$
$981.2 \div 44 = 22.3$

Tell the children they are going to work in pairs to check if the calculations are correct. Allow them one or two minutes to discuss with their partners how they are going to undertake this task. At the end of this time, choose a pair to explain how they are going to make the checks. If necessary, ask other pairs if the correct method is not given first time. Elicit that they will need to use the inverse operation for each calculation, for example for the first one it will be $3 \times 2.3 = 6.9$. Tell the children to work through each one, recording their work on their whiteboards. Check answers and establish that $2.4 \div 4 = 0.6$, not 0.7.

Show the following calculation and ask the children to check using the inverse operation: $348 \div 27 = 12.89$. Establish that 12.89×27 does not give 348 exactly (it gives 348.03). Discuss why this is so. Establish that 12.89 was an approximate answer.

Write the following on the board and ask the children to work in pairs to work out the answers:

$26.3 + ? = 98.2$ $203.6 - ? = 72.4$ $0.53 \times ? = 6.36$ $? - 25.45 = 16.38$

Discuss the answers to each question, ensuring that children can explain what they had to do in each case.

Independent work: Give the children further examples to be solved.

Review

Ask children from the more confident group to write some of their made-up calculations on the board. Ask the children to estimate answers and then check using their calculators. Choose one or two children to explain how to check that calculations are correct. Ensure they use the word 'inverse' in their explanation.

Differentiation

Less confident learners: As the focus is on using inverse operations, give whole number calculations only so that the children can concentrate solely on choosing the appropriate operation.

More confident learners: This group could make up calculations for each other to solve.

Lessons 11-15

Preparation
Lesson 11: Display the 2D shapes on the board, OHP or interactive whiteboard.
Lesson 12: Write on the board the sets of numbers for the Starter.
Lesson 14: Display the 3D shapes on the board, OHP or interactive whiteboard.

You will need
Photocopiable pages
'Visualising shapes' (page 61), one per child
CD resources
Support and extension versions of 'Visualising shapes'. General resource sheets: 'Dotty paper'; 'Triangular dotty paper (small)' or 'Triangular dotty paper (large)', for support; '2cm squared paper', copied onto thin card.
Equipment
Plastic 2D and 3D shapes; poster showing 2D drawings of 3D shapes; art straws; sticky tape or Blu-Tack; rulers; scissors; construction equipment such as Polydron and Clixi; cardboard boxes of different shapes and sizes; glue.

Learning objectives

Starter
● Solve multi-step problems, and problems involving fractions, decimals and percentages; choose and use appropriate calculation strategies at each stage, including calculator use. (Revision of Block A)
● Use decimal notation for tenths, hundredths and thousandths; partition, round and order decimals with up to three places, and position them on the number line. (Revision of Block A)
● Make and draw shapes with increasing accuracy and apply knowledge of their properties.
● Calculate mentally with integers and decimals: U.t ± U.t, TU × U, TU ÷ U, U.t × U, U.t ÷ U. (Revision of Block A)

Main teaching activities
2006
● Describe, identify and visualise parallel and perpendicular edges or faces; use these properties to classify 2D shapes and 3D solids.
● Make and draw shapes with increasing accuracy and apply knowledge of their properties.
1999
● Describe and visualise properties of solid shapes such as parallel or perpendicular faces or edges.
● Classify quadrilaterals, using criteria such as parallel sides, equal angles, equal sides...
● Make shapes with increasing accuracy.

Vocabulary
parallel, perpendicular, regular, irregular, face, edge, vertex, vertices, polyhedron, quadrilateral, polygon, names of 2D and 3D shapes

Lesson 11 (Apply)

Starter
Revisit: Ask the children to draw quickly on their whiteboards the grid shown here. Then ask them to fill it in with the appropriate amounts. Discuss strategies used, for example halving numbers, quartering numbers, adding two columns together.

	100%	50%	25%	12½%	75%	10%
£4000						
£12,000						
£28,000						
£46,000						

Main teaching activities
Whole class: Display the following shapes: parallelogram, kite, trapezium, square, rectangle, rhombus. Ask the children to name each shape. Remind them that the shapes are all quadrilaterals. Recap vocabulary such as perpendicular, parallel, acute angle, obtuse angle, symmetrical. Tell the children they are going to list the properties of each shape using the criteria of sides, angles and lines of symmetry.
Independent work: Ask the children to list the properties of the shapes in their books using the method described above.

Differentiation

Less confident learners: Work with this group using large plastic shapes as a visual aid.
More confident learners: When the task is completed, ask this group to draw some quadrilaterals of their own (eg parallelogram, kite, trapezium) using rulers and protractors.

Review

Choose a set of properties (for example, angles) and read them out to the class. Ask the children which shapes these could describe. Now read out another set of properties, such as sides, and ask: *Which shapes are now eliminated? Why? Which shapes remain?* If more than one shape is left, read out the symmetry properties to establish which shape you were describing.

Lesson 12 (Review and apply)

Starter

Revisit: Write the following numbers on the board in this order: 3.270, 3.720, 3.027, 3.727, 3.702. Tell the children that the numbers have been ordered from lowest to highest but that two of them have been put in the wrong place. Ask: *Which two are incorrect? Why are they in the wrong order?* Ensure the children can explain why that is, using the correct place value terminology (for example, tenths, hundredths, thousandths). Repeat with similar lists, such as: 26.317, 26.137, 26.731, 27.317 and 26.713.

Main teaching activities

Whole class: Recap on parallel and perpendicular, drawing lines on the board to illustrate. Make the statement: *All trapeziums have one pair of parallel sides and one pair of sides of equal length. Is this statement true or false?* (False.) Working in pairs, ask the children to respond to this investigation, backing up their conclusions with drawn evidence. At the end of the allocated period of time, ask them to come to a conclusion, explaining why the statement is false and producing their evidence.

Tell the children they are going to draw a quadrilateral on their whiteboard based on given information: *My quadrilateral has two sets of parallel sides. What could it be?* They should produce a range of squares, rectangles and parallelograms. Ask: *What further information would be needed to make the description of a shape more precise, for example for a square?* Elicit that you would need the following information: all four sides are equal; all four angles are right angles.

Try another one: *My quadrilateral has only one set of parallel lines.* The children should produce a range of trapeziums. Ask: *What other information could be given to identify the type of trapezium?* This could include, for example, non-parallel sides of equal length, two acute angles, two obtuse angles.

Independent work: Give out the 'Dotty paper' general resource sheet and the 'Visualising shapes' activity sheet. Explain that the instructions given could produce more than one type of quadrilateral.

Differentiation

Less confident learners: Let this group work from the support version of 'Visualising shapes', where the instructions are more precise and less open to interpretation.
More confident learners: This group should work from the extension version of the activity sheet, where the instructions include visualising shapes through the properties of the diagonals.

Review

Ask a child to give instructions for visualising a shape and invite the rest of the class to draw it. Repeat with other volunteers.

Lesson 13 (Apply)

Starter

Reason: Give out the 'Dotty paper' general resource sheet. Tell the children you are going to describe some shapes, which they should draw on the paper. Explain that for some of the shapes, there will be more than one possibility.
Shape 1: a pentagon with two right angles and one pair of parallel sides
Shape 2: a quadrilateral with one set of parallel sides and two right angles
Shape 3: a kite with two inside dots
Shape 4: a quadrilateral with two sets of parallel sides
Shape 5: a pentagon with three sets of perpendicular lines and one set of parallel sides

Share the shapes constructed and discuss the different outcomes.

Main teaching activities

Whole class: Give out copies of the 'Triangular dotty paper (small)' general resource sheet. Ask the children to draw a rhombus with sides of 1 unit on their paper. Explain that this is the basic shape they will be using for the following investigation. Tell them they are going to investigate how many different shapes they can make using two... three... four... five... rhombuses. The rhombuses must join edge to edge, and may not overlap. A shape cannot be counted twice if it is rotated.

Independent work: Encourage the children to be systematic in their investigation, rather than just drawing shapes randomly. Encourage the completing of a table as they go along to record their findings. Allow 15 minutes to complete task.

Review

Discuss findings. Ask: *Is there a pattern to how many shapes can be made according to how many rhombuses are used?* Ask the children to look at all the shapes they have made. *Which other quadrilateral can be made using two or more rhombuses?* (Parallelogram.)

Differentiation

Less confident learners: This group might find it easier to use the 'Triangular dotty paper (large)' general resource sheet.
More confident learners: Encourage the children to use their completed table to produce a formula for finding how many shapes can be made.

Lesson 14 (Teach and apply)

Starter

Revisit: Begin by revising doubling and halving two-digit numbers. This should include whole numbers and decimals. Also include some odd numbers in the halving process, even though they will produce a half. Examples might include: *Double and halve 45* (90 and 22½)... *56* (112 and 28)... *72* (144 and 36)... *88* (176 and 44)... *3.4* (6.8 and 1.7)... *7.8* (15.6 and 3.9)... *9.6* (19.2 and 4.8). With decimal numbers, some children find it easier to treat them as whole numbers and reinstate the decimal point at the end.

Main teaching activities

Whole class: Start with a display of 3D shapes, including a cube, cuboid, a selection of prisms and pyramids, sphere, cylinder, cone and so on. Show the children plastic, wooden or cardboard models of the shapes, but also try to have examples of these shapes as they occur in everyday situations, for example: cylinder (drinks can), sphere (ball), cuboid (cereal packet), triangular prism (chocolate bar). Discuss key words like face, edge and vertex, and examine the properties of each shape on display. Ask: *How many faces does it have? What shape(s) are the faces? How many edges are there? How many vertices are there? Which shapes are regular polyhedra?* (ie all their faces are the same shape and size). Also discuss the meaning of the terms 'parallel' and 'perpendicular' when applied to faces and/or edges.

Group work: The children should work in mixed-ability pairs or small groups on the following tasks. Provide them with art straws, sticky tape or Blu-Tack, rulers and scissors and ask them to make skeletal models of some of the straight-sided shapes on display. This will require careful measuring, cutting and fixing. Display the poster showing 2D drawings of 3D shapes. Ask the children to identify the shapes and then write a short description of each one. Also make available construction equipment like Polydron and Clixi. Using a colour coding system (such as red face is parallel to blue face), ask them to produce models of polyhedra, noting particular sets of parallel and perpendicular faces for each one.

Differentiation

Less confident learners: Focus particularly on the skeletal models of 3D shapes and talk through their properties, especially for children who have difficulty calculating the number of edges and vertices of shapes. Edges have to be measured and cut before assembly and vertices become automatic fixing points.
More confident learners: Set this group investigations involving the set of shapes known as the Five Platonic Polyhedra because all their faces are the same shape and size. These are: the cube (six square faces), the tetrahedron (four triangular faces), the octahedron (eight triangular faces), the icosahedron (twenty triangular faces) and the dodecahedron (twenty pentagonal faces).

Review

Play a game of 'Back-to-back', where a child sits back-to-back with a partner, chooses a shape and describes it to the other to guess. Display the large poster to check that children can recognise 3D shapes from 2D drawings.

Lesson 15 (Apply and evaluate)

Starter
Revisit: This time, work on doubles and corresponding halves of multiples of 10 up to 1000. For example, say: *Double and halve 40* (80 and 20)... *120* (240 and 60)... *260* (520 and 130)... *510* (1020 and 255).

Main teaching activities
Whole class: Explain that in this lesson the children will continue to explore the characteristics and properties of 3D shapes. Ensure first that the children appreciate the meaning of the word 'net' when applied to 3D shapes. Revise using several types of cardboard box. Demonstrate how they can be flattened out to show how they were made. Reassemble the shape to illustrate how it fits together. Then show the children a large version of one of the nets of a closed cube on the whiteboard or the OHP. Explain that this shape is called a hexomino because it has an area of six squares. Demonstrate how this shape makes a closed cube.

Group work: Provide the children with the '2cm squared paper' general resource sheet and ask them to investigate and find all the nets of a cube that will make a closed box. There should be a total of 11 different nets. Remember that if the nets are likely to be fixed permanently, then gluing flaps will need to be included.

Review
Invite volunteers out to the front of the class to demonstrate how some nets successfully made closed cubes while others did not. Mount a classroom display of the successful ones. Also share the results achieved by the more confident group in finding the nets of other 3D shapes.

Invite the children to write what they have learned from this unit of work and which aspects they feel they need to study further in order to become competent.

Differentiation
Less confident learners: It may be quicker and easier to provide this group with a series of hexominoes already drawn and cut out, so that the children can focus on making them up to see which nets produce a closed cube.

More confident learners: Expand the 'net' theme by challenging this group to find successful nets for other well-known 3D shapes, especially the tetrahedron (triangular-based pyramid), the Egyptian pyramid (square-based) and the triangular prism.

Name _____   Date _____

What's it worth?

Fact box: Use this important information to help you.

$$3 \times n = 3n \qquad n \div 5 = \frac{n}{5} \qquad n \times n = n^2 \qquad a \times b = ab \qquad 6 \times n \times n = 6n^2$$

Section 1

Find the value of each equation if $a = 4$, $b = 6$, $c = 5$, $d = 9$ and $e = 3$.

ab _____

$2c$ _____

$\dfrac{d}{e}$ _____

$7b^2$ _____

$cd + de$ _____

c^2 _____

$\dfrac{bc}{10}$ _____

$40 - a^2$ _____

Section 2

Find the value of n in each of these equations.

$4n - 3 = 21$ _____

$\dfrac{n}{5} = 40$ _____

$6n + 12 = 48$ _____

$42 = n - 9$ _____

$9n = 108$ _____

$n^2 = 121$ _____

$n = \dfrac{16}{4} + 18$ _____

$3n^2 = 75$ _____

BLOCK B

Securing number facts, understanding shape

Name _____   Date _____

Five square

You are going to investigate the patterns in the squares of numbers ending in 5.
Look carefully at the pattern below:

$$15^2 = 225$$

$$25^2 = 625$$

$$35^2 = 1225$$

$$45^2 = 2025$$

Do you notice anything about the answers? Is there a common pattern?

With your partner, can you work out how these answers were calculated?

HANDY HINT

Look carefully at the ten's digit in the question.
What do you have to do to make it into the first digit or digits of the answer?

Once you have worked out the method, write the answer to these squares:

$55^2 =$ _____

$65^2 =$ _____

$85^2 =$ _____

$105^2 =$ _____

Choose two more numbers to square.

_____

_____

Now check your results using a calculator.

Name _____   Date _____

Jake's clever thoughts

$1.2 \times 6 = 7.2$

$360 \div 9 = 40$

$7.2 \div 9 = 0.8$

$4.8 \div 0.6 = 8$

$2 \div 10 = 0.2$

$0.75 \times 4 = 3$

Jake knows these number facts.

Can you find the answers to the questions below using his thoughts?

1. Find 9×0.8. _____

2. Divide 3 by 4. _____

3. What is $7.2 \div 6$? _____

4. Find $7.2 \div 0.8$. _____

5. How many 0.2s make 2? _____

6. What is $360 \div 40$? _____

7. What is $\frac{1}{8}$ of 4.8? _____

8. How many 1.2s in 7.2? _____

Now use the following numbers to write four different number statements: 0.7, 0.6 and 0.42.

1. _____

2. _____

3. _____

4. _____

Name _____   Date _____

Division bingo

A game for two players

Preparation

Cut out the two game cards, the divisor cards and the number cards. Give a game card to each player, and put the divisor cards and number cards face down in two separate piles.

How to play

Take it in turns to pick up a divisor card and a number card. Divide the number by the divisor. If you have the answer on your game card, cross it out. Put the divisor and number cards back at the bottom of each pile. The winner is the first to cross out all the numbers on their card.

Game card 1

1.76	1.36	4.9	187	0.34
17.1	0.593	0.117	34	9.78

Game card 2

3.4	18.7	0.136	49	5.93
17.6	0.49	1.17	1.71	0.978

Divisor cards

10	100	1000

Number cards

340	176	490	593	171
1870	13·6	11.7	59.3	97.8

Name _____   Date _____

Visualising shapes

Read carefully each of the descriptions below. Visualise each shape, then draw it accurately on your dotty paper.

Remember: There are alternatives, so you may have different answers from others in your group. Always use a ruler.

1. Three quadrilaterals that have just one set of parallel sides.

2. A quadrilateral that has two sets of parallel sides of equal length.

3. A quadrilateral that has two obtuse angles and two acute angles.

4. Two quadrilaterals that have four right angles.

5. A quadrilateral that has only two right angles.

6. Two quadrilaterals that have two sets of parallel sides.

7. A quadrilateral with no parallel sides (a challenge!).

BLOCK B

Securing number facts, understanding shape

Securing number facts, understanding shape

Lesson	Strands	Starter	Main teaching activities
1. Teach	Use/apply	Calculate mentally with integers and decimals: U.t ± U.t, TU × U, TU ÷ U, U.t × U, U.t ÷ U. (Revision of Block A)	Represent and interpret sequences, patterns and relationships involving numbers and shapes; suggest and test hypotheses; construct and use simple expressions and formulae in words then symbols (eg the cost of c pens at 15 pence each is 15c pence).
2. Teach	Use/apply	Find the difference between a positive and a negative integer, or two negative integers, in context. (Revision of Block A)	As for Lesson 1
3. Teach	Use/apply	**Use knowledge of place value and multiplication facts to 10 × 10 to derive related multiplication and division facts involving decimals (eg 0.8 × 7, 4.8 ÷ 6).**	Tabulate systematically the information in a problem or puzzle; identify and record the steps or calculations needed to solve it, using symbols where appropriate; interpret solutions in the original context and check their accuracy.
4. Apply	Use/apply	Order a set of fractions by converting them to fractions with a common denominator. (Revision of Block E)	• Tabulate systematically the information in a problem or puzzle; identify and record the steps or calculations needed to solve it, using symbols where appropriate; interpret solutions in the original context and check their accuracy. • Represent and interpret sequences, patterns and relationships involving numbers and shapes; suggest and test hypotheses; construct and use simple expressions and formulae in words then symbols (eg the cost of c pens at 15 pence each is 15c pence).
5. Apply	Use/apply	• Tabulate systematically the information in a problem or puzzle; identify and record the steps or calculations needed to solve it, using symbols where appropriate; interpret solutions in the original context and check their accuracy. • Use a calculator to solve problems involving multi-step calculations.	As for Lesson 4
6. Practise	Knowledge Use/apply	**Use knowledge of place value and multiplication facts to 10 × 10 to derive related multiplication and division facts involving decimals (eg 0.8 × 7, 4.8 ÷ 6).**	• Use knowledge of multiplication facts to derive quickly squares of numbers to 12 × 12 and the corresponding squares of multiples of 10. • Represent and interpret sequences, patterns and relationships involving numbers and shapes; suggest and test hypotheses; construct and use simple expressions and formulae in words then symbols (eg the cost of c pens at 15 pence each is 15c pence).
7. Review	Knowledge Use/apply	As for Lesson 6	As for Lesson 6
8. Review	Knowledge	**Select and use standard metric units of measure and convert between units using decimals to two places.** (Revision of Block C)	**Use knowledge of place value and multiplication facts to 10 × 10 to derive related multiplication and division facts involving decimals (eg 0.8 × 7, 4.8 ÷ 6).**
9. Apply	Knowledge	Solve simple problems involving direct proportion by scaling quantities up or down. (Revision of Block E)	• **Use knowledge of place value and multiplication facts to 10 × 10 to derive related multiplication and division facts involving decimals (eg 0.8 × 7, 4.8 ÷ 6).** • Use approximations, inverse operations and tests of divisibility to estimate and check results.
10. Apply	Knowledge	Use knowledge of multiplication facts to derive quickly squares of numbers to 12 × 12 and the corresponding squares of multiples of 10.	Recognise that prime numbers have only two factors and identify prime numbers less than 100; find the prime factors of two-digit numbers.
11. Review	Knowledge	Order a set of fractions by converting them to fractions with a common denominator. (Revision of Block E)	Use approximations, inverse operations and tests of divisibility to estimate and check results.
12. Teach	Knowledge Calculate	**Find equivalent percentages, decimals and fractions.** (Revision of Block E)	• Tabulate systematically the information in a problem or puzzle; identify and record the steps or calculations needed to solve it, using symbols where appropriate; interpret solutions in the original context and check their accuracy. • Use a calculator to solve problems involving multi-step calculations.
13. Apply	Shape	Make and draw shapes with increasing accuracy and apply knowledge of their properties.	Describe, identify and visualise parallel and perpendicular edges or faces; use these properties to classify 2D shapes and 3D solids.
14. Apply	Shape	**Find equivalent percentages, decimals and fractions.** (Revision of Block E)	As for Lesson 13
15. Apply and evaluate	Shape	Calculate mentally with integers and decimals: U.t ± U.t, TU × U, TU ÷ U, U.t × U, U.t ÷ U. (Revision of Block A)	Make and draw shapes with increasing accuracy and apply knowledge of their properties.

Unit 2 — 3 weeks

Speaking and listening objectives
- Use a variety of ways to criticise constructively and respond to criticism.

Introduction
There are a total of 15 lessons in this block. Using and applying mathematics is integrated into all lessons through discussion and application of problem solving skills. Children investigate sequences, patterns and relationships. They use their knowledge of multiplication facts to find square numbers and to derive related multiplication and division facts for decimal numbers. They investigate prime numbers and use inverse operations and tests of divisibility.

The latter part of the unit focuses on understanding shape. Children use properties to investigate 2D shapes. They make and draw shapes accurately using a range of mathematical equipment.

Opportunities to respond to the suggestions of others are found in many of the lessons (see speaking and listening objective).

Use and apply mathematics
- Represent and interpret sequences, patterns and relationships involving numbers and shapes; suggest and test hypotheses; construct and use simple expressions and formulae in words then symbols (eg the cost of c pens at 15 pence each is $15c$ pence).

Lessons 1–12

Preparation
Lesson 1: Draw patterns on the board for the main activity.
Lesson 4: Write the fractions on the board for the Starter activity. Draw the diagram on the board for the Review activity.
Lesson 5: Copy 'Hundred square' onto OHT if you are not using the interactive resource.
Lesson 8: Write the equivalent measures on the board for the Starter activity.
Lesson 9: Write up the information for the Starter activity. Write up the questions for the main activity.

You will need
Photocopiable pages
'Monty the match snake' (page 75), 'Formula 1' (page 76) and 'Number sequence' (page 77), one per child.
CD resources
Support and extension versions of 'Formula 1' and 'Number sequence'; core, support and extension versions of 'Brackets first', 'Fact finder', 'Be reasonable' and 'Check it'. General resource sheet: 'Hundred square', for display and one per child. Interactive resource: 'Number grid'.
Equipment
Used matchsticks or similar, for support; table squares, for support; pegboards and pegs, for support; counting stick; individual whiteboards and pens; calculators.

Learning objectives

Starter
- Calculate mentally with integers and decimals: U.t $\pm$ U.t, TU $\times$ U, TU $\div$ U, U.t $\times$ U, U.t $\div$ U. (Revision of Block A)
- Find the difference between a positive and a negative integer, or two negative integers, in context. (Revision of Block A)
- Use knowledge of place value and multiplication facts to 10 $\times$ 10 to derive related multiplication and division facts involving decimals (eg 0.8 $\times$ 7, 4.8 $\div$ 6).
- Order a set of fractions by converting them to fractions with a common denominator. (Revision of Block E)
- Tabulate systematically the information in a problem or puzzle; identify and record the steps or calculations needed to solve it, using symbols where appropriate; interpret solutions in the original context and check their accuracy.
- Use a calculator to solve problems involving multi-step calculations.
- Select and use standard metric units of measure and convert between units using decimals to two places. (Revision of Block C)
- Solve simple problems involving direct proportion by scaling quantities up or down. (Revision of Block E)
- Use knowledge of multiplication facts to derive quickly squares of numbers to 12 $\times$ 12 and the corresponding squares of multiples of 10.
- Find equivalent percentages, decimals and fractions. (Revision of Block E)

Main teaching activities
2006
- Represent and interpret sequences, patterns and relationships involving numbers and shapes; suggest and test hypotheses; construct and use simple expressions and formulae in words then symbols (eg the cost of c pens at 15 pence each is $15c$ pence).
- Tabulate systematically the information in a problem or puzzle; identify and record the steps or calculations needed to solve it, using symbols where appropriate; interpret solutions in the original context and check their accuracy.
- Use knowledge of multiplication facts to derive quickly squares of numbers to 12 $\times$ 12 and the corresponding squares of multiples of 10.

- Use knowledge of place value and multiplication facts to 10 × 10 to derive related multiplication and division facts involving decimals (eg 0.8 × 7, 4.8 ÷ 6).
- Recognise that prime numbers have only two factors and identify prime numbers less than 100; find the prime factors of two-digit numbers.
- Use approximations, inverse operations and tests of divisibility to estimate and check results.
- Use a calculator to solve problems involving multi-step calculations.

1999
- Recognise and extend number sequences.
- Solve mathematical problems or puzzles, recognise and explain patterns and relationships, generalise and predict.
- Make and investigate a general statement about familiar numbers or shapes by finding examples that satisfy it; develop from explaining a generalised relationship in words to expressing it in a formula using letters or symbols (eg the cost of n articles at 15p each).
- Recognise squares of numbers to at least 12 × 12.
- Derive quickly squares of multiples of 10 (eg 60 × 60).
- Use factors; use known number facts and place value to consolidate mental multiplication and division.
- Recognise prime numbers; factorise numbers to 100 into prime factors.
- Check results of calculations.
- Know and apply simple tests of divisibility.

Vocabulary

problem, solution, calculate, calculation, equation, reasoning, predict, rule, formula, relationship, sequence, pattern, classify, criterion, criteria, generalise, construct, integer, decimal, fraction, square number, multiple, factor, factorise, divisor, divisible, prime, prime factor, consecutive, inverse, operation, product, quotient, estimate, approximate

Lesson 1 (Teach)

Starter
Reason: Tell the children they are going to use the digit 4 and the four operations +, −, × and ÷ to make the numbers 1 to 5. The digit can be used as often as needed and brackets can be used to identify the order of calculation if needed. Encourage a range of strategies, including using indices. Solutions may include:

$4 \div 4 = 1$

$(4 + 4) \div 4 = 2$

$(4 + 4 + 4) \div 4 = 3$

$4^2 \div 4 = 4$

$4 + (4 \times 4) \div 4 = 5$

Main teaching activities
Tell the children they are going to investigate growing patterns and will need to be able to explain how each pattern is generated. Draw these two patterns on the board:

Unit 2 ▢ 3 weeks

▷

Ask the children to draw the next pattern on their whiteboards or in their books, thus:

◆ ◆

◆ ◆ ◆

◆ ◆ ◆

◆ ◆ ◆

Explain that pattern 1 (the first term) can be written as (3 × 1) + 2. In pairs, ask children to work out how the second and third terms should be written: (3 × 2) + 2; (3 × 3) + 2. Ask the children to explain what is happening in the pattern. Using the formula they have created, what would be the tenth term (3 × 10) + 2 = 32; thirtieth term (3 × 30) + 2 = 92; hundredth term (3 × 100) + 2 = 302. Show how this formula can be written as 3N + 2 to work out any term in the pattern.

Ask the children to work in pairs to construct a similar pattern, for example 6N + 4. They should draw the first three sequences and then produce a formula. Ask pairs to swap their patterns with another pair and find the tenth and hundredth terms. Choose one or two pairs to explain to the rest of the class their growing patterns.

Independent work: Give out the activity sheet 'Monty the match snake', which gives practice in investigating growing patterns.

Review

Discuss the formula needed to solve the problem of Monty's body. Elicit 4 + 3*n*, 4 being the head of the snake. Ask: *What is the total number of matches in the tenth term?* 4 + (3 × 10) = 34... *the hundredth term?* 4 + (3 × 100) = 304. Can the children work out the twenty-fifth term and fiftieth term?

Differentiation

Less confident learners: This group should continue the patterns using used matchsticks or similar as a practical aid. They should find the eighth, tenth and twentieth segments.
More confident learners: You may wish to give this group a different shape to investigate, such as hexagons.

Lesson 2 (Teach)

Starter

Recall: Pose the following question: *My freezer has broken down. It was -6°C but has now risen to 14°C. What is the rise in temperature? After being repaired, the temperature starts to fall at a rate of 1°C per 15 minutes. How long does it take for my freezer to be back at -6°C?* Pose similar questions to allow practice at finding the difference between positive and negative integers in context.

Main teaching activities

Whole class: Point out to the children that in mathematics, relationships between numbers can be written using symbols – often letters of the alphabet – and that these are often used in simple formulae to help us with certain rules and calculations. Write up a simple example on the whiteboard or flipchart. Say: *We could denote a packet of sweets by the letter 'p'. The cost of each individual packet could be shown by the letter 'c'. If we wanted to find the total cost (t) of a number of packets of sweets we could use the formula t = p × c, or, in full, total cost (t) = numbers of packets (p) × cost of one packet (c).* Use another example. Remind the children that the area of a rectangle or square can be calculated by multiplying the length by the width. In formula terms this could be written as *a* (area) = *l* (length) × *w* (width). Ask the children what other formulae could be developed from this. They should respond that *l* = *a* ÷ *w* and *w* = *a* ÷ *l*. Then ask the class if they can give a formula for finding the perimeter of a rectangle or square. They should produce several alternatives. They could use *l* + *w* + *l* + *w* in various forms, or (*l* + *w*) × 2 or 2 (*w* + *l*). From this last example, emphasise that in these types of formulae a letter and a number next to each other with no visible sign always means multiply. So, for example, 2*t* = 2 × *t* and 5*n* = 5 × *n*.
Group work: Provide the children with copies of the 'Formula 1' activity sheet to work through.

Differentiation

Less confident learners: Provide this group with the support version of 'Formula 1', which deals with using the formula area = length × width only. Support may be needed when the formula is expressed in other ways, such as *w* = *a* ÷ *l*.
More confident learners: This group should work on the extension version of the activity sheet, where they use other formulae, namely, circumference of a circle = pi × diameter, and converting degrees in Fahrenheit into degrees in Celsius (F = 9C ÷ 5 + 32).

▷

▷ ### Review

Check through calculations that the children have carried out on the activity sheets and ensure figures have been correctly matched to letters in formulae. Select a formula and ask: *Can you explain what this formula means?*

Lesson 3 (Teach)

Starter
Recall: Explain that you would like the children to use multiplication table facts to derive the answers to division questions. Say, for example: *I have 36 apples to share between six children. How many do they each receive? The total cost of tickets for a pop concert was £72. If there are eight tickets, how much did each cost?* Ask other division questions set in context. Include decimals, such as: *Six children share £3.60 between them. How much does each get? Hair bows are made from 0.4m of ribbon. How many bows can I make with 4.8m?*

Main teaching activities
Explain to the children that they are going to investigate how brackets are used in calculations. Put the following calculation on the board and ask the children to find the answer: $12 \times 6 \div 3$. Ask for solutions. The majority of children will respond with the answer 24. Tell them that the answer you were looking for is 24. Can they see how you got to this answer? Show how brackets can be used to tell us which operation to carry out first – the answer 24 was arrived at using the calculation $12 \times (6 \div 3) = 24$. Show other examples, such as $25 + 5 \times 3 = \square$ or $14 + 12 \div 2 \times 4 = \square$. Ask the children to find all possible solutions. Encourage them to set their work out systematically so that they can check that they have included all solutions. List all possible solutions on the whiteboard.
Group work: Let the children work through the 'Brackets first' activity sheet.

Review
Go through the activity sheets, marking them with the children. Reinforce that operations in brackets must be carried out first. Tell the children that if brackets are not shown, there is an agreed order in which operations should be carried out. This can be shortened to BODMAS (brackets, of (^{2}), division, multiplication, addition and subtraction) to help them remember. Ask for some examples to test this out.

Differentiation
Less confident learners: This group should work on the support version of 'Brackets first', with only one set of questions. Provide table squares if necessary, so multiplication and division problems can be solved quickly.
More confident learners: Provide this group with the extension version of the activity sheet. In the second section children, working in pairs, can devise their own problems involving brackets, where the answers are given and they have to provide the variables. How many different solutions for each can they find?

Lesson 4 (Apply)

Starter
Reason: Write on the board the following fractions: $^1/_4$, $^1/_2$, $^3/_8$, $^7/_8$. Ask: *How can we order these fractions?* Encourage the children to find a common denominator and then to order the fractions. Draw an empty number line labelled 0 at one end and 1 at the other. Invite children to place each fraction where they estimate it belongs. Repeat this for another family of fractions, such as $^1/_3$, $^4/_5$, $^5/_6$, $^2/_5$.

Main teaching activities
Whole class: Explain that, during the main part of the lesson, groups will be working on different number puzzles involving number sequences and patterns. Stress that in solving these puzzles it is important to work from the known to the unknown. Emphasise the importance of looking for relationships between numbers that will help to make generalisations about which rules are being applied. Once rules have been established, this should be used to predict what form the pattern or sequence is taking.
Group work: Let the children work on the 'Number sequence' activity sheet. They have to work out the patterns involved in making balanced triangles using single-digit numbers.

Differentiation

Less confident learners:
Provide plenty of equipment like straws, matchsticks, pegboards and so on, so that children can work with patterns and sequences in a concrete way first. This will help them make the link between the spatial and the numerical pattern. They then work on the support version of 'Number sequence'.

More confident learners:
Encourage this group to extend their own number sequences as far as they can once they have completed the extension version of the activity sheet, which deals with the number sequence associated with Leonardo Fibonacci.

Review

Draw the following diagram on the board:

☺	☺	☺	☺	= 32
♡	☾	☾	☺	= 26
♡	♡	✸	☾	= 38
☺	✸	☾	♡	= 36

Tell the children that each shape stands for a number. Ask them to work out the value of each shape and the total of each line. At the end of the time limit, check answers (face = 8, heart = 10, moon = 4, flash = 14.) Ask the children to explain how they worked it out. Ensure all understand that there is an order to working out the solution (start with the top row as they are all smiley faces, so 32 ÷ 4 = 8).

Lesson 5 (Apply)

Starter

Reason: Give out calculators. Pose the question: *You have won first prize in a competition. You have a choice of prize: either £2500 in cash or £10 for each minute you spend in school today. Which will you choose and why?* The children should first estimate which they think will be the best option before starting their calculations. Encourage a systematic approach, where they list their calculations as each stage of the problem is worked through. Share answers. Did anyone make the right choice? Was anyone surprised at the outcome?

Differentiation

Less confident learners: Give out smaller number grids, such as a 6 × 6 grid numbered 1–36. Ask children to colour in multiples of 3. What do they notice? If they carried on, would 39/42/52 be in the sequence? How do they know?

More confident learners: Once their patterns are complete, pose questions such as: *If this pattern were continued, would 120 (or any chosen number) be in this sequence? Explain your reasoning.*

Main teaching activities

Whole class: Display the 'Number grid' interactive resource and highlight every multiple of 2 (or use the 'Hundred square' general resource sheet). Ask the children why this has given this type of pattern (because it is the ×2 table and every other number is coloured in). Ask the children to predict which tables would produce horizontal lines/vertical lines/diagonal lines.
Independent work: Ask the children to test their hypotheses using copies of the 'Hundred square'.

Review

Ask a selection of children to come forward with their completed hundred squares. They should explain the patterns they have discovered and how they could use this pattern to predict which other numbers would be in the sequence if the number square was extended.

Lesson 6 (Practise)

Starter

Revisit: Chant the ×8 table backwards and forwards, and starting at different points. Use this to count in 80s and then 0.8s. Use a counting stick as a visual aid. Point to selected divisions and ask what the division would represent if you were counting in any of these multiples.

Main teaching activities

Whole class: Recap on square numbers. Ask: *What are the square numbers to 100?* Working in pairs, ask the children to investigate what happens if you add two consecutive square numbers. What do they notice? (Answer is always an odd number.) Can they say why this is? (An odd + an even number is always an odd answer.)

Paired work: Tell the children they are going to investigate the sums of two square numbers, for example $2^2 + 6^2 = 40$. Explain that you want them to think about how they could record what they are doing in order to ensure that every combination is included.

The table shown below could be used to systematically record combinations:

	2^2	3^2	4^2	5^2	6^2	7^2	8^2	9^2	10^2
2^2									
3^2									
4^2									
5^2									
6^2									
7^2									
8^2									
9^2									
10^2									

Differentiation

Less confident learners: Ask children to find all the sums up to 100 only.
More confident learners: Encourage the children to work out a method of recording that tabulates every combination systematically, for example:

$2^2 + 3^2$	$3^2 + 4^2$	$4^2 + 5^2$
$2^2 + 4^2$	$3^2 + 5^2$	$4^2 + 6^2$
$2^2 + 5^2$	$3^2 + 6^2$	$4^2 + 7^2$

(or they could use the table shown right).

Review

Ask the children to share the numbers they made. Shade these in on a 'Hundred square' or on the 'Number grid' interactive resource. Ask questions such as: *How many numbers up to 100 can be made? Which ones cannot? Why?* Encourage the children to share the methods they used to ensure they had found all the combinations.

Lesson 7 (Review)

Starter

Revisit: Repeat the Starter for Lesson 6, but choose a different multiple, for example 6/60/0.6.

Main teaching activities

Whole class: Remind the children of work they did in Unit 1, when they found squares of multiples of 10. As a class, find 20^2, 30^2 and 40^2. Ask them to use this information to estimate what 21^2, 31^2 and 41^2 might be. Take some suggestions and write them on the board. Ask the children to work in pairs to calculate 21^2. Share methods. Establish that an efficient method is $(21 \times 10) + (21 \times 10) + 21$ or $21 \times 10 = 210$, $210 \times 2 = 420$, $420 + 21 = 441$. Ask the children to find the answer to 31^2 and 41^2.

Record answers on the board in column form:
$21^2 = 441$
$31^2 = 961$
$41^2 = 1681$

Paired work: Explain that there is a pattern to working out the square of a number ending in 1. Ask the children to work in pairs to find the method. Emphasise that they need to look closely at not just the answers already given, but at the relationships between the number being squared and the answer.

Collect responses and discuss. The first part of the answer is the square of the tens digit. The middle number is the tens digit doubled, and lastly the answer will always end in 1. Thus, 31^2 is 9 in the hundred column (3^2) and 6 in the tens column (3 doubled) and a 1 in the units column. Try this for 51^2 together:

Square the tens digit = 25__
Put a 1 on the end = 25__1
Find the middle digit by doubling the 5 = 10. Cannot put a 10, so put a 0 and change 25__1 to 26__1 = 2601.

Unit 2 ▢ 3 weeks

Ask the children to work out 61^2, 71^2, 81^2 and 91^2. This table could be used to help with calculations:

	Tens squared	Tens doubled	1 on the end	
61^2	36	12	1	= 3721

Review
Check answers. Ask the more confident group to disclose their findings. Ask: *Does this work for numbers over 100 if they end in a 1?* (Yes it does.)

Lesson 8 (Review)

Starter
Revisit: Remind the children that 1kg = 1000g, 1l = 1000ml and 1km = 1000m. Ask them to convert between units of measurement. For example: *Write 4.2l in millilitres. Write 2032m in kilometres.* Give a range for the children to convert.

Main teaching activities
Whole class: Recap on previous work. Write up 56 ÷ 7 = 8 and ask: *What are the other known facts that can be derived from this?* (7 × 8 = 56; 8 × 7 = 56; 56 ÷ 8 = 7) *What about 5.6 ÷ 7? What are the associated facts?*

Try 4.8 ÷ ▢ = 0.8. Ask the children to write the associated facts. Check answers.

Lastly, ask the children to explain to their partner why the following sum is incorrect: 0.9 × 8 = 72.

Then ask a selection of partners to relay back the explanations that they were given. How well did their partner explain? Were they listening to their partner fully? Check that all the children understand why 0.9 × 8 = 7.2, not 72.
Individual work: Provide each child with a copy of the 'Fact finder' activity sheet, which requires them to find related facts.

Review
Write the following on the board:

2.65 × 18 = 47.7
6.75 ÷ 1.35 = 5
0.8 × 18 = 14.4

Ask the children the following questions, and ask which fact would help them answer the question:
● *I have £14.40. I buy bags of sweets costing 80p each. How many can I buy?*
● *A length of ribbon measuring 6.75m is cut into five lengths. How long is each length?*
● *How heavy will 18 parcels, each weighing 800g, be altogether?*
● *A shop sells chocolate sponge cakes. Eighteen people buy them. The shop takes £47.70. How much does each cost?*

Lesson 9 (Apply)

Starter
Reason: Show this recipe for leek soup:

4 leeks
2 onions
½ l water
100ml cream
Serves two

Ask:
● *How many leeks will I need for soup for six people?*
● *If I have 1l of water, how many onions will I need?*
● *I have three onions. How many leeks should I use?*
● *I want to make soup for five people. What quantity of ingredients should I use?*
● *If I use six leeks in my soup, how much cream should I use?*

Main teaching activities

Whole class: Write the following question: *A cake uses 0.4kg of flour. As I have 1½ kg of flour, I can make four cakes. True or false?* Ask the children to discuss in pairs and feedback to the class, explaining their reasoning and rectifying the error.

Write the next question: *Is it true that 10 20cm lengths of string can be cut from a piece 2m long?* Again, ask children to explain their reasoning.

Independent work: Tell the children they are going to answer a selection of similar questions, for which they must explain their reasoning. Give out copies of the 'Be reasonable' activity sheet. Remind the children that they need to estimate where appropriate in order to check that their answers are feasible.

Review

Choose one question from each ability group to work through as a class.

Differentiation

Less confident learners: Provide the support version, which uses less challenging numbers that allow children to concentrate on the methods they have used to check the answers to the word problems.

More confident learners: Provide the extension version, which requires children to use decimals to 2dp.

Lesson 10 (Apply)

Starter

Recall: Pose a selection of questions relating to previous work on square numbers, for example: *What number multiplied by itself makes 400? What is the square root of 900? What is 21²? If 14 × 15 = 210, what is 15²?*

Main teaching activities

Whole class: Recap on the prime numbers between 0 and 100 and check that the children remember what a prime factor is. Try a few together such as the prime factors of 16 and 36. Ask the children what numbers have the prime factors 3 and 5.

Show how you could use prime factors to help you multiply, for example, 36 × 18. Find the prime factors of 18: 2 and 3².

36 × 3 = 108   108 × 3 = 324   324 × 2 = 648

Repeat for 25 × 28. The prime factors of 28 are 2² and 7.

25 × 7 = 175   175 × 2 = 350   350 × 2 = 700

Paired work: In pairs, ask the children to use prime factors to find 42 × 32 and 21 × 56. Check answers and ensure that the children are accurately finding the prime factors. Explain that it does not matter which number they break down in to the prime factors.

Independent work: Give examples for the children to work through in their books.

Differentiation

Less confident learners: This group should be supported to find the prime factors of the multiplier.

More confident learners: Include three-digit by two-digit numbers.

Review

Pose the following questions to assess children's understanding:
● *Which prime numbers are greater than 30 but less than 50?*
● *Tell me why 81 is not a prime number.*
● *What are the prime factors of 64? How can you use this information to multiply amounts by 64?*

Lesson 11 (Review)

Starter

Revisit: Write the following fractions on the board:

$$\frac{2}{9} \quad \frac{5}{18} \quad \frac{1}{2} \quad \frac{4}{6} \quad \frac{17}{18} \quad \frac{1}{3} \quad \frac{7}{9}$$

Ask the children to estimate, then order, from smallest to largest. Working in pairs, ask them to change each fraction to a common denominator and order. Were they correct?

Main teaching activities

Recap on tests of divisibility. Ask the children how to check that a number is divisible by 3, 4, 6 and 8. Give pairs time to check by trying examples on their whiteboards.

Elicit the following:

- A number can be divided by 3 if the sum of its digits is divisible by 3.
- A number can be divided by 6 if a number is even and can be divided by 3.
- A number can be divided by 4 if its last two digits are divisible by 4.
- A number is divisible by 8 if half of it is divisible by 4 or, with larger numbers, if the last three digits are divisible by 4.

Ask questions such as:

- *Is 362 divisible by 4? What about 932?*
- *Is 271 divisible by 3? What about 507?*
- *Will 2008 be a leap year? Explain your answer.*

Tell the children that tests of divisibility can be used to check results of calculations. Ask: *What other strategies could be used?* (Approximating.) Ask the children what they would do when estimating 3926×7? Elicit 4000×7. What about 6291×51? Elicit 6000×50.

Independent work: Give out copies of the activity sheet 'Check it'. Tell the children that they need to use the tests of divisibility, and approximations, to find answers to the questions.

Review

Recap on tests of divisibility and make a display of these on the maths wall so that the children can use them when necessary.

Write up the following numbers:

702   7992   162   8244   2214

Explain that all these numbers can be divided by 9. Ask the children if they can work out the divisibility rule. (The sum of the digits must be divisible by 9.)

Differentiation

Less confident learners: Provide the support version of 'Check it', which uses numbers to 9999 only, as it focuses more on practical understanding of tests of divisibility rather than complex calculations.

More confident learners: Provide the extension version, which includes decimals to 1 dp.

Lesson 12 (Teach)

Starter

Revisit: Recap on decimal/fraction/percentage equivalents: for example, ¼ = 0.25 = 25%. Check other common equivalents.

Write a number such as 260 on the board. Ask questions such as: *What is ¼... ¾... 20%... of this number?* Repeat for other numbers.

Main teaching activities

Whole class: Give out calculators to each child. Pose the following question: *Three consecutive square numbers total 110. What are they?* Ask the children to investigate using their calculators. Check that they record their results systematically to inform the next attempts. Check answers (25 + 36 + 49). Ask them how they arrived at the answer, looking for answers that relate to the fact that the numbers needed to be less than 50 and that approximating 35 + 35 + 35 = 105 would help to establish which square numbers would fit.

Differentiation

Less confident learners:
Multiplication questions should initially be two digits by one digit, with two-digit × two-digit calculations for those children who show good understanding.

More confident learners:
Devise questions that require multiplication of three-digit by two-digit integers and, in the case of using the inverse operation with decimals, ensure that both numbers use decimals to one place.

Write the next question: 23 ☐ × 5 ☐ = 12,561. Ask the children to work this out on their calculators. Discuss how they found the two missing digits. Elicit that they needed to find two digits that made an answer with 1 in the units column, hence 3 and 7. These digits then needed to be tried in each position to find the final solution.

Finally, ask the children to solve 52.4 × ☐ . ☐ = 445.4. Check answers. Ask them to explain how they arrived at 8.5. (By using the inverse operation 445.4 ÷ 52.4.)

Independent work: Give the children similar examples to work through in their books.

Review

Talk through some of the examples set and discuss strategies. Then pose the question: *Three consecutive numbers total 2280. What are they?* Discuss the starting point. Establish that the children know 10 × 10 × 10 = 1000, so the number must be bigger than 10. 20 × 20 × 20 = 8000 so numbers must be smaller than 20. Now it is easier to find the correct numbers needed. Encourage the children to use their calculators to find the answer.

Lessons 13-15

Preparation

For some lessons, you will need to draw, or import from whiteboard programs, 2D and 3D shapes as visual prompts.

You will need

CD resources
'Shape symmetry'.
Equipment
Plastic 2D and 3D shapes; opaque bag; OHP/board/interactive whiteboard protractor; protractors; nail boards and elastic bands; compasses; rulers; individual whiteboards and pens.

Learning objectives

Starter

● Make and draw shapes with increasing accuracy and apply knowledge of their properties.
● Find equivalent percentages, decimals and fractions. (Revision of Block E)
● Calculate mentally with integers and decimals: U.t ± U.t, TU × U, TU ÷ U, U.t × U, U.t ÷ U. (Revision of Block A)

Main teaching activities

2006
● Describe, identify and visualise parallel and perpendicular edges or faces; use these properties to classify 2D shapes and 3D solids.
● Make and draw shapes with increasing accuracy and apply knowledge of their properties.

1999
● Describe and visualise properties of solid shapes such as parallel or perpendicular faces or edges.
● Classify quadrilaterals, using criteria such parallel sides, equal angles, equal sides...
● Make shapes with increasing accuracy.

Vocabulary

parallel, perpendicular, regular, irregular, face, edge, vertex/vertices, polygon, names of 2D and 3D shapes including quadrilateral, rhombus, kite, parallelogram, trapezium, rectangle, parallelogram, triangle, isosceles, equilateral, scalene, radius, diameter, circumference, intersecting, intersection, bisect, plane, properties, angle, symmetry, diagonal

Lesson 13 (Apply)

Starter

Reason: Hide a selection of 2D shapes and 3D solids in a bag. Describe one at a time using properties such as angles and lines of symmetry. Ask the children to draw what each shape could be. Reveal the shapes to see how many they recognised.

Main teaching activities

Whole class: Draw a square on the board. Ask the children how many lines of symmetry it has, and draw them in. Using a board protractor, or interactive protractor, measure the angles between each line of symmetry. Establish that each angle is 90°. There are four angles which total 360°.

Independent work: Tell the children that they are going to investigate the measurements of angles between the lines of symmetry of different shapes. Give out activity sheet 'Shape symmetry' and protractors for each child. Tell them to draw the lines of symmetry on each shape. Ask them to design a table whereby they record the angle sizes and totals for each of the shapes. Ask them to measure the angles and record in their table.

Review

Invite children to share their results. What did they notice about the totals of the angles in each shape? (All = 360°). Did they notice any patterns or any links between the angles sizes? Discuss all their findings.

Differentiation

Less confident learners: This group may need to be supported in their use of a protractor.

More confident learners: Challenge the children to draw their own symmetrical shape as accurately as possible, and to repeat the angle-measuring activity for this shape.

Lesson 14 (Apply)

Starter

Revisit: Explain that you will say a fraction and the children should write the corresponding percentage on their whiteboards. Ask them to hold these up when you say *Show me*. Say, for example: $1/2$, $1/4$, $3/4$, $1/3$, $2/3$, $1/10$, $7/10$.

Main teaching activities

Whole class: Tell the children they are going to investigate the diagonals of quadrilaterals. Draw two squares of different size on the board and draw in the diagonals. Ask for the properties: for example, in each square, the diagonals are the same length and they intersect at right angles. They also bisect at the centre of the square.

Group work: Using dotty paper, the children should draw three different examples of each of the following: rhombus, rectangle, kite, trapezium and parallelogram. For each shape ask: *What is the common property?* Encourage children to come up with a general statement for each shape. For example: the diagonals of a kite intersect at right angles.

Review

Ask: *Which quadrilaterals have diagonals that intersect at right angles? Which quadrilaterals have diagonals which bisect at the centre point?*

Differentiation

Less confident learners: Some children may find it easier to construct their quadrilaterals on nail boards with elastic bands. Alternatively, they could use an ITP or other interactive program to help them generate the shapes needed.

More confident learners: Challenge the children to draw an irregular quadrilateral and to comment on the intersection of its diagonals.

Lesson 15 (Apply and evaluate)

Starter

Recall: Explain that you are going to ask division facts which children can derive from the multiplication tables. Ask questions such as: 40 ÷ 8, 81 ÷ 9, 72 ÷ 8, 720 ÷ 8, 36 ÷ 9, 360 ÷ 9 and so on.

Main teaching activities

Whole class: Give out compasses, protractors and rulers. Tell the children you are going to show them how to construct a triangle using a ruler and compass. Your triangle will be isosceles with sides 12cm, 8cm and 8cm. Explain that yours on the board will not be to scale as it would be too small for everyone to see!

Draw a line to represent the base. Label it 12cm. Open a board compass and show how the children would open theirs at 8cm. Place the compass at the end of one line and draw an arc above the base line. Put the compass to the other end of the base line and repeat. Where the two arcs cross, this will be the top of the triangle. Join either end of the base line to the top point to produce the triangle. Ask the children to draw the same triangle in their books using the same method.

As they are working, check that the children understand the method. Ask them to get their partners to check their measurements.

Paired work: Tell the children that they are going to teach their partner how to draw a shape using set items of equipment. Give each pair two tasks from the list below, according to ability. Each one of the pair should choose one of the tasks and work out what to do before explaining to their partner.

Sample tasks:

1. Draw a triangle with angles of 40°, 70° and 70° using a ruler and protractor.

2. Draw a rhombus using a ruler and protractor.

3. Draw a rectangle using a ruler and set square.

4. Draw a hexagon using a ruler and protractor.

5. Draw a kite using a ruler and protractor.

6. Draw a right-angled triangle with sides 10cm, 8 cm and 7cm. Choose your equipment.

Upon completion, partners should provide feedback about the quality of the instructions given so that the recipient can adapt their instructions.

Review

Choose one or two children to say their instructions to the rest of the class. The class should then follow them and construct the shape. Give opportunities for feedback about the quality of the instructions.

Now ask the children to write down what they have learned from this unit of work and which aspects they need to study further in order to become competent.

Differentiation

Less confident learners: Decide whether to work with these children as a group. Encourage them to explain what they are doing (and why) as they make each shape.

More confident learners: Ask these children to choose one of their shapes and to write instructions for drawing it which others can follow.

Name _____   Date _____

Monty the match snake

Monty the snake is made of matchsticks.

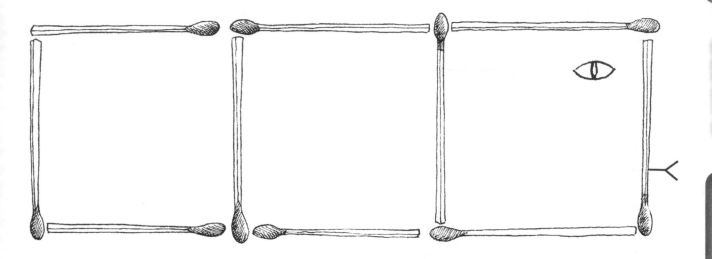

Count the number of matches that make up his head, and how many make each segment of his body. Can you write this as a formula? (Don't forget to include his head).

_____

If Monty has 10 segments in his body, how many matches will he be made of altogether?

_____

If he has 100 segments, how many matches altogether?

_____

Each time, show how you used the formula.

How would the formula change if Monty's body was made of pentagons rather than squares?

_____

_____

Name _____   Date _____

Formula 1

- **Match the expressions that mean the same thing.**

one less than t	t × l
double t	3t
t times itself	t − l
t	2 × t
treble t	t^2

- **Using the formulae area (a) = length (l) × width (w), l = a ÷ w and w = a ÷ l, solve these rectangle problems.**

1.
l = 12cm

w = 5.5cm

Find the area.

_____

2.
a = 52cm²

l = 8cm

Find the width.

_____

3.
a = 57.6cm²

w = 7.2cm

Find the length.

_____

- **Using the formula area of a triangle (a) = base (b) x height (h) ÷ 2, solve these triangle problems.**

1.
h = 10cm

b = 8cm

Find the area.

_____

2.
a = 35cm²

h = 7cm

Find the base.

_____

3.
a = 48cm²

b = 6cm

Find the height.

_____

BLOCK B Securing number facts, understanding shape

Name _____   Date _____

Number sequence

- **Use the digits 1 to 6 to make each side of the triangle total 9.**

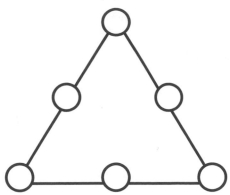

- Rearrange the digits to make balanced triangles with other totals for the three sides

- **Make more balanced triangles here using the digits 1 to 9.**
  Start with making the total for each of the three sides 17.

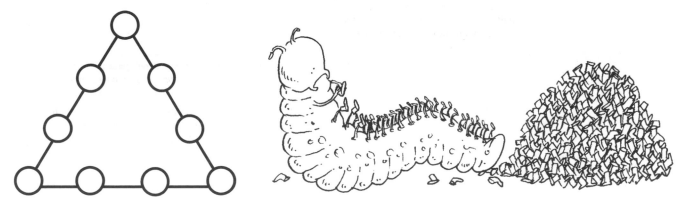

- **This shape is made up of two triangles. Use the digits 1 to 7.**
  Each straight line should total 12.

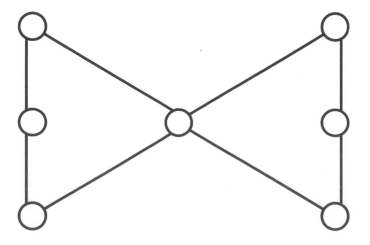

Securing number facts, understanding shape

Lesson	Strands	Starter	Main teaching activities
1. Teach	Use/apply	Tabulate systematically the information in a problem or puzzle; identify and record the steps or calculations needed to solve it, using symbols where appropriate; interpret solutions in the original context and check their accuracy.	Tabulate systematically the information in a problem or puzzle; identify and record the steps or calculations needed to solve it, using symbols where appropriate; interpret solutions in the original context and check their accuracy.
2. Practise and apply	Use/apply	**Use knowledge of place value and multiplication facts to 10 × 10 to derive related multiplication and division facts involving decimals (eg 0.8 × 7, 4.8 ÷ 6).**	As for Lesson 1
3. Teach	Use/apply	As for Lesson 1	Represent and interpret sequences, patterns and relationships involving numbers and shapes; suggest and test hypotheses; construct and use simple expressions and formulae in words then symbols (eg the cost of c pens at 15 pence each is 15c pence).
4. Practise	Use/apply	Represent and interpret sequences, patterns and relationships involving numbers and shapes; suggest and test hypotheses; construct and use simple expressions and formulae in words then symbols (eg the cost of c pens at 15 pence each is 15c pence).	As for Lesson 3
5. Review	Knowledge	**Use efficient written methods to add and subtract integers and decimals, to multiply and divide integers and decimals by a one-digit integer, and to multiply two-digit and three-digit integers by a two-digit integer.** (Revision of Block A)	Use knowledge of multiplication facts to derive quickly squares of numbers to 12 × 12 and the corresponding squares of multiples of 10.
6. Teach	Knowledge	Calculate mentally with integers and decimals: U.t ± U.t, TU × U, TU ÷ U, U.t × U, U.t ÷ U. (Revision of Block A)	**Use knowledge of place value and multiplication facts to 10 × 10 to derive related multiplication and division facts involving decimals (eg 0.8 × 7, 4.8 ÷ 6).**
7. Apply	Knowledge	Use a calculator to solve problems involving multi-step calculations.	**• Use knowledge of place value and multiplication facts to 10 × 10 to derive related multiplication and division facts involving decimals (eg 0.8 × 7, 4.8 ÷ 6).** • Use a calculator to solve problems involving multi-step calculations.
8. Review	Knowledge	Tabulate systematically the information in a problem or puzzle; identify and record the steps or calculations needed to solve it, using symbols where appropriate; interpret solutions in the original context and check their accuracy.	Recognise that prime numbers have only two factors and identify prime numbers less than 100; find the prime factors of two-digit numbers.
9. Review	Knowledge	Use approximations, inverse operations and tests of divisibility to estimate and check results.	Use approximations, inverse operations and tests of divisibility to estimate and check results
10. Teach	Shape	Describe, identify and visualise parallel and perpendicular edges or faces; use these properties to classify 2D shapes and 3D solids.	Describe, identify and visualise parallel and perpendicular edges or faces; use these properties to classify 2D shapes and 3D solids.
11. Practise	Shape	As for Lesson 10	As for Lesson 10
12. Review	Shape	As for Lesson 10	Make and draw shapes with increasing accuracy and apply knowledge of their properties.
13. Review	Shape	Represent and interpret sequences, patterns and relationships involving numbers and shapes; suggest and test hypotheses; construct and use simple expressions and formulae in words then symbols (eg the cost of c pens at 15 pence each is 15c pence).	As for Lesson 12
14. Teach	Shape	Calculate the perimeter and area of rectilinear shapes; estimate the area of an irregular shape by counting squares. (Revision of Block D, Unit 1)	As for Lesson 12
15. Apply and evaluate	Shape	As for Lesson 13	As for Lesson 12

Unit 3 ▢ 3 weeks

Speaking and listening objectives

● Use a range of oral techniques to present persuasive arguments and engaging narratives.

Introduction

There are a total of 15 lessons in this block. Using and applying is integrated into all lessons through discussion and application of problem solving skills. Children investigate sequences, patterns and relationships. They use their knowledge of multiplication facts to find square numbers and to derive related multiplication and division facts for decimal numbers. They investigate prime factors and use inverse operations and tests of divisibility. They use calculators to solve multi-step problems. The latter part of the unit focuses on shape. Children use properties to investigate 3D solids. They make and draw shapes accurately using a range of mathematical equipment.

The speaking and listening objective is covered in many lessons, but particularly in Lesson 10.

Use and apply mathematics

● Represent and interpret sequences, patterns and relationships involving numbers and shapes; suggest and test hypotheses; construct and use simple expressions and formulae in words then symbols (eg the cost of *c* pens at 15 pence each is 15*c* pence).

Lessons 1–4

Preparation

Lessons 1 and 2: Display the question for the main teaching activities.
Lesson 3: Before the lesson check the euro to sterling and US dollars to sterling exchange rates on the internet.
Lesson 4: Display the information needed for the Starter activity.

You will need

Photocopiable pages
'Sports kit' (page 92), 'Andrew's party' (page 93) and 'Foreign currency' (page 94), one per child.
CD resources
Support and extension versions of 'Andrew's party' and 'Foreign currency'. Interactive resource: 'Graphing and charting tool'.
Equipment
OHP/interactive whiteboard calculator; calculators; graph paper (preferably 1cm divided into 1mm intervals).

Learning objectives

Starter

● Tabulate systematically the information in a problem or puzzle; identify and record the steps or calculations needed to solve it, using symbols where appropriate; interpret solutions in the original context and check their accuracy.
● Use knowledge of place value and multiplication facts to 10 × 10 to derive related multiplication and division facts involving decimals (eg 0.8 × 7, 4.8 ÷ 6).
● Represent and interpret sequences, patterns and relationships involving numbers and shapes; suggest and test hypotheses; construct and use simple expressions and formulae in words then symbols (eg the cost of *c* pens at 15 pence each is 15*c* pence).

Main teaching activities

2006
● Tabulate systematically the information in a problem or puzzle; identify and record the steps or calculations needed to solve it, using symbols where appropriate; interpret solutions in the original context and check their accuracy.
● Represent and interpret sequences, patterns and relationships involving numbers and shapes; suggest and test hypotheses; construct and use simple expressions and formulae in words then symbols (eg the cost of *c* pens at 15 pence each is 15*c* pence).
1999
● Solve mathematical problems or puzzles, recognise and explain patterns and relationships, generalise and predict. Suggest extensions asking 'What if...?'
● Make and investigate a general statement about familiar numbers or shapes by finding examples that satisfy it; develop from explaining a generalised relationship in words to expressing it in a formula using letters as symbols (eg the cost of *n* articles at 15p each).

Vocabulary

problem, solution, calculate, calculation, tabulate, systematically, reasoning, predict, rule, formula(e), relationship, sequence, pattern, classify, criterion, criteria, generalise, construct, conversion, integer, decimal, multiple, factor, inverse, operation

Lesson 1 (Teach)

Starter
Reason: Tell the children that the number 786 has a digit sum of 21. *What other three-digit number has a digit sum of 21?* Ask for a few examples. Tell them that they are going to list all the three-digit numbers they can that have a digit sum of 21. Collect answers. How many can be made? How can the children be sure they have not missed any? Discuss how a systematic approach is needed. For example, list all the numbers starting with 99, then 98, then 97..., then 89, 88, 87 and so on. (Note: There are 28 solutions, 7 beginning with 9, 6 beginning with 8, 5 beginning with 7 and so on – the children should be able to see a pattern forming here as to how they can check all numbers have been generated.)

Main teaching activities
Whole class: Write the following on the board: 'In a local football league, there are 6 teams. If each team plays each other once, how many games will be played?' Ask the children to work in pairs to find the solution. Establish that there will be 15 games. Ask the children how they made sure that all the games were included. Share their methods. If not elicited, then show two possible methods:
1. Teams cannot play themselves, so 6 teams × 5 teams = 30, then halve this because teams only play each other once.
2. A systematic method such as

1 v 2   2 v 3   3 v 4
1 v 3   2 v 4   3 v 5
1 v 4   2 v 5   3 v 6 etc
1 v 5   2 v 6
1 v 6

   Discuss the importance of tabulating all possibilities when finding solutions to problems.
Paired work: Give out the 'Sports kit' activity sheet. Tell the children they must find out all the possibilities available for a group of sports teams who are buying new kit. In order for all possible outcomes to be listed, they should design a table to list results. The majority of the class should start on question 2.

Review
Show a selection of charts and tables produced and discuss the different layouts used. Decide on the most effective and discuss how easy it is to read the information to check that all possibilities have been included..

Differentiation
Less confident learners: This group should concentrate on question 1, which has fewer possibilities and requires a less sophisticated table.
More confident learners: This group should concentrate on question 3, which will need a more organised approach.

Lesson 2 (Practise and apply)

Starter
Rehearse: Chant the 4-times table. Ask the children to work in pairs to explain how the 4-times table can help when multiplying a number by 0.4. Share answers, establishing that you would multiply by 4 then divide by 10, so 4 × 8 = 32, and 0.4 × 8 = 3.2. Encourage the children to use this to produce a 0.6 table of answers and a 0.8 table of answers.

Main teaching activities
Whole class: Remind the children of the work covered in Lesson 1, and how charts or tables are needed when solving a problem to help record the information generated.
   Pose the following problem: 'In a doughnut factory, they make chocolate doughnuts and vanilla doughnuts, each with a choice of fillings: cream, jam, chocolate sauce or honey. The doughnuts are sprinkled in either sugar or nuts. Chocolate doughnuts cannot have jam, and vanilla doughnuts cannot have nuts. How many different kinds of doughnuts can be made?' Tell the children to work in pairs to find the answer, recording their work in a

systematic way. Share answers, asking the children to explain their methods. Establish that ten different types of doughnut can be made. Some children may have used a table, some a numerical formula. Again, remind them of the importance of recording results in an organised way in order to check results. The following table could be used to show children how the information could be arranged:

	Jam/sug	Jam/nuts	Honey/sug	Honey/nuts	Cream/sug	Cream/nuts	Choc/sug	Choc/nuts
Choc d'nut	×	×	✓	✓	✓	✓	✓	✓
Vanilla d'nut	✓	×	✓	×	✓	×	✓	×

Differentiation

Less confident learners: Provide the support version of the activity sheet, which has a limited set of possibilities.

More confident learners: Provide the support version of the activity sheet, which has a more sophisticated table of possibilities.

Independent work: Give out the activity sheet 'Andrew's party'. Explain to the children that Andrew's mum is preparing for Andrew's 11th birthday party. She has two tasks left to do and needs some help. Each task has more than one answer and she needs to know all the possibilities.

Review

Discuss the possibilities available for each of the questions. Ask a selection of children to explain how they set out their information. Invite the children to explain why they think their method is a particularly effective way to record results.

Lesson 3 (Teach)

Starter

Reason: Show the following calculation:

```
   795
 + 846
 ─────
  1641
```

Ask the children to work in groups to find out how many different calculations can be generated by using the digits 4, 5, 6, 7, 8 and 9 in three-digit add three-digit calculations. Encourage them to work as a group in a structured way by assigning different tasks to each child: for example, child A finds all the possibilities when the digit 9 is in the hundreds column of the top row, child B finds all the possibilities when 8 is in that position, and so on. State that the answers need not be found.

Check results. How many calculations can be generated? Which calculation is likely to give the biggest/smallest answer? How did each group approach the task?

Main teaching activities

Whole class: Remind the children about previous work on converting pounds to foreign currencies. Talk about exchange rates and why they are needed. Demonstrate, using an OHP/interactive whiteboard calculator, how to change from euros to pounds, or vice versa, by dividing or multiplying by the exchange rate. For example, 144 euros can be bought for £100. Ask questions for the children to work on in pairs using written methods or calculators, such as:
● *I have £50. How much is that in euros?*
● *A CD costs 20 euros. How much is that in pounds?*

Paired work: Give each pair a copy of the 'Foreign currency' sheet. Ask them to discuss methods of calculation and to work out each answer.

Differentiation

Less confident learners: Provide the support version of the activity sheet, which uses a tabular format.

More confident learners: Provide the extension version of the activity sheet, which uses more challenging amounts.

Review

Collect answers, discuss the children's methods and correct errors. Ask further questions based on exchange rates and challenge the children to ask

BLOCK B

Securing number facts, understanding shape

▷ and answer their own exchange rate questions. Supply the current exchange rates. Set homework: ask the children to find the exchange rates of three other currencies in preparation for Lesson 4.

Lesson 4 (Practise)

Starter
Revisit: Write on the board: '$3n - 2 = 10$'. Ask: *What is the value of n?* Establish that $n = 4$. Now try this one:

$$\frac{2n \times 4}{2} = 12$$

Remind the children that they can use simple expressions involving letters to record formulae. For example: *If pencil top erasers cost 20p, I can use the expression 20n pence to find out the cost of however many I wish to buy. If I buy five erasers, n would be 5, so 20 × 5 = 100p.*

Tell the children they are going to convert the following statements to simple expressions:
- The cost of *n* erasers at 9p each
- The cost of *n* apples at 26p each
- The cost of *n* bananas at 17p each

Ask the children to work out the cost of 13 erasers, 7 apples, 6 bananas, if *n* is the number bought.

Main teaching activities
Whole class: Remind the children of the currency conversion they undertook in Lesson 3. Explain that a conversion graph can also be used to work out exchange rates. Tell them that the currency on Mars is the zygot. There are 2.25z to £1. Draw the following graph on the board (or use the 'Graphing and charting tool' interactive resource):

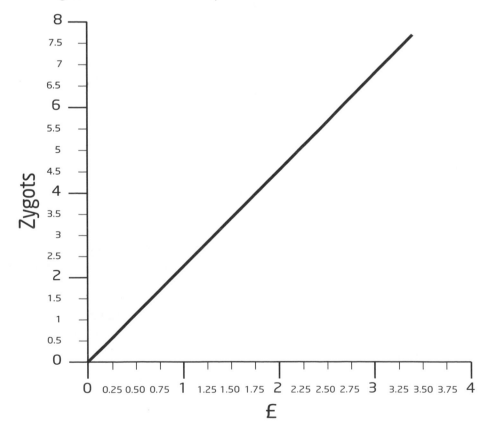

Show how to chart the relationship on the graph, and how to read from the conversion line. Ask: *How many zygots in £3? How much is 8 zygots worth?*

Unit 3 ⬛ 3 weeks

Paired work: Provide graph paper and tell children they are going to produce a conversion graph for the currency they investigated for homework (alternatively, you may wish to give out currency rates for children to use). Remind them to think very carefully about the scales they are using on each axis.

Once they have completed their graph, ask the children to compose five questions for another pair to answer and swap graphs with someone on their table.

Review

Ask pairs to evaluate the graphs they were given to use and feed back to the rest of the class on their effectiveness. Discuss any problems the children encountered, such as choosing a suitable scale, accuracy of graphs and so on, and discuss how these can be overcome.

Lessons 5-9

Preparation

Lesson 5: Draw the calculation outline several times on the board or on an OHT.
Lesson 6: Write on the board the question for the Starter activity.

You will need

CD resources
Core, support and extension versions of 'Finding solutions 1' and 'Finding solutions 2'.
Equipment
Calculators.

Learning objectives

Starter

● Use efficient written methods to add and subtract integers and decimals, to multiply and divide integers and decimals by a one-digit integer, and to multiply two-digit and three-digit integers by a two-digit integer. (Revision of Block A)
● Calculate mentally with integers and decimals: U.t ± U.t, TU × U, TU ÷ U, U.t × U, U.t ÷ U. (Revision of Block A)
● Use a calculator to solve problems involving multi-step calculations.
● Tabulate systematically the information in a problem or puzzle; identify and record the steps or calculations needed to solve it, using symbols where appropriate; interpret solutions in the original context and check their accuracy.
● Use approximations, inverse operations and tests of divisibility to estimate and check results.

Main teaching activities
2006
● Use knowledge of multiplication facts to derive quickly squares of numbers to 12 × 12 and the corresponding squares of multiples of 10.
● Use knowledge of place value and multiplication facts to 10 × 10 to derive related multiplication and division facts involving decimals (eg 0.8 × 7, 4.8 ÷ 6).
● Use a calculator to solve problems involving multi-step calculations.
● Recognise that prime numbers have only two factors and identify prime numbers less than 100; find the prime factors of two-digit numbers.
● Use approximations, inverse operations and tests of divisibility to estimate and check results.
1999
● Recognise squares of numbers to at least 12 × 12.
● Derive quickly squares of multiples of 10 (eg 60 × 60).
● Use factors; use known number facts and place value to consolidate mental multiplication and division.
● Develop calculator skills and use a calculator effectively.
● Recognise prime numbers; factorise numbers to 100 into prime factors.
● Check results of calculations
● Know and apply simple tests of divisibility.

Vocabulary

problem, solution, calculate, calculation, tabulate, systematically, reasoning, decimal, square number, multiple, factor, divisible, test of divisibility, prime, prime factor, inverse, operation, estimate, approximate

Lesson 5 (Review)

Starter

Revisit: Write the digits 1 to 9 on the board. Ask a child to call out six digits at random (say, 1, 4, 3, 9, 8, 2). The children should arrange the digits as an addition or subtraction sentence by filling in the boxes in this diagram:

Ask the children to arrange the six digits given previously so as to give a number as near to 10 as possible. Check answers. (Nearest answer is 8.94 + 1.23 = 10.17. Next best answer is 8.49 + 1.32 = 9.81.) Call out six more random digits. Ask for an answer as near to 2 as possible. Repeat for different totals.

Main teaching activities

Whole class: Recap on previous work covered in Block B. Ask: *How can we use 4^2 to find 40^2 and 400^2? How can we find 700^2?* Ask: *How can we use 30^2 to work out 30×32?* Elicit $30 \times 30 = 900$; $30 \times 2 = 60$; and $900 + 60 = 960$. *How about 20×26?* $20^2 = 400$; $20 \times 6 = 120$; and $400 + 120 = 520$. Give the children a similar selection to work out in their book, reminding them to use their knowledge of square numbers to help them.

Review

Discuss how using square numbers can help with multiplying. Pose this question: *A farmer has to quickly estimate the area of his field. He knows it measures 78m × 82m. What calculation would you advise him to use to work it out quickly?* Establish that 80^2 would be a good estimate. Work out 78 × 82. *How close is this to the estimate of $80^2 = 6400$?*

Differentiation

Less confident learners: Support this group with their calculations, ensuring that the correct number of zeros are used in the answer.
More confident learners: You may wish to include calculations to three digits such as 400 × 420.

Lesson 6 (Teach)

Starter

Reason: Write the digits 6, 5 and 9 on the board. Ask the children to arrange them as a U.t × U calculation to make as near to a whole number as possible. (Answer: 9.5 × 6 or 9.6 × 5, which both give whole-number answers.) Give out three more digits to investigate, for example 1, 4 and 7. Repeat as required. Ask: *In order to make an exact whole number, what digits are needed?* Elicit that a 5 and an even number are needed as the multiplier and the tenth.

Main teaching activities

Whole class: Pose this question: *Bathroom blinds are made using 1.5m of wire. I have 12.2m of wire. How many blinds can I make? How much more wire will be needed to make one more set?* Discuss the steps needed for solving written problems: read question; highlight information; choose method of calculation; estimate answer; calculate; check. As a class, solve the question. Ask for an estimation of how many 1.5m are in 12.2m and write it on the board. Encourage the children to use jottings to work out the actual answer. Establish that 1.5 × 8 = 12, therefore eight blinds can be made. Remind them to check the requirements of the question – they also need to find out how much more wire is needed to make one more blind. Establish that there is 0.2m of wire left, so a further 1.3m is needed.

Work though the next question: *My pet rabbit eats 160g of rabbit food a day. I open a 5kg bag on 1 June. Will I have enough food to last until 1 July, when I buy a new bag?* Again, discuss what information is needed to solve this problem and what methods the children need to use. (Answer: yes, I will have enough as I will have used 4800g.)

Individual work: Give out copies of 'Finding solutions 1'and ask the children to work individually on the sheet.

Review

Choose a selection of the children's own problems that they were asked to make up. Evaluate their success. Were the figures given used appropriately? Can the problem be solved with the information given?

Lesson 7 (Apply)

Starter

Refine: Give out calculators. Write on the board: 'I buy 2 bags of marbles. Each bag costs £1. There are 25 marbles in each bag. How much does it cost for 1 marble?' Ask the children to use their calculators to find the answer. Discuss the display and establish that 0.04 in the context of money means 4p. Ask the children what 0.04 would be if the question had been about litres (40ml) *What about kg?* (40g) *Metres?* (4cm) Check that all are able to interpret a calculator display correctly. Give additional practice if needed.

Main teaching activities

Whole class: Pose this problem: *Jars of toffees are packed in boxes of 10. A full box weighs 2.55kg. If an empty jar weighs 75g, what is the weight of toffees in each jar?* Work through the question together, establishing what needs to be found out with each step. Elicit that there are ten jars so you need to divide 2.55kg by 10. (0.255kg) Next, you need to subtract the weight of the jar. Establish that 0.255kg = 255g, so 255g – 75g = 180g. Therefore, the toffees weigh 180g. Ensure workings are shown on the board so that the children can see the importance of working in an organised manner, and that workings can be used to track back to any mistakes.

Pose the next question: *Each jar of toffees costs £5.40. I can buy identical toffees loose from the sweet shop. They cost £1.75 per 50g. Is it cheaper to buy the jar containing 180g or buy 180g loose from the shop?* Ask the children to discuss the problem in pairs and establish a method of calculation. Share ideas. Establish that they will need to find the cost of 1g of sweets by each method first. Encourage the children to work out the answer using their calculators.

£5.40 ÷ 180g = 0.03 = 3p per gram
£1.75 ÷ 50g = 0.035 = 3 ½p per gram

(More confident children may suggest finding 10g, therefore dividing by 18 and by 5.)

Establish that it is cheaper to buy toffees in the jar. Ask the children how much it would cost to buy 180g of toffees loose. Establish £6.30, 90p dearer than the jar.

Independent work: Give out the activity sheet 'Finding solutions 2'. Tell the children they are going to work through similar problems using their calculators. Explain that as they work through each stage of the problems, they should record their methods.

Review

As for Lesson 6, choose a selection of problems invented by the children and ask the rest of the class to solve them. Did the problems require more than one step in calculation? Were calculator displays read correctly?

Lesson 8 (Review)

Starter

Reason: Show the children how to find the digital root of a number: the digital root of 67 is 4, found by adding the digits together until a single digit answer is reached: 67 → 13 (6 + 7) → 4 (1 + 3). Ask half of the class to find

Differentiation

Less confident learners:
Provide the support version of the activity sheet.
More confident learners:
Provide the extension version of the activity sheet.

Differentiation

Less confident learners:
Provide the support version of the activity sheet.
More confident learners:
Provide the extension version of the activity sheet.

BLOCK B

Securing number facts, understanding shape

the digital roots of answers from the 3-times table up to ×12. Ask the other half to find the digital roots of the answers in the 6-times table up to 3 ×12.

Write each digital root sequence on the board. What do they notice? Why is this? (Both have the same digital roots. This is because all numbers which are multiples of 6 are also multiples of 3.)

Now ask the children to find the digital roots of the answers in the 8-times table up to ×12. What do they notice about the sequence? How would it continue? (8, 7, 6, 5, 4, 3, 2, 1, 9, 8, 7 and so on.)

Main teaching activities

Whole class: Recap on previous work in Units 1 and 2. Ask the children to write down the prime numbers to 100. Give them five minutes, working in groups, to do this.

Recap on prime factors and find the prime factors of 14, 16 and 27. Establish that for 14 they are 2 and 7, for 16 they are $2^2 \times 2^2$ and for 27 they are 3^3. Ask what the children notice about the prime factors of 16 and 27. Elicit that they have squares and cubes as their prime factors.

Paired work: Tell the children they are going to investigate which numbers have only squares and cubes as their prime factors. Ask them to find all these numbers up to 30.

Review

Share findings. Invite the children to explain how they were able to predict which numbers would only have square and cube prime factors.

Lesson 9 (Review)

Starter

Reason: Pose this question: *I think of a number, add 12 then divide by 8. My answer is 6. What was my starting number?* Ask the children to solve and explain how they would work it out. Elicit that they needed to use inverse operations. Pose similar problems such as:

- *I think of a number, subtract 17, then multiply by 4. My answer is 320.*
- *I think of a number, add 10 and multiply by 6. My answer is 153.*

Main teaching activities

Whole class: Tell the children they are going to revise tests of divisibility from an earlier unit. Ask them to tell you how they know a number is divisible by 10, 5, 2 and 25.

Tell the children they are going to investigate the test of divisibility for 9. Ask them to write down the digital roots of numbers in the 9-times table up to 9 × 10. What do they notice about the digital root? (The pattern is 9, 9, 9, 9, 9...) Ask them to check the digital root of 9 × 12 and 9 × 13. *Does the pattern continue?* (Yes.) Ask: *How can this pattern help us to check if any number can be divided by 9?* Elicit that if the digital root of a number is 9, then it can be divided by 9.

Put the following numbers on the board and ask the children to use the test of divisibility to see which numbers can be divided by 9.

945   206   2610   3753   1417

Paired work: Tell the children they are going to find the digital root of the 3-times table and use the answers to establish how to find out if a number is divisible by 3.

Review

Share results. Establish that a number is divisible by 3 if its digital root is 3, 6 or 9. A number is divisible by 6 if it is even and has a digital root of 3, 6 or 9. Put a selection of numbers on the board and check if they can be divided by 3 or 6.

BLOCK B
Securing number facts, understanding shape

Differentiation
Less confident learners: This group should work to 20.
More confident learners: This group should work to 60. Having found the answers to 30, encourage them to predict what the next set will be and then check their predictions.

Differentiation
Less confident learners: Provide adult support for this group in this investigation.
More confident learners: Ask this group to undertake the task with the 6-times table to find the test of divisibility for 6. They will need to test some numbers as the test of divisibility has two aspects to it and is not as straightforward as it first appears.

Lessons 10-15

Preparation

Lesson 10 : Display shapes on an interactive whiteboard.
Lesson 11: Display shapes on an interactive whiteboard. Also display the chart, leaving room for a number of rows.
Lesson 13: Display a net of a cuboid.
Lesson 14: Display the cuboid described in the Starter activity.
Lesson 15: Display the tables for the Starter activity.

You will need
Equipment
Plastic 2D and 3D shapes; images of shapes to display; access to a drawing program such as SuperLogo; one computer between two; thin card; scissors; glue or sticky tape; protractors; string, board compasses; compasses; rulers.

Learning objectives

Starter

● Describe, identify and visualise parallel and perpendicular edges or faces; use these properties to classify 2D shapes and 3D solids.
● Represent and interpret sequences, patterns and relationships involving numbers and shapes; suggest and test hypotheses; construct and use simple expressions and formulae in words then symbols (eg the cost of c pens at 15 pence each is $15c$ pence).
● Calculate the perimeter and area of rectilinear shapes; estimate the area of an irregular shape by counting squares. (Revision of Block D, Unit 1)

Main teaching activities
2006
● Describe, identify and visualise parallel and perpendicular edges or faces; use these properties to classify 2D shapes and 3D solids.
● Make and draw shapes with increasing accuracy and apply knowledge of their properties.
1999
● Describe and visualise properties of solid shapes such as parallel or perpendicular faces or edges.
● Classify quadrilaterals, using criteria such parallel sides, equal angles, equal sides.
● Make shapes with increasing accuracy.

Vocabulary
parallel, perpendicular, regular, irregular, face, edge, vertex, vertices, plane, polyhedron, prism, quadrilateral, polygon, names of 2D and 3D shapes, diagonal, circumference, diameter, radius, pi, net

Lesson 10 (Teach)

Starter
Recall: Play 'Guess the shape'. Hide a selection of 2D shapes in a bag. Describe one at a time using properties such as: *My shape has one pair of parallel sides and no perpendicular sides. What am I?* (Trapezium.)

Main teaching activities
Whole class: Give out a selection of cubes and triangular prisms on each table and, if possible, display these solids on an interactive whiteboard. (There are many programs that display solid shapes so that all faces can be seen.) Ask the children to describe the cube by referring to how many faces are parallel to the base and perpendicular to the base. Ask: *If the cube is moved on to a different face, does this information change? How many parallel faces does it have? How many perpendicular? What about the edges? How many are perpendicular to the base? What shape are its faces?*

Repeat for the triangular prism. Ask the children to imagine the prism has been sliced through in a plane parallel to the triangular face. *What is the result?* Explain that a prism is the same all the way through its length.
Paired work: Give out a selection of 3D solids such as a tetrahedron, square based pyramid, cuboid and hexagonal prism. Tell the children they are going to present a short narrative to the others in the group describing the properties of their shape in relation to parallel and perpendicular faces and edges. They will also need to explain what happens to their solid if it is cut through a variety of planes. If necessary, to ensure everyone is clear about the outcome, give a short narrative yourself, using the properties of the cube used earlier.

BLOCK B

Securing number facts, understanding shape

Differentiation

Less confident learners: Give this group the triangular prism so they can reinforce the properties learned earlier.
More confident learners: Give this group solids such as an octahedron or dodecahedron.

Differentiation

Less confident learners: This group should be able to complete the chart independently, but may need help in discovering the relationship between the vertices, faces and edges.
More confident learners: Include a dodecahedron and octahedron in their shapes and ask them to record their findings as a simple expression.

Review

Ask the children if any of them were given a particularly good presentation by a pair from their table. Ask these pairs to come to the front and present their narratives to the rest of the class.

Lesson 11 (Practise)

Starter

Refine: Repeat as for Lesson 10, but using 3D solids and giving clues relating to parallel and perpendicular faces and edges.

Main teaching activities

Whole class: Draw the following chart on the board:

Solid	Vertices	Faces	Edges
Cube			
Triangular prism			

Hold up a cube and triangular prism or display on the whiteboard and ask the children to help you fill in the information.
Paired work: Tell the children they will be given a selection of 3D solids (cuboid, tetrahedron, square-based pyramid, variety of prisms) and that they need to continue the table for each solid. Once finished, they need to explore the relationship between the vertices, faces and edges of each shape. What do they discover?

Review

Fill in the rest of the chart on the whiteboard for the additional solids. Ask the children what they found out about the relationship between the vertices (V), faces (F) and edges (E). Elicit that the number of edges can be found by adding the faces and vertices together and then subtracting 2. Ask the more confident group if they were able to write this as an expression. Elicit $(V + F) - 2 = E$.

Lesson 12 (Review)

Starter

Reason: Draw the following Carroll diagram on the board:

	Perpendicular faces	No perpendicular faces
Parallel faces	Cube	Triangular prism
No parallel faces	Square-based pyramid	Tetrahedron

Ask: *Are all the solids correctly positioned? If not, which should be moved and to where?* Ask the children to also correctly place a hexagonal prism and a cuboid.

Main teaching activities

Whole class: For this lesson, you will need access to computers (preferably one between two children). Use a drawing program such as SuperLogo. This lesson may need to be adapted depending upon the children's familiarity with the chosen computer program and their previous knowledge. Use the drawing program to demonstrate how to draw a kite. Discuss on-screen controls, angle of turn, and so on. In pairs, ask the children to describe how they would use the program to draw a parallelogram. One child should pretend to be the turtle and follow their partner's instructions. Encourage

▶ them to give feedback to their partner about how successful the instructions were.

Paired work: Tell the children they are going to program the on-screen turtle to produce given polygons. Assign a trapezium and a regular hexagon to the majority of the class. (Note: if children are familiar with using the program to draw polygons, you may wish to challenge them to produce 3D representations of solids.)

Review

Ask the children to give you sets of instructions for drawing their shapes. Follow them on the whiteboard as they give them out. Are they easy to follow? Are they successful? If they do not produce the required shape, ask the rest of the class to find and correct the errors.

Differentiation

Less confident learners: Give this group an equilateral triangle and a rhombus to draw.
More confident learners: Give this group an octagon and regular pentagon to draw.

Lesson 13 (Review)

Starter

Revisit: Write the following expressions on the board: $3a = 12$; $2n = 18$; $37 - y = 25$. Ask the children to find the values of a, n and y. (4, 9 and 12.) Write the following expressions on the board and ask the children to use the information above to solve them:

$(4 \times 6) \div a =$

Pencils cost n pence. What is the cost of $8n$ pencils?

$a^2 + n^2 =$

$(y - 8) \times (3n) =$

$$\frac{4y}{6} =$$

Main teaching activities

Whole class: Draw a net of a cuboid on the whiteboard. Ask the children to reproduce this on paper or thin card and work out the minimum number of tabs, and their positions, needed in order to be able to construct the cuboid. Ask the children to cut out their nets and see if the tabs are correctly positioned. Ask: *Were all the edges sealed correctly? Did anyone have too many/not enough tabs?*

Independent work: Give out protractors. Tell the children that they are going to work out the net of a triangular prism which has equilateral triangular faces of 7cm and rectangular faces of 10cm in length. Tabs must be included so that the net can be stuck together.

Differentiation

Less confident learners: Assign a square-based pyramid to this group and support them when drawing the triangular faces.
More confident learners: Assign this group a different solid such as a hexagonal prism or tetrahedron.

Review

Share the nets for the different solids. Set homework: ask children to choose a solid and produce a set that will fit inside each other as a nesting set.

Lesson 14 (Teach)

Starter

Recall and refine: Recap on the formula for finding the area of a rectangle (Year 5). Elicit $A = l \times b$. Draw a cuboid on the board (not to scale) with the dimensions labelled: length 12cm, breadth 6cm and height 4cm. Ask the children to use this information to work out the surface area of the cuboid (Year 6 progression to Year 7). Discuss methods used. Establish that you find the area of the large rectangular faces and multiply by 4. You then find the area of the small rectangular faces and multiply by 2. Both are then added together. (Answer: 240cm²)

Ask what would be a quick method of finding the surface area of a cube. Elicit the answer: finding the area of one face and multiplying by 6.

Main teaching activities

Whole class: Give out rulers, compasses and string. Draw a circle on the board and label the circumference, diameter and radius. Check all the children can use compasses accurately by asking them to draw circles with radii 4cm and 6cm in their workbooks. Ensure that they understand that if a circle needs a radius of 4cm, they need to open their compasses to 4cm.

Independent/paired work: Explain to the children that they are going to explore the relationships between the circumference, diameter and radius of a circle. Ask them to copy the table below into their books:

Radius	Diameter	Circumference

Ask the children to draw a series of circles in their work book with radii of 3cm, 5cm, 7cm and 9cm. For each circle, they should fill in the chart to show radius, diameter and circumference. The circumference can be found by using the string. Once the table is completed, ask the children to work in pairs to find the relationship between the radius and diameter, the radius and circumference and the diameter and circumference.

Review

Ask the children for their findings and establish that:
- the diameter is twice the radius
- the circumference is approximately three times the diameter
- The circumference is approximately six times the radius.

Differentiation

Less confident learners: This group may need extra practice in using compasses accurately. They may also need support in finding the relationships between the radius, diameter and circumference.

More confident learners: Once they have discovered the relationships, introduce these children to the sign for pi (π). Tell them that the relationship between the circumference and diameter of a circle is called pi and is approximately 3.142.

Lesson 15 (Apply and evaluate)

Starter

Revisit: Tell the children that a function machine multiplies a number by 9 then adds 6. This is written as $9n + 6$. Show the following table and ask the children to find out which answers are correct:

In	Out
6	60
3	31
8	78
4	52
2	25
12	114

Now show the next table, asking the children to work out the rule ($5n + 2$):

In	Out
5	27
11	57
4	22
15	77
30	152
2.5	14.5

Unit 3 ◻ 3 weeks

▷ ## Main teaching activities
Whole class: Tell the children they are going to investigate how to draw shapes accurately within circles. Explain that they can use the relationships between the radius, diameter and circumference discovered in Lesson 14 to help them.

Show how to draw an equilateral triangle within the circle. On the whiteboard draw a circle with board compasses. Tell the children you need to make three points at equal distances apart on the circumference. Remind them that the diameter of a circle fits into the circumference approximately three times. Draw a diameter across the circle. Open the compasses to the length of the radius (half diameter). Place the point of the compasses on one end of the diameter and swing the compasses in two directions to mark two points on the circumference of the circle. Using a ruler, draw lines to join the end of the diameter to the two marked points, and the two marked points to each other. Measure the sides of the triangle to check it is equilateral.
Independent work: Tell the children that they are going to construct their own shapes within a circle, ensuring that the vertices of the shape are on the circumference of the circle. Ask them to draw a circle in their book and investigate how to draw a regular hexagon inside.

Review
Ask individual children to show their shapes and describe how they constructed them.

Set homework: challenge the children to produce other designs within their circles using compasses and rulers. Examples could be:
● marking six points on the circumference and joining these points with arcs going across the circle to produce a six-petalled flower;
● drawing concentric circles then ruling lines across the circle, which produces a chequerboard effect when coloured alternately with two colours.

Invite the children to write down what they have learned from this unit of work and for which aspects they need more experience in order to become competent.

Differentiation
Less confident learners: Work with this group, reminding the children that the radius fits into the circumference six times. Ensure that they use this information as a starting point for their investigation.
More confident learners: Assign a regular pentagon to this group.

Name _____   Date _____

Sports kit

Three sports teams have asked their local sports shop to produce some new kit for next season. The shop has given them several options. Can you help them make their choice? Think carefully about how you are going to present your results, so that you can check that all possibilities have been covered.

Diamonds Netball Team need new skirts, tops and bibs. Here are their choices. What different kits can they have?

● Skirts: Skirts come in two designs – pleated or straight. Colours available are black, blue, green, red and grey.

● Tops: Tops can be short sleeved or cap sleeved. They come in white, yellow, pale blue or pink.

● Bibs: Bibs are either black or navy blue. They can have white or red letters on them.

Rovers Football Club need new shorts, shirts and socks. Here are their choices. What different kits can they have?

● Shorts: Shorts come in two designs – plain or with a stripe down the side. Colours available are white, black or blue. White shorts do not come with a stripe.

● Shirts: Shirts can be long sleeved or short sleeved. They come in red, blue, yellow, black or white. The red and blue are also available with stripes.

● Socks: Socks are white, red or black.

● Black socks cannot be worn with black shorts, and white shorts cannot be worn with white tops.

All-Stars Ice Hockey Team need new trousers, shirts, helmets and gloves. What different kits can they have?

● Trousers: Trousers can be black, red or blue. The red and black trousers also come with stripes down the side, and the blue ones can also be patterned with stars.

● Shirts: Shirts can be white, red, blue or green. Each colour (except white) can also be patterned with white stars. The white shirts can come with red stars.

● Helmets: Helmets can be white or black. The black helmets can have red stars printed on them.

● Gloves: Gloves are either black, brown or red.

● After looking at the kit, the team decide that they do not want striped trousers to be paired with the tops that have stars. Green shirts cannot be worn with blue trousers and white helmets cannot be worn with white tops. They do not like the red gloves at all!

Name _____   Date _____

Andrew's party

It is Andrew's 11th birthday and his mum is planning a party. Can you help her with the last two tasks?

For each task, show your results in a clear and organised way.

1. Andrew's mum has to make several plates of sandwiches. Here are her ingredients:

Type of bread	Filling	Accompaniment
brown	ham	tomato
white	cheese	cress
rolls	egg	cucumber
	tuna	lettuce

What different types of sandwich can she make, using just one ingredient from each list each time?

2. Andrew's mum would like to give every guest a party bag. Each bag should have 5 items in it and should cost no more than £2.50. What different combination of bags can she make?

Items:

pencil............................ 20p

magic trick.................. 90p

balloon......................... 20p

whistle 30p

sweets........................... 55p

yo-yo 65p

comic 50p

pack of cards 80p

Name _____   Date _____

Foreign currency

1. Complete the exchange rate table below, which shows pounds to euros.

Pounds sterling (£)	Euro (€)
£1.00	€1.44
	€28.80
£50.00	
	€93.60
£75.00	

2. Mrs Muller needs £250.00 in cash for her holiday. How many euros will she need to buy this amount?

_____

3. Jamie buys two souvenirs of his trip to Paris. They each cost €5.76. How much did he spend altogether in pounds?

_____

4. Last week the exchange rate was £1.00 = €1.37. If I changed £50.00 last week and again this week, what would be the difference in the value of the euros I would receive?

_____

5. A camera is available this week in London for £199.00. The same camera is available in Madrid for €270.00. Which is the best deal? Why?

_____

    PHOTOCOPIABLE ◖◗SCHOLASTIC

Handling data and measures

Key aspects of learning
- Enquiry
- Information processing
- Evaluation
- Communication
- Creative thinking
- Empathy

Expected prior learning
Check that children can already:
- construct frequency tables, pictograms, bar charts and line graphs to represent the frequencies of events and changes over time
- collect, select and organise data to answer questions; draw conclusions and identify further questions to ask
- use ICT to collect, analyse, present and interpret information
- find and interpret the mode of a set of data
- describe the occurrence of familiar events using the language of chance or likelihood.

Objectives overview
The text in this diagram identifies the focus of mathematics learning within the block.

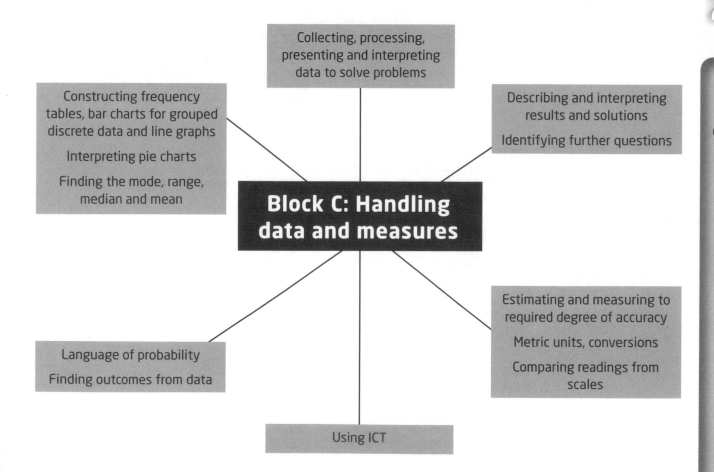

Collecting, processing, presenting and interpreting data to solve problems

Constructing frequency tables, bar charts for grouped discrete data and line graphs

Interpreting pie charts

Finding the mode, range, median and mean

Describing and interpreting results and solutions

Identifying further questions

Block C: Handling data and measures

Language of probability

Finding outcomes from data

Estimating and measuring to required degree of accuracy

Metric units, conversions

Comparing readings from scales

Using ICT

Handling data and measures

Speaking and listening objectives

- Make notes when listening for a sustained period and discuss how note-taking varies depending on context and purpose.

Introduction

The using and applying mathematics lessons that start this unit deal with the construction and interpretation of different forms of graphs, especially pie charts and line graphs. Children are also shown the importance of graphs in other curriculum areas, particularly science and geography. In addition, the unit explains the terms median, range, mode and mean and allows children to use them in context. Lessons towards the end of the unit provide practical opportunities to revise the use of metric units of measurement and to check children's ability to read a variety of measuring scales.

Use and apply mathematics

- Suggest, plan and develop lines of enquiry; collect, organise and represent information, interpret results and review methods; identify and answer related questions.

Lesson	Strands	Starter	Main teaching activities
1. Teach	Data	**Select and use standard metric units of measure and convert between units using decimals to two places (eg change 2.75 litres to 2750ml, or vice versa).**	Construct and interpret frequency tables, bar charts with grouped discrete data, and line graphs; interpret pie charts.
2. Teach and apply	Data	As for Lesson 1	As for Lesson 1
3. Apply	Data	As for Lesson 1	As for Lesson 1
4. Practise and apply	Data	Describe and interpret results and solutions to problems using the mode, range, median and mean.	• **Solve problems by collecting, selecting, processing, presenting and interpreting data, using ICT where appropriate; draw conclusions and identify further questions to ask.** • Describe and interpret results and solutions to problems using the mode, range, median and mean.
5. Practise and apply	Data	**Select and use standard metric units of measure and convert between units using decimals to two places (eg change 2.75 litres to 2750ml, or vice versa).**	Construct and interpret frequency tables, bar charts with grouped discrete data, and line graphs; interpret pie charts.
6. Teach	Data	Find the difference between a positive and a negative integer, or two negative integers in context. (Revision of Block A)	Describe and interpret results and solutions to problems using the mode, range, median and mean.
7. Apply	Use/apply	Calculate mentally with integers and decimals: U.t ± U.t, TU × U, TU ÷ U, U.t × U, U.t ÷ U. (Revision of Block A)	Suggest, plan and develop lines of enquiry; collect, organise and represent information, interpret results and review methods; identify and answer related questions.
8. Review and teach	Measure	Use approximations, inverse operations and tests of divisibility to estimate and check results. (Revision of Block B)	**Select and use standard metric units of measure and convert between units using decimals to two places (eg change 2.75 litres to 2750ml, or vice versa).**
9. Review and teach	Measure	Read and interpret scales on a range of measuring instruments, recognising that the measurement made is approximate and recording results to a required degree of accuracy; compare readings on different scales, for example when using different instruments.	As for Lesson 8
10. Teach and evaluate	Measure	As for Lesson 9	Read and interpret scales on a range of measuring instruments, recognising that the measurement made is approximate and recording results to a required degree of accuracy; compare readings on different scales, for example when using different instruments.

Lessons 1-7

Preparation
Lesson 1: Prepare a copy of 'Space days' for display.
Lesson 2: Prepare a copy of 'Charity graph' for display.
Lesson 4: Children will need data on weather from newspapers and other sources including the internet.
Lesson 6: Write the sets of numbers on the board for the main teaching activities.

You will need
Photcopiable pages
'Zarg the alien' (page 105) and 'What's the weather?' (page 106), one per child.
CD resources
'Cool down', 'What's the weather?' and 'Varik and friends'; 'Space days' and 'Charity graph' for display; support and extension versions of 'Zarg the alien'; core, support, extension and template versions of 'Money matters'. Interactive resource: 'Graphing and charting tool'.
Equipment
Access to internet for weather data; calculators; audio tape recorder; centimetre squared paper.

Learning objectives

Starter
● Select and use standard metric units of measure and convert between units using decimals to two places (eg change 2.75 litres to 2750ml, or vice versa).
● Describe and interpret results and solutions to problems using the mode, range, median and mean.
● Find the difference between a positive and a negative integer, or two negative integers, in context. (Revision of Block A)
● Calculate mentally with integers and decimals: U.t ± U.t, TU × U, TU ÷ U, U.t × U, U.t ÷ U. (Revision of Block A)

Main teaching activities
2006
● Solve problems by collecting, selecting, processing, presenting and interpreting data, using ICT where appropriate; draw conclusions and identify further questions to ask.
● Describe and interpret results and solutions to problems using the mode, range, median and mean.
● Construct and interpret frequency tables, bar charts with grouped discrete data, and line graphs; interpret pie charts.
● Suggest, plan and develop lines of enquiry; collect, organise and represent information, interpret results and review methods; identify and answer related questions.
1999
● Solve a problem by representing, extracting and interpreting data in tables, graphs, charts and diagrams, including those generated by a computer, eg line graphs (eg for distance/time, for a multiplication table, a conversion graph, a graph of pairs of numbers adding to 8); frequency tables and bar charts with grouped discrete data (eg test marks 0-5, 6-10, 11-15...).
● Find the mode and range of a set of data; begin to find the median and mean of a set of data.

Vocabulary
problem, solution, calculate, calculation, method, explain, reasoning, reason, predict, pattern, relationships, classify, represent, analyse, interpret, estimate, approximate, measure, millimetre (mm), centimetre (cm), metre (m), kilometre (km), gram (g), kilogram (kg), tonne (t), millilitre (ml), centilitre (cl), litre (l), data, information, survey, questionnaire, graph, chart, table, scale, interval, division, horizontal axis, vertical axis, axes, label, title, pictogram, bar chart, bar line chart, line graph, pie chart, frequency, mode, maximum, minimum, value, range, mean, average, median, statistics

Lesson 1 (Teach)

Starter
Recall and refine: Explain that you will write on the board some abbreviations for metric units. Ask the children to give each unit's full name, and give an example of how it could be used. Use km, m, cm, mm, kg, g, l, ml and cl. Now say: *Convert 2.125km to metres. How many metres is it? Change 500ml to litres.*

Main teaching activities
Whole class: Display the 'Space days' activity sheet. Explain that the data is represented by sectors – like the pieces of a pie. Each sector represents

BLOCK C

Handling data and measures

the proportion of items in that sector. Ask: *What proportion of a Monday does Zarg spend in each lesson?* Establish that ¼ or 25% of the time is spent learning Martian (two hours). This leaves six hours spent equally on astrophysics and intergalactic travel (three hours each). Now show how Zarg's friend on Pluto spends his day. Ask: *What fraction of a Monday does Yardok spend on each subject? Which of the two spends more time learning astrophysics?* Establish that we cannot tell because we do not know how long a school day is on Pluto. Tell the children a school day is 18 hours. Ask: *Now is it possible to find out who spends more time on each subject?* Stress that although the sector on Zarg's chart is bigger that on Yardok's, this does not mean it is a greater amount. It needs to be related to the overall amount in the whole chart.

Individual work: Give out copies of the 'Zarg the alien' activity sheet, which provides practice in interpreting and drawing pie charts.

Review

Check the children's understanding of pie charts by revisiting the 'Space days' activity sheet. This time change the number of hours in each school day and ask the children to give the value of each sector.

Lesson 2 (Teach and apply)

Starter

Revisit: Revise that children can convert quickly and mentally both ways between metric units to two decimal places. For example: 2.45m = 245cm, 407cm = 4.07m, 2.65l = 2650ml, 4750ml = 4.75l, 4500g = 4.50kg and 8.35kg = 8350g.

Main teaching activities

Whole class: Display the 'Charity graph' activity sheet. Explain that the graph shows the amount of money collected by a group of children who are raising funds for charity. Point out that the data is grouped and that each block shows a range of amounts. Ask the children to tell you the range for each block on the graph. Follow this up with other questions: *How many children collected between £15 and £19.99? Look at the block £0 to £4.99. What is the largest amount that could have been collected by this group?* (£4.99 × 5.) *What is the smallest amount?* (0 × 5.) Point out that the graph cannot tell us exactly how much was raised, as each block does not give an exact amount. Establish how many children were collecting for charity altogether. (50)

Paired/independent work: Encourage the children to imagine that the group has been collecting for a further two months. *What could the graph look like now?* Ask them to produce a graph of their predictions.

Review

Display the 'Charity graph' sheet again and revise the data shown. Then review the children's predictions as to how it might have changed. Establish that more children will appear in the last three blocks and fewer in the first three blocks, as the amount of money raised will have increased. Draw the predictions on the resource sheet. Explain that there is not a set answer as it is not possible to predict the outcome accurately. Establish that the number of children still adds up to 50. More able children may have added one or more blocks, £30-£34.99 and £35-£39.99.

Lesson 3 (Apply)

Starter

Reason: Ask the children what kind of metric units they would need to use to measure a number of different items. They should always give reasons for their answers. Use the following examples to start them off: the weight of an eating apple (g); the distance between two towns (km); the capacity of

▷ a glass tumbler (ml); the weight of an adult (kg); the length of a pencil (cm/mm); the length of a motor car (m); the capacity of a fish tank (l).

Main teaching activities

Whole class: Give out copies of the 'Cool down' activity sheet. Tell the children that the graph shows the results of a science experiment comparing how quickly hot water cools in different containers. A is a metal mug and B is a plastic disposable cup. Ensure that the children understand how to read the graph. Then ask them to fill in the missing information on the chart. Ask the following questions: *How many minutes does it take for A to reach 50°C?* (19 minutes approximately.) *How many minutes does it take for B to reach the same temperature?* (12 minutes approximately.) *For how many minutes is the temperature in container A above 45°C?* (25 minutes.)

Discuss what might happen if the temperature of each container was measured for a further 20 minutes. Ask: *Would there be a point at which A and B were the same temperature? Would the temperatures eventually drop to 0°C?* Establish that temperatures would become equal to room temperature and would fall no lower.

Group work: Ask the children to plot another set of data on the graph for container C, an insulated foam cup with a lid, using the data shown here.

Differentiation

Less confident learners: Provide adult support to ensure children plot the points in the correct positions on the graph. **More confident learners:** Do not provide this group with figures. Challenge them to plot what they think the rate of cooling would be and complete their own chart.

Time (minutes)	0	10	15	20	30	40	50	60
Container C (temperature in °C)	90	85	82	77	68	59	50	45

Review

Show on the displayed resource sheet the results produced by the groups. Ask the children to pose questions about the results for others in the class to answer.

Lesson 4 (Practise and apply)

Starter

Rehearse: The children will each need individual whiteboards. Give them four numbers to add together. Ask them to write the answer on their whiteboards and show it. They then have to divide the total by 4 to find the mean. For example: 25, 14, 26 and 31; total = 96, mean = 24. Repeat this with different sets of numbers

Main teaching activities

Whole class: Explain to the children that over the next two lessons they will be looking at planning for a holiday in the sun. Today you will be checking weather information. Discuss where this kind of information may be obtained, for example, five-day weather forecasts for some cities in Europe can be obtained from CEEFAX (BBC1) and from the internet.

Show the data in the table below and explain that this is the five-day weather forecast for Malaga for the first week in June. Ask the children if they can remember how to find the mean maximum daytime temperature (add the five entries and then divide the total by 5: total = 139, mean = 27.8). This will give the average or mean daytime temperature. Ask about the range of temperatures. Remind the children that this is the difference between the greatest and least of the data (30 – 26 = 4). Remind them that the median is the middle value (28). Go through the same process looking at the night-time temperatures

Paired work: Hand out copies of 'What's the weather?' and ask the children to find the range, the mode and the mean for each data set. Working with

	Daytime maximum	Night-time minimum
Monday	27	18
Tuesday	28	17
Wednesday	28	17
Thursday	30	19
Friday	26	14

Differentiation

Less confident learners: Let this group work with just one destination. Allow them to use a calculator. They may make a tape recording of their weather forecast rather than write it.
More confident learners: Make sure these children use all the information for their destination in their weather script.

a partner they should discuss what the weather would be like for the week.

Review

Ask the children to think about what the data tells them. Let some children read or play their weather forecaster's script. Compare scripts. Ask: *Have you interpreted the information in the same way? If there are differences, why? How might the script change if it was for a holiday programme promoting the resort?*

Lesson 5 (Practise and apply)

Starter

Refine: Provide the children with examples of measuring problems in which they have to convert units to find the solutions. Start with these examples: *A bottle holds one litre of water. David fills five glasses with water. He puts 120ml in each glass. How much water is left in the bottle?* (400ml.) *Four parcels weigh 0.4kg, 350g, 0.65kg and 245g. How much do they weigh altogether?* (1645g or 1.645kg.) Ask the children to make up their own puzzles that involve converting units in some way.

Main teaching activities

Whole class: Tell the children that if we are travelling abroad we need to be able to convert currency as well as metric and imperial units. Remind them that we tend to measure in miles, but in continental Europe they use kilometres. We use pounds sterling, but much of Europe uses euros.

Explain that the children are going to draw a conversion graph to help them to convert kilometres into miles and vice versa. If we know that 100km = 62 miles, we can easily draw a conversion graph. Use the 'Graphing and charting tool' interactive resource to draw the graph as a class. Say: *We are going to label the vertical axis miles, and put in the values from 0 to 100, in steps of 10. The horizontal axis will be kilometres from 0 to 100. We know that 0km = 0 miles, so we can mark the point 0,0. We also know that 100km = 62 miles.*

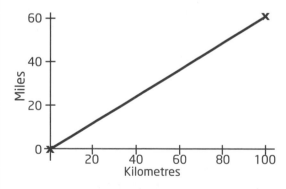

Ask a child to show you where 100km is on the horizontal axis, and where 62 miles is on the vertical axis. Say: *This gives us the point on the graph where we know the values are equal. We can now draw a line from 0, 0 to 100, 62. At any point on that line we can find the relative values for kilometres and miles.*

Demonstrate finding values for conversions from kilometres to miles and vice versa. Ask children to come out and find conversion values. Check that they are able to convert from kilometres to miles and vice versa.
Individual/paired work: The children should work individually or in pairs to draw their own conversion graphs, then answer the questions on 'Money matters' related to the graph. Remind them that there are 100 cents in one euro, and that this makes conversion simpler. They then make up conversion questions to ask their partner.

Review

Discuss any difficulties that the children have had. Ask the children how

Differentiation

Less confident learners: Give this group the support version of 'Money matters', where the conversion rate chosen is simpler (1.4 euros to the pound) and the questions use amounts that will convert easily using the graph.
More confident learners: Give this group the extension version of 'Money matters', where the questions are more complex and involve amounts outside the range of the graph. Children will have to break down these amounts in order to convert them. ▷

they could convert a larger amount of currency, such as £350 (it could be broken down into smaller amounts). Ask: *How would you convert values less than £1? Would the graph you have drawn be accurate enough?* Suggest to children that they draw another graph for values up to £1. Ask them to suggest the values to use and invite a child to draw the graph on the board. Use this to convert small amounts of money, such as 35p or 28 cents.

Lesson 6 (Teach)

Starter
Recall: Explain that you will write a list of integers onto the board, including negative numbers. Write up, for example, -25, 8, 15, -31, -14. Ask the children to order these, lowest number first. Repeat for other examples, such as 21, -21, 13, 27, -4, -19.

Main teaching activities
Whole class: Write the following numbers on the whiteboard: 3, 7, 2, 5, 3, 2, 1, 2, 4. Ask: *Which number appears the most?* (2) Explain that this is the 'mode' or the most frequent number. Write the following sets of numbers on the whiteboard: 11, 12, 13, 11, 10, 9, 11, 7 (11); 4, 3, 3, 3, 2, 4, 3, 4, 4, 6, 5, 6, 5 (3 and 4). Ask: *Which is the mode of each set?*

Explain that sometimes data is in groups, known as 'modal groups'. Draw this pocket-money chart on the whiteboard. Then ask: *Which amount of pocket money do most children receive?* (£4) Say: *This is the modal group.*

Amount of pocket money	£2	£4	£5	£6	£10
Number of children	5	8	4	3	3

Look at the first set of numbers again. Explain that you are now going to find the 'range'. Ask for the smallest number. (1) Ask for the largest number. (7) Ask: *What is the difference between them?* (6) *This is the 'range'.* Go on to find the range of the other three sets of data that have already been used.

Explain that yet another way of interpreting data is to find the 'median'. To do this the data has to be arranged in order of size. For example, for the numbers 1, 7, 12, 8, 13, 3, 1, the order would be 1, 1, 3, 7, 8, 12, 13. The median would be 7 because it is the middle number. Then find the medians of the other sets of data used previously. Explain what happens when there are two middle numbers because there is an even set of numbers in the group. In this case add the middle numbers and divide by 2.

Lastly, tell children they are going to find the 'mean' or 'average' of a set of data. Ask them to imagine that a parent wants to know how well their child is doing in spelling tests. It would take too long to go through every result, so the teacher would give an average score. For example, Shannon's test scores over a week were 13/20, 16/20, 12/20, 19/20 and 15/20. Ask the children to estimate her average score. Then show them how to work it out. Add the scores (75). Divide by the number of tests (5): 75 ÷ 5 = 15. So, on average Shannon gets 15/20. Sometimes she is below her average (13 and 12) and sometimes she is above her average (16 and 19).
Independent work: Let the children work on the 'Varik and friends' activity sheet, which contains questions relating to mode, range and median.

Review
Ask for volunteers to explain the meaning of the words 'mode', 'median', 'range' and 'mean'. Encourage them to give real-life contexts in which they would be used – for example, the mode of a group of children's trainers sizes, the median in a survey of children's heights.

Differentiation
Less confident learners: This group should focus on questions 1 to 4 of the activity sheet. Work with them to ensure they receive support, particularly with questions 3 and 4.
More confident learners: Encourage this group to work through the activity sheet as quickly as possible so they can move on to question 5, which deals with finding the mean.

BLOCK C

Handling data and measures

Lesson 7 (Apply)

Starter
Revise: Play the game 'Show me' on individual whiteboards. Ask the children to show the double of each number you call out. Start with these examples: 72, 126, 3.8, 0.7, 0.15. Explain that one way to solve these questions is to double the most significant figure first.

Main teaching activities
Whole class: Examine the following statement: *Sanjay tells everyone that the 'e' and 'o' keys on the keyboard of his word processor will wear out first because these are the commonest two vowels that you use in written text.* Ask the children to suggest ways in which they could investigate to see if this statement is true. What information will they need to collect? How will they collect it? What will be the best way of displaying the information? Elicit that they will need to study a range of passages of text to see if the statement is true. To make the enquiry fair, every piece of text should contain the same number of words (say, 100). Also that the best way to show the information would be a bar graph to display how often vowels occur each time.

Paired work: Pair up the children and ask them to select a page of text at random from a book, newspaper or magazine. They should identify a passage of 100 words and then count up the number of times a, e, i, o, u have been used. Suggest they use a tally system of counting. The results should then be recorded in the form of a bar graph.

Review
Look at the examples of graphs that the children have produced. Make a class display of them. Discuss with the children how they carried out the enquiry. *Was Sanjay's statement correct? Which vowels had been used most? Which vowel had been used fewest times?*

Differentiation
Less confident learners: Check that this group have selected the 100-word passage carefully, that they are able to record the information on squared paper including the correct use of scale, suitable labelling, etc.
More confident learners: This group could check to see if results remain the same if the length of passage is increased to, say, 200 words. Or they could investigate the frequency of use of consonants, ie letters that are not vowels.

Lessons 8-10

Preparation
Lessons 8 and 9: Have available the various types of equipment needed for practical measuring tasks.
Lesson 10: Collect food and drink packaging.

You will need
Photocopiable pages
'Measure by measure' (page 107), one per child.
CD resources
Support, extension and template versions of 'Measure by measure'; core, support, extension and template versions of 'On the line'.
Equipment
Measuring equipment including rulers, measuring sticks, tapes, trundle wheels, weighing scales, spring balances, measuring jugs and cylinders; suitable small objects for measuring; selection of food and drink packaging.

Learning objectives

Starter
● Use approximations, inverse operations and test of divisibility to estimate and check results. (Revision of Block B)
● Read and interpret scales on a range of measuring instruments, recognising that the measurement made is approximate and recording results to a required degree of accuracy; compare readings on different scales, for example when using different instruments.

Main teaching activities
2006
● Select and use standard metric units of measure and convert between units using decimals to two places (eg change 2.75 litres to 2750ml, or vice versa).
● Read and interpret scales on a range of measuring instruments, recognising that the measurement made is approximate and recording results to a required degree of accuracy; compare readings on different scales, for example when using different instruments.
1999
● Use, read and write standard metric units, including their abbreviations, and relationships between them; convert smaller to larger units and vice versa.
● Suggest suitable units and measuring equipment to estimate or measure length, mass and capacity.
● Record estimates and readings from scales to a suitable degree of accuracy.

BLOCK C Handling data and measures

▷ **Vocabulary**
estimate, measure, standard metric units of measurement and their abbreviations

Lesson 8 (Review and teach)

Starter
Reason: Tell the children that if they wanted to work out the calculation 602 – 287, they could first estimate the answer by rounding the integers to 600 and 300. The answer will therefore be about 300. Ask the children to find the approximate answers to the following questions, rounding off numbers to the nearest 10, 100, 1000 or whole number as appropriate: 36.9 – 8.6; 779 – 213; 7.6 × 3.9; 1872 + 3899; 41.7 ÷ 5.8, 492 + 89 + 503; 27.4 × 3.8; 50.2 – 9.6; 2046 – 205; 63.9 ÷ 7.7. Discuss answers and ask the children to explain their choices when rounding up or down.

Main teaching activities
Whole class: Remind everyone that there are 1000m in a kilometre, 1000ml in a litre, 1000g in a kilogram, 1000mm in a metre and 100cm in a metre. Show the children that 3kg 125g can be written in two other ways, by converting to grams (3125g) or as a decimal fraction of a kilogram (3.125kg). If written as a decimal fraction, only the kg unit is used, not the g. Ask the children to write 4732g in two other ways on their whiteboards. Discuss the answers. Then try the following as a whole class.

465m	=	km	or	km	m
1.25l	=	ml	or	l	ml
76m	=	cm	or	km	
2km 5m =		km	or	m	

For each of these, stress the importance of place value, especially the use of zero as a place holder. You may need to draw a place value chart on the board as each measurement is converted. For example, 2km 5m:

T	U	.	t	h	th
	2	.	0	0	5

Repeat this activity, if necessary, for kilograms and litres. By the end of the lesson, the children should know the equivalent of one thousandth of a kilometre, a kilogram and a litre in metres, grams and millilitres.

Independent work: Provide the children with the 'Measure by measure' activity sheet, which gives them practice in converting measurements. You will also need to provide rulers, tape measures and weighing scales, plus a measuring jug and some plastic cups for children to use for question 4. Explain to the children how they should use these.

Review
Display a place value chart. Ask the children where they would place 1m, 10m, 100m and 1000m. Repeat the process for 1g, 10g, 100g and 1000g and for 1ml, 10ml, 100ml and 1000ml. Check that they understand the importance of the zero when writing these measurements, for example 1m = 0.001km.

Differentiation
Less confident learners: Provide this group with the support version of 'Measure by measure', which contains examples relating to the conversion of larger units to smaller units.
More confident learners: This group should work on the extension version of 'Measure by measure', which will extend their thinking about converting smaller to larger units.

Lesson 9 (Review and teach)

Starter
Review: Provide the children with two measurement points from a scale and ask them to give you a measurement that would come between them. Put the points on the whiteboard as a scale if it helps. Try these examples: 4cm and 6cm (one decimal place), 1.7m and 1.9km (two decimal places), 4.6km and 5.6km (two decimal places), 3kg and 5kg (two decimal places) and 7l and 10l (two decimal places).

Main teaching activities
Whole class: Ask the children to list common units of length. Look for

BLOCK C

Handling data and measures

kilometre, metre, centimetre, decimetre and millimetre. Tell the children that these are all metric measurements. Rehearse the relationship between them. Remind the children that 1000m = 1km, 100cm = 1m, 10cm = 1dcm and 10mm = 1cm. Also explain the vocabulary. Say: *'Kilo' means 1000, 'centi' means* $^1/_{100}$*. This helps us to know how big units are. A centimetre is* $^1/_{100}$ *of a metre. If 'milli' means* $^1/_{1000}$*, how many millimetres are there in 1 metre?* Then ask some quick-fire questions relating to converting smaller into larger units. Use the following examples. *How many centimetres are there in ¾ of a metre? How many millimetres are there in 6 metres? How many centimetres are there in 3.6 metres? How many millimetres are there in 12.5 centimetres? How many metres are there in 4.2 kilometres?* Remind the children of previous work, when they wrote measurements in different ways, such as: 9076m = 9km 76m = 9.076km. Try a few as revision. For example, write these measurements in two different ways: 126cm, 1.3m, 2km 5m.

Paired work: Provide a range of measuring equipment, such as rulers, metre sticks, tape measures and so on. Tell the children they are to measure a range of objects in the classroom, such as the height of the table, length of books, circumference of a friend's head. Stress that they need to choose the correct equipment for the task. Tell them also that the measurements need to be recorded in two different ways using the type of chart shown below. Encourage accuracy, ie measuring to the nearest millimetre. Ensure that the children estimate lengths before measuring each object.

Object	Estimate	Measurement 1	Measurement 2
Maths book	25cm	25cm	0.25m

Review
Recap on the relationships between the metric units of length. Say: *A table is 1200mm in length. How would this be written in (a) centimetres; (b) metres?* Check that the children can convert between the units.

Lesson 10 (Teach and evaluate)

Starter
Review: Ask the children to tell you the value of each interval on certain scales found on the sides of measuring cylinders. Draw the scales on the whiteboard for the children to look at, such as: 0–500ml, four divisions (100ml); 0–100ml, three divisions (25ml); 0–100ml, one division (50ml); 0–100ml, nine divisions (10ml); 0–100ml, four divisions (20ml).

Main teaching activities
Whole class: Show the children a collection of food packets, containers and so on that are clearly labelled with metric units. Talk about the amounts of grams, litres and millilitres that are shown. Highlight any that have the letter 'e' on them either before or after the weight. Explain that the letter 'e' stands for 'excluding' and means the weight or capacity of the food item inside the packaging but not including the weight of the tin, jar, carton, box or bottle. Also display a variety of measuring instruments used for finding length (rulers, tapes), mass (weighing scales, spring balances) and capacity (measuring cylinders). Look carefully at the scales shown on them and discuss how they are organised. Enlarged versions of some of these should be displayed on the OHP for discussion purposes.

Paired work: Let the children work in pairs on 'On the line', where they have to read amounts from a variety of scales showing length, mass and capacity.

Review
Ask children from the more confident group to make a short presentation to the class. What objects did they choose? What equipment did they use? Which units were the most suitable? What results did they obtain? Ask: *What have you learned in this unit? Which aspects do you need to practise more?*

Differentiation
Less confident learners: Ensure this group is confident about using the equipment available. Check that measurements start from zero and not from the edge of the ruler, for example.
More confident learners: Encourage this group to find the perimeters of large objects, such as the playground, with tape measures and trundle wheels and then show their results in scale drawings.

Differentiation
Less confident learners: Give this group the support version of 'On the line', with simpler problems. Give them practice filling in scales with some of the numbers missing. Initially measurements can be rounded off, for example to the nearest half-centimetre (length), nearest quarter of a kilogram (mass) and nearest 100 millilitres (capacity).
More confident learners: Start this group with the extension version of 'On the line'. Then work with them while they measure the length, mass and capacity of selected objects in the classroom, using a variety of equipment with a range of different scales.

Name _____   Date _____

Zarg the alien

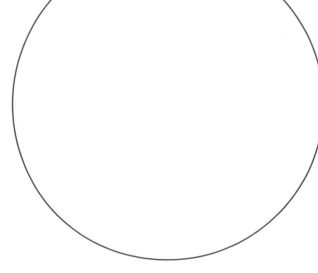

This is a pie chart to show the lesson plan for a Martian school on a Wednesday.

A typical school day for Zarg lasts 8 hours.

1. What fraction of the day does Zarg spend on each lesson?

_____   _____

_____   _____

2. How long, in hours, does each lesson last?

_____   _____

_____   _____

3. What percentage of the time is spent on maths? _____

Complete the pie chart, which shows the lesson plan for a Plutonian school on a Wednesday.

A typical school day for Yardok lasts 12 hours.

4. Fill in Yardok's typical school day if Triludian maths lasts for $\frac{3}{12}$ of the day, modern foreign languages lasts for $\frac{2}{12}$ of the day, time travel takes up $\frac{6}{18}$ of the day and the rest of the day is spent learning hover-boarding skills.

5. How long does Yardok spend on each subject?

_____   _____

_____   _____

6. Who has the longest maths lesson, Zarg or Yardok? _____

Name _____   Date _____

What's the weather?

Here are some five-day weather forecasts for temperatures (°C) in some cities in Europe.

Lisbon

| Maximum | 27 | 28 | 29 | 30 | 26 |
| Minimum | 13 | 15 | 19 | 17 | 16 |

Amsterdam

| Maximum | 21 | 22 | 23 | 25 | 23 |
| Minimum | 4 | 10 | 11 | 12 | 13 |

Rome

| Maximum | 25 | 26 | 26 | 21 | 25 |
| Minimum | 14 | 16 | 17 | 18 | 17 |

Athens

| Maximum | 27 | 27 | 28 | 28 | 24 |
| Minimum | 18 | 15 | 18 | 19 | 17 |

- Calculate the mean, mode and range for each city, for both the maximum and minimum temperatures.

	mean	mode	range
Lisbon Maximum			
Lisbon Minimum			
Amsterdam Maximum			
Amsterdam Minimum			
Rome Maximum			
Rome Minimum			
Athens Maximum			
Athens Minimum			

- Choose one destination and write a script for the television weather forecaster to describe the expected weather for the week.

Name _____   Date _____

Measure by measure

1. Write each of the measurements in two other ways.

2kg 36l g   = _____ and _____

4726g   = _____ and _____

36cm   = _____ and _____

146m   = _____ and _____

6km 860m   = _____ and _____

27ml   = _____ and _____

3060ml   = _____ and _____

2. Measure the length of your exercise book. Write the answer in these three different ways.

_____ cm   _____ mm   _____ m

3. Measure the height of your table. Write the answer in these three different ways.

_____ cm   _____ mm   _____ m

4. Estimate how much water the plastic cup holds. Use the measuring jug to check your answer. Write the answer in three different ways.

_____ estimate   _____ ml   _____ l   _____ ?

5. Choose two items to weigh, such as your exercise book or pencil case. Write the answers below.

Item 1 _____ g _____ kg

Item 2 _____ g _____ kg

BLOCK C

Handling data and measures

Handling data and measures

Speaking and listening objectives
● Use a range of oral techniques to present a persuasive argument.

Introduction
Initially this unit of ten lessons provides opportunities for children to use and apply their mathematical skills by reading and interpreting straight-line conversion graphs and pie charts. They also have the chance to experience solving problems by looking for and interpreting clues found in certain types of data. There is also revision of key data handling terms like mode, range, median and mean and practical work that explores probability, likelihood and chance. Working with metric units is revisited, and there are also comparisons with imperial units still in use.

Use and apply mathematics
● Solve problems by collecting, selecting, processing, presenting and interpreting data, using ICT where appropriate; draw conclusions and identify further questions to ask.

Lesson	Strands	Starter	Main teaching activities
1. Teach	Data	Calculate mentally with integers and decimals: U.t ± U.t, TU × U, TU ÷ U, U.t × U, U.t ÷ U. (Revision of Block A)	Construct and interpret frequency tables, bar charts with grouped discrete data, and line graphs; interpret pie charts.
2. Teach and apply	Data	Use approximations, inverse operations and tests of divisibility to estimate and check results. (Revision of Blocks A and B)	As for Lesson 1
3. Review	Data	Use decimal notation for tenths, hundredths and thousandths; partition, round and order decimals with up to three places, and position them on the number line. (Revision of Block A)	**Solve problems by collecting, selecting, processing, presenting and interpreting data, using ICT where appropriate; draw conclusions and identify further questions to ask.**
4. Teach and apply	Data	Calculate mentally with integers and decimals: U.t ± U.t, TU × U, TU ÷ U, U.t × U, U.t ÷ U. (Revision of Block A)	As for Lesson 3
5. Review	Data	As for Lesson 4	Describe and interpret results and solutions to problems using mode, range, median and mean.
6. Teach	Data	Use a calculator to solve problems involving multi-step calculations.	Describe and predict outcomes from data using the language of chance or likelihood.
7. Practise	Data	As for Lesson 6	As for Lesson 6
8. Apply	Measure	Read and interpret scales on a range of measuring instruments, recognising that the measurement made is approximate and recording results to a required degree of accuracy; compare readings on different scales, for example when using different instruments.	Read and interpret scales on a range of measuring instruments, recognising that the measurement made is approximate and recording results to a required degree of accuracy; compare readings on different scales, for example when using different instruments.
9. Review	Measure	**Select and use standard metric units of measure and convert between units using decimals to two places (eg change 2.75 litres to 2750ml, or vice versa).**	**Select and use standard metric units of measure and convert between units using decimals to two places (eg change 2.75 litres to 2750ml, or vice versa).**
10. Review and evaluate	Measure Calculate	As for Lesson 9	**• Select and use standard metric units of measure and convert between units using decimals to two places (eg change 2.75 litres to 2750ml, or vice versa).** • Use a calculator to solve problems involving multi-step calculations.

Lessons 1-4

Preparation

Lesson 1: Check current rates of exchange.

Lesson 2: Prepare 'Conversion graphs' for display and write conversion questions on the whiteboard.

Lesson 3: Prepare general resource sheets 'Pie charts 1–4' for display.

Lesson 4: Note that if a different time-zone map is used or if the website worldtimezone.com is accessed, the time zones may be marked differently from those on the resource sheet. Before the lesson draw the table templates on the whiteboard.

You will need

Photocopiable pages

'Conversion graphs' (page 117), one per pair.

CD resources

'World time zones'. General resource sheets: 'Pie chart 1', 'Pie chart 2', 'Pie chart 3' and 'Pie chart 4'. Interactive resource: 'Graphing and charting tool'.

Equipment

Counting stick; centimetre squared paper; 360° protractors; globe.

Learning objectives

Starter

● Calculate mentally with integers and decimals: U.t ± U.t, TU × U, TU ÷ U, U.t × U, U.t ÷ U. (Revision of Block A)

● Use approximations, inverse operations and tests of divisibility to estimate and check results. (Revision of Blocks A and B)

● Use decimal notation for tenths, hundredths and thousandths; partition, round and order decimals with up to three places, and position them on the number line. (Revision of Block A)

Main teaching activities

2006

● Construct and interpret frequency tables, bar charts with grouped discrete data, and line graphs; interpret pie charts.

● Solve problems by collecting, selecting, processing, presenting and interpreting data, using ICT where appropriate; draw conclusions and identify further questions to ask.

1999

● Solve a problem by representing, extracting and interpreting data in tables, graphs, charts and diagrams, including those generated by a computer, eg line graphs (eg for distance/time, for a multiplication table, a conversion graph, a graph of pairs of numbers adding to 8); frequency tables and bar charts with grouped discrete data (eg test marks 0–5, 6–10, 11–15…).

Vocabulary

graph, chart, table, scale, interval, division, horizontal axis, vertical axis, axes, label, title, pictogram, bar chart, bar line chart, line graph, pie chart, conversion graph, constant proportion, GMT (Greenwich Mean Time), IDL (International Date Line)

Lesson 1 (Teach)

Starter

Refine: Provide the children with the answer to a division calculation (eg 9). They have to write on their whiteboards as many facts as possible that will have this answer, for example, 63 ÷ 7 = 9. Give them a time limit (say, 45 seconds), then share the responses. Move on to other numbers (eg 6 or 8). Encourage use of fractions, decimals and percentages, such as $^3/_9$ of 27.

Main teaching activities

Whole class: Use the 'Graphing and charting tool' interactive resource to draw the following conversion graph: Josh and Sarah take part in a charity bicycle ride at a steady rate of 2km per half-hour. Plot the journey over 180 minutes. (See diagram.) Explain that points in between each marked division have a value. Ask questions such as: *How long did it take for the children to travel 6km? How long did it take the children to travel 11km?* Explain that this is a conversion graph to show the relationship between two units of measurement and that intermediary points have values.

Independent work:

Give out current rates of exchange from the local bank or the internet, or cut out the details from

▶

Differentiation

Less confident learners: Choose a currency for this group that will be straightforward to convert.
More confident learners: When this group has completed the graph, challenge them to make up questions based on it for the rest of the class to answer.

a newspaper. Ask the children to plot their own conversion graph to change £s to another currency (avoid using the euro as this is featured in the next lesson). Calculators can be used with conversions. (They could use the 'Graphing and charting tool' to do this if appropriate.)

Review

Use the graph from the main teaching activities. Tell the children that another child has joined the charity ride. Although she travels at 2km per ½ hour, she takes a 15-minute break after each hour of cycling. How would this be plotted on the graph? (It would be plotted as a straight line, keeping the same distance value, for 15 minutes of time.)

Lesson 2 (Teach and apply)

Starter

Recall: Write on the board a three-digit number such as 456 and ask: *Will this number divide exactly by 4? How can you tell? What about by 8?* Encourage the children to explain how they worked this out. Revise other tests for divisibility, such as for dividing 348 by 2, 3, 4, 5, 6, 7, 8, 9 and 10.

Main teaching activities

Whole class: Display the 'Conversion graphs' activity sheet. Explain that these types of graphs are called conversion graphs because they are used to change one system of units into another. These particular conversion graphs are very useful when working out the distances involved in foreign travel and the value of money when visiting or taking a holiday in Europe. Emphasise that both graphs must start at zero, as either no distance has been travelled at that point or no money has been exchanged. Stress also that both graphs are straight lines because the distances or amounts of money increase by the same quantity each time. This is known in maths as 'constant proportion'. Tell the children that points should be located as accurately as possible and then connected by a line drawn with a ruler.

Differentiation

Less confident learners: Provide help with the construction of the graphs, such as drawing axes, deciding on scale and marking points.
More confident learners: Encourage this group to make other examples of conversion graphs based on topics already worked on in class, such as changing temperatures from °C into °F, converting kilograms into pounds and litres into pints/gallons.

Paired work: Working in pairs, the children construct the two conversion graphs from the data. Provide them with centimetre squared paper and copies of the 'Conversion graphs' sheet. Write the following questions on the OHP or whiteboard:

● *How many kilometres are these distances?* 10 miles, 15 miles, 20 miles, 35 miles, 45 miles.
● *How many miles are these distances?* 16km, 48km, 100km, 115km.
● *Change these pounds to euros:* £2, £5, £8, £9, £25.
● *Change these euros to pounds:* €3.20, €8, €12.80, €16, €60.

Review

Ask the children: *What do we mean by the term 'conversion graph'? What does the phrase 'constant proportion' mean?* Ask for volunteers to provide answers to the questions set on the conversion graphs.

Lesson 3 (Review)

Starter

Reason: Label one end of the counting stick 0 and the other end 1. Count in steps of 0.4 along and back on the stick. Point to any point on the stick and ask the children to say what decimal fits there. Repeat, labelling the stick in steps of 0.6, 0.8, and so on.

Main teaching activities

Whole class: Tell the children they are going to revisit pie charts (see Block C, Unit 1, Lesson 1). Explain that this time they are going to gather information to make their own simple pie charts on the grids provided. Stress that pie charts are increasingly popular as a way of conveying information because of their visual appeal. Remind the children that the complete area

▶

of the circle represents all the information and is divided into sectors, each of them showing certain categories. Say: *This type of graph is especially good at showing how part of something relates to the whole.* On the OHP, show the children examples of the grids they can use for their pie charts (using 'Pie chart 1'). They could have eight sections (45° angles), 10 sections (36° angles), 12 sections (30° angles) or 24 sections (15° angles). Discuss possible topics, including types of trees, surveys of favourite television programmes, or time spent on different activities during the day, with each hour represented by a 15° angle (360° ÷ 24 = 15°). Stress that, to make amounts easy to show, some rounding may be necessary.

Paired work: Ask the children to choose a topic for which to construct a pie chart. Provide pairs with an appropriate pie-chart grid from the range provided in the general resources. Once the chart has been completed, ask them to interpret the information shown and write as many statements about it as possible. These should include smallest and largest amounts, amounts that are the same, comparison between amounts, and so on.

Review
Look at the examples of the pie charts the children have produced. Mount them on a class display.

Lesson 4 (Teach and apply)

Starter
Refine: Explain that you will ask division facts which the children can derive from the multiplication tables. Ask: *What is 49 divided by 7? 81 divided by 9? 64 divided by 8?* Ask the children to say the square of the number that you say, for example: *What is the square of 4, 2, 9, 7, 11, 8, 12...* including all the squares up to 12 × 12.

Main teaching activities
Whole class: Give out copies of the 'World time zones' activity sheet. Explain to the children that there are different time zones around the world. Show the globe to reinforce understanding of the fact that when it is daylight in the British Isles it will be dark in places like New Zealand and Australia. Refer to the activity sheet, explaining that times are recorded as before or after GMT. Also that the time zones on the sheet show how many hours before or after GMT the time is, according to the country's position east or west of the International Date Line. To the west it is earlier than GMT (–) and to the east it is later (+). Ask questions relating to the sheet, such as: *It is 3.00pm in France. What time is it in New York?* Draw the following chart on the board. Ask the children to copy it onto their whiteboards and fill in the missing information (alternatively, complete it with the whole class).

GMT	2.00pm	6.30pm	3.30am
Brazil			
Los Angeles			
China			

Independent work: Ask each child to complete a simple timetable of a typical day, such as: *I get up at 7.00am. I eat breakfast at 8.00am. I start school at 9.00am.* They should then choose a country and list what time it would be there as they are doing each activity. Record as follows:

Activity	Time in the UK	Time in ....

Differentiation
Less confident learners: Recommend that this group works on pie chart grids with only eight or ten sections. Provide support with rounding numbers, calculating sectors and drawing lines in the correct places.
More confident learners: Challenge this group to make their own pie charts from blank circles, calculating their own angles and marking them using a 360° protractor.

BLOCK C

Handling data and measures

Unit 2 2 weeks

Review

Using the 'World time zones' activity sheet, choose a city where the time difference from London is considerable – for example, Los Angeles (8 hours earlier) or Sydney (10 hours later). Discuss what problems this may cause in an international context. For example, businesses around the world find it hard to communicate, families have to arrange phone calls at mutually appropriate hours, and so on.

Invite children from the more confident group to report back on their investigation of time zones in the USA. Ensure that the discussions help the children to understand and appreciate time zones and that they can use the time-zone chart accurately.

Lessons 5-7

Preparation
Lesson 5: Draw a measuring cylinder on the board for the Starter.
Lesson 6: Write up some statistics on the board.
Lessons 6 and 7: It may save time if duplicated sheets are provided for children to record results of investigations.

You will need
Photocopiable pages
'Number sets' (page 118), one per child.
CD resources
Support, extension and template versions of 'Number sets'.
Equipment
Calculators; coins (some copper, some silver); 1-6 dice.

Learning objectives

Starter
- Calculate mentally with integers and decimals: U.t ± U.t, TU × U, TU ÷ U, U.t × U, U.t ÷ U. (Revision of Block A)
- Use a calculator to solve problems involving multi-step calculations.

Main teaching activities
2006
- Describe and interpret results and solutions of problems using mode, range, median and mean.
- Describe and predict outcomes from data using the language of chance or likelihood.

1999
- Use the language associated with probability to discuss events, including those with equally likely outcomes.
- Find the mode and range of a set of data; begin to find the median and mean of a set of data.

Vocabulary
frequency, mode, range, mean, average, median, statistics, fair, unfair, risk, doubt, likely, unlikely, equally likely, likelihood, certain, uncertain, probably, possible, impossible, chance, good chance, poor chance, no chance, equal chance, even chance, outcome, biased, random

Lesson 5 (Review)

Starter
Revise: Draw a large measuring cylinder on the whiteboard complete with a scale going vertically down the side. Label the scale from 0 to 5 litres. Mark in the litres and each litre divided equally into five parts, 200ml each. Ask children to come out to the board to mark in the following measurements: 600ml, 1l 400ml, 2l 200ml, 3l 800ml, 4l 600ml, and so on. Also indicate points between the marked measures and ask children to round them first to the nearest litre and then to the nearest 200ml.

Main teaching activities
Whole class: Revise the meaning of the words 'mode' and 'range' as applied to sets of data (Block C, Unit 1). Write a list of statistics on the board, such as the scores achieved by a darts player with his first six darts: 36, 5, 14, 9, 14, 3. Ask: *What is the range of these scores?* (It is the difference between the highest and lowest scores, so 36 - 3 = 33. The highest score is 33 more than the lowest score.) *What does mode mean?* (It is the most frequent value in the list. In this case it is 14.) Discuss when knowing the mode of a set of data would be useful. For example, a children's clothing firm knowing which sizes

are bought most frequently, and a paint company knowing what colour of paint is the most popular. Then go on to consider 'median' and 'mean'. Again, use a set of data written on the board to explain the meanings. For example, use 10, 2, 7, 9 and 2. Explain that to find the median we put all the numbers in order, smallest to largest, and then find the middle value. The order would be 2, 2, 7, 9 and 10, and the median would be 7. Also explain that to find the mean we divide the total by the number of members in the list. So, 2 + 2 + 7 + 9 + 10 = 30, 30 ÷ 5 = 6. The mean is 6. Explain that if there is no middle value in a set of numbers the median is halfway between the two middle numbers. For example, the median of 5, 9, 11 and 15 is 10, because 10 comes halfway between 9 and 11. Explain that the mean is sometimes referred to as the average, but that this is not technically correct because it is only one type of average. Median and mode are also types of average.

Paired work: Set the children to work in pairs on the 'Number sets' activity sheet. Once the sheets have been distributed, quickly revise the processes involved in finding the range, the mode, the median and the mean.

Review
Ensure that the children fully understand the terms used in the lesson. Ask: *How would you find the range of a set of numbers? What do you understand by the term 'mode'? What do we mean by the term 'median'? What calculations are needed to find the mean of a set of numbers?* Remind them that mode, median and mean are all types of average and suit certain situations better than others – for example, cricket batters' scores (mean), the most common children's shoe sizes in a class (mode), the halfway point in a group of children's heights (median).

Lesson 6 (Teach)

Starter
Review: Ask the children to work out 2 + 4 × 3 on the calculator. Discuss the two possible answers, 18 and 14. Remind the children of the meaning of brackets in a calculation. Work through examples on the calculators where brackets are put in different places, such as 7 × (8 + 6) and (7 × 8) + 6. Also get children, in pairs, to put in the missing brackets, for example 3 × 6 + 4 = 30 and 3 × 6 + 4 = 22. Discuss solutions. Stress that multiplying is completed before addition but that brackets help to avoid misunderstandings.

Main teaching activities
Whole class: Tell the children they are going to investigate probability (the likelihood that something will or will not happen). First discuss the concepts of 'impossible' and 'certain'. If a ball is thrown into the air, for example, it is impossible for it to continue moving upwards. On the other hand, it is certain that the sun will rise tomorrow. Show the children an example of a simple probability scale in which impossible is 0, certain is 1 and all other probabilities lie somewhere between these two. These can be described using other phrases such as 'likely', 'unlikely', 'equally likely', 'no chance', 'good chance', 'poor chance', 'even chance'. Explain that probability and its connection with the study of statistics is an important area of mathematics and can be applied to many ordinary situations like the outcome of sports events, weather conditions, insurance claims and traffic movements.

Paired work: Start with an activity that has only two possible outcomes. When a coin is tossed, it is equally likely to come down heads or tails. This is known as an even chance. Invite the children to predict how many heads and how many tails they would expect to get if the coin was tossed ten times. *What result might be expected if the number of tosses was increased to 20, 50 or 100?* Encourage pairs to test out their theories and record the results.

Review
Review the outcomes of the paired work. How close were the results to their predictions? Did the number of tosses significantly affect the findings?

Differentiation
Less confident learners: This group should work from the support version of 'Number sets', where each of the four terms is dealt with separately. Check at the end of each section that the children have carried out the correct processes and calculations.

More confident learners: Children in this group should work on the extension version of the activity sheet, where the problems are more word-based. Point out that some of the answers will produce decimal numbers but calculations should not require a calculator. Encourage the children to gather their own data for interesting range, mode, median and mean calculations.

Differentiation
Less confident learners: Keep the number of attempts down to small manageable amounts. Assist with methods of recording or provide this group with recording sheets that have already been prepared.

More confident learners: Let this group experiment with two coins (perhaps one copper and one silver). Ask: *How many different ways are there for the coins to settle now? What is the probability of throwing a pair of heads or a pair of tails?*

Lesson 7 (Practise)

Starter
Read: Show the children how to use the MC key on the calculator to clear the memory, the M+ and M– to store and amend stored calculations and the MR button to retrieve stored calculations. Ask them, in pairs, to find the missing operations in these calculations using their knowledge of the four operations. (48 ? 20) ÷ (10 ? 3) = 4; (352 ? 32) ? (416 - 338) = 858; (472 ? 8) + (1116 ? 106) = 1069; (483 ? 20) × (119 ? 7) = 8551. Take feedback and discuss the strategies used.

Main teaching activities
Paired work: Pairs of children should work with six-sided dice. They should investigate the likelihood of throwing odd/even numbers and the likelihood of throwing individual numbers 6, 4, 1.

Review
Discuss the results of the investigation carried out in the main teaching activities. Draw a 0 to 1 probability scale and ask children to plot the results on it.

Lessons 8-10

Preparation
Lesson 8: Prepare the 'Weighing scales' activity sheet for display.
Lesson 9: Enlarge the 'Metric abbreviations and equivalents' general resource sheet for use as a wall chart. Prepare the 'Conversion tables' general resource sheet for display.
Lesson 10: Prepare the 'Kilometres-miles conversion chart' resource sheet for display.

You will need
Photocopiable pages
'Weighing scales' (page 119), one per pair.
CD resources
Support version of 'Weighing scales'; core, support, extension and template versions of 'All change'; 'Driving distances'. General resource sheets: 'Conversion tables', 'Metric abbreviations and equivalents', 'Kilometres-miles conversion chart'. ITP: 'Measuring scales' and 'Thermometer'.
Equipment
OHP/whiteboard calculator; calculators.

Learning objectives

Starter
● Read and interpret scales on a range of measuring instruments, recognising that the measurement made is approximate and recording results to a required degree of accuracy; compare readings on different scales, for example when using different instruments.
● Select and use standard metric units of measure and convert between units using decimals to two places (eg change 2.75 litres to 2750ml, or vice versa).

Main teaching activities
2006
● Read and interpret scales on a range of measuring instruments, recognising that the measurement made is approximate and recording results to a required degree of accuracy; compare readings on different scales, for example when using different instruments.
● Select and use standard metric units of measure and convert between units using decimals to two places (eg change 2.75 litres to 2750ml, or vice versa).
● Use a calculator to solve problems involving multi-step calculations.
1999
● Use, read and write standard metric units (km, m, cm, mm, kg, g, l, ml, cl), including their abbreviations, and relationships between them. Convert smaller to larger units (eg m to km, cm or mm to m, g to kg, ml to l) and vice versa.
● Suggest suitable units and measuring equipment to estimate or measure length, mass or capacity.
● Record estimates and readings from scales to a suitable degree of accuracy.
● Develop calculator skills and use a calculator effectively.

Vocabulary
estimate, approximate, measure, millimetre (mm), centimetre (cm), metre (m), kilometre (km), gram (g), kilogram (kg), tonne (t), millilitre (ml), centilitre (cl), litre (l)

Lesson 8 (Apply)

Starter

Revise: Draw a long horizontal line on the whiteboard to represent 0–5cm. Mark in each of the centimetre points and also the millimetre marks between each centimetre. Ask children to come to the board and mark in given measurements, such as 0.4cm, 1.9cm, 2.6cm, 3.1cm, 4.7cm and so on. Also indicate other points marked and ask children to read them off, first to the nearest centimetre, then to the nearest half centimetre and finally to the nearest millimetre.

Main teaching activities

Whole class: Emphasise to the children that reading the scale on a measuring instrument is similar to reading a number line. It is important to realise that there are numbers in between the main numbers that are marked. Display the 'Weighing scales' activity sheet. Discuss how the measurements are given on the weighing scales, the first three in kilograms and the other two in grams. Explain that scales are organised in different ways – they can be horizontal, vertical or curved. Ask the children to work out the value of the interim markers in each case. For example: *If the pointer came to here what weight would be shown? Where would 2.5kg come on scales 1, 2 and 3? Where would 350g come on scales 4 and 5?* Ask for volunteers to mark the following measurements on scales 1, 2 and 3: 2.7kg, 4100g, 1.8kg, 3300g and 3.4kg. *Which weights can be shown exactly, which have to be estimated?*

  Then ask for volunteers to mark these measurements on scales 4 and 5: 60g, 490g, 180g and 325g. Again, check to see which can be measured exactly and which have to be estimated. Alternatively, use the ITPs 'Measuring scales' and 'Thermometer' on the interactive whiteboard and ask children to find various values, changing the scale periodically.

Paired work: Provide each pair with a copy of the 'Weighing scales' activity sheet. Ask one child to think up a secret weight and then mark it with an arrow on one of the scales 1, 2 and 3. The other child should identify what the weight is and mark it on one of the other scales. Encourage the children to check each other's work and then swap over. Repeat the process using scales 4 and 5.

Review

Check through the children's work with them. Which of the scales did they find easiest to read? Which was most difficult? How did they manage when the weights had to be estimated? Try to have some other examples of weighing instruments for the children to see so they can compare different scales.

Differentiation

Less confident learners: Provide the support version of the activity sheet, on which some of the halfway markers have been included.

More confident learners: Ask these children to work out the value of unnumbered markers on a measurement scale. Encourage them to devise and label measurement scales of their own. On the scales used in class, ask them to convert the kilogram readings to grams, and vice versa.

Lesson 9 (Review)

Starter

Revisit: Check first that the children remember the main fractional parts of 10, 100 and 1000 (one-quarter of 10 is $2^1/_2$, half of 10 is 5, three-quarters of 10 is $7^1/_2$, one-tenth of 10 is 1; for 100 the fractions would be 25, 50, 75 and 10 and so on). Count on or back in different increments related to metric units including decimal equivalents – for example, centimetres to metres (10cm, 20cm, 30cm or 0.1m, 0.2m, 0.3m). Move on to metres to kilometres: counting in hundreds, this would be 100m, 200m, 300m or 0.1km, 0.2km, 0.3km; counting in tens, this would be 10m, 20m, 30m or 0.01km, 0.02km, 0.03km. Repeat these counting activities using grams to kilograms and millilitres to litres.

Main teaching activities

Whole class: Display the 'Conversion tables' general resource sheet and go through it with the children, first working from smaller to larger units

Differentiation

Less confident learners: Provide this group with the support version of 'All change', where children have to write length, mass and capacity in three different ways. Display the OHT of 'Metric abbreviations and equivalents'.

More confident learners: Let this group work on the extension version of 'All change'. Ask them to make up more conversions involving kilograms/tonnes and centilitres/litres, such as 680kg = ? tonne, 4.3 tonne = ? kg, 75cl = ? l and 3.24l = ? cl.

and then vice versa. Also demonstrate what happens to the position of the decimal point when changing very small units into larger ones. For example, 200ml = 0.2l, 20g = 0.020kg and 2m = 0.002km. Also make sure the children are conversant with the facts that 1000kg = 1 tonne, 100 centilitres = 1 litre and 1 centilitre = 10 millilitres.

Independent work: Working individually, the children should focus on the 'All change' activity sheet. Length and capacity measurements have to be changed into either smaller or larger units while mass measurements, written in a variety of ways, have to be ordered from smallest to largest.

Review

Focus on questions where the children have to order a group of measurements, smallest to largest, by putting them into the same family of metric units. Use the following examples:

- Length: 2.45m, 260cm, 2$\frac{1}{2}$m, $\frac{3}{4}$km, 0.76km, 850m.
- Mass: 1$\frac{1}{2}$kg, 1.400kg, 1600g, 1.4800 tonne, 1500kg, 1 tonne 450kg.
- Capacity: 3.800l, 3l 750ml, 3850ml.

Lesson 10 (Review and evaluate)

Starter

Revisit: Revise the conversion of smaller units into larger units and vice versa. Include examples involving length, mass and capacity. Expect the children to be able to give measurements in at least one other way, and in most cases two alternatives, eg: 57mm = 5cm 7mm = 5.7cm; 1753m = 1km 753m = 1.753km; 2560g = 2kg 560g = 2.560kg; 5004ml = 5l 4ml = 5.004l.

Main teaching activities

Whole class: Remind the children that metres, kilometres, litres and so on, are units within the metric system, and talk about the relationships between m and km. For example, ask: *What units are used in the imperial system?* Collect responses and record these on the board (check in particular that the children know that length is measured in inches, feet, yards and miles).

Write on the board a range of different metric/imperial conversions, for example:

8 kilometres = 5 miles   1 metre = 3 feet 3 inches
1 kilogram ≈ 2.2lb   30 grams ≈ 1oz
4.5 litres ≈ 1 gallon (and 8 pints in 1 gallon).

Remind the children about the use of the approximation sign (≈) in these examples. Ask some questions about these conversions, using the OHP calculator to check answers. For example: *How many millilitres in 1 pint?* (570 millilitres.) *How many miles in 100 kilometres?* (66 miles.)

Focus the children on miles and kilometres and build a conversion chart on the board (use the 'Kilometres–miles conversion chart' general resource if required).

Group work: Give each group a copy of the 'Driving distances' activity sheet, which includes distances from channel ports in kilometres. Ask the children to fill in the blank table by converting the distances from kilometres to the nearest whole mile. Allow the groups to use calculators for this purpose. Encourage the children to approximate their answers before using the calculators.

Differentiation

Less confident learners: Provide adult support for this activity. Suggest that the children multiply by 0.62 and then round to the nearest mile. For example: Calais to Cologne is 421 kilometres. 421 × 0.62 is 261.02, so the distance is rounded to 261 miles.

More confident learners: After completing the activity, provide the children with a road atlas and challenge them to use its distance chart to calculate kilometres to miles or miles to kilometres conversions.

Review

Discuss the conversions the children made and address any difficulties they had with the calculations. Review other conversions, for example: 2.54 cm = 1 inch. Discuss real-life uses for imperial units, such as buying petrol and cooking. If you have time, go through a recipe with items in ounces and ask individual children to convert into grams.

Invite the children to discuss in pairs what they have learned during this unit. They can write an evaluation of their learning, including that which they still find difficult.

Name _____   Date _____

Conversion graphs

Miles to kilometres:

miles	10	20	30	40	50	60	70	80
km	16	32	48	64	80	96	112	128

Pounds to euros:

£	1	2	3	4	5	6	7	8	9	10
€	1.60	3.20	4.80	6.40	8	9.60	11.20	12.80	14.40	16
£	11	12	13	14	15	16	17	18	19	20
€	17.60	19.20	20.80	22.40	24	25.60	27.20	28.80	30.40	32

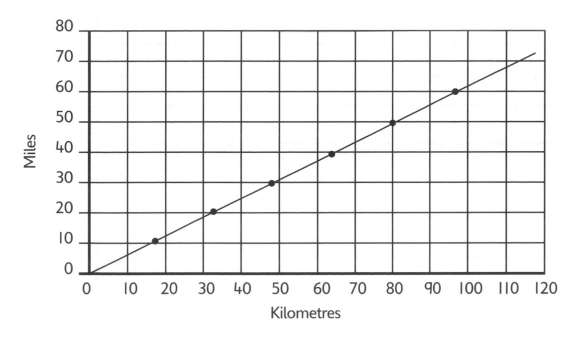

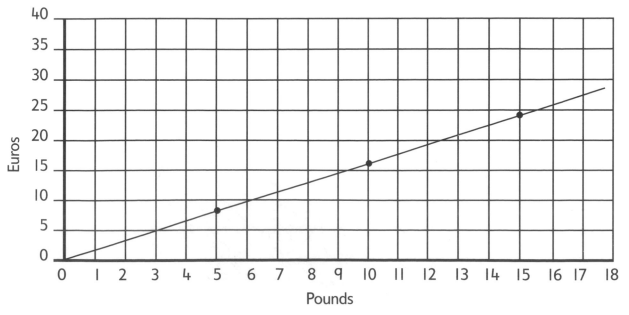

Name _____   Date _____

Number sets

Find the range, mode, median and mean of these sets of numbers.

		range	mode	median	mean
1	9, 7, 2, 2, 10				
2	6, 9, 5, 4, 6				
3	12, 15, 17, 12				
4	9, 21, 20, 18, 9, 9				
5	18, 32, 28, 18, 54				

Make up your own sets of numbers for finding the range, mode, median and mean.

1				
2				
3				
4				
5				

Name _____   Date _____

Weighing scales

1.

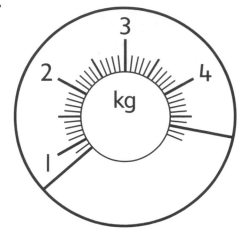

2.

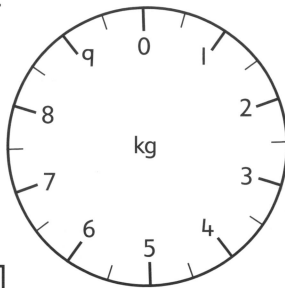

3.

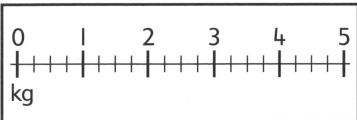

4.

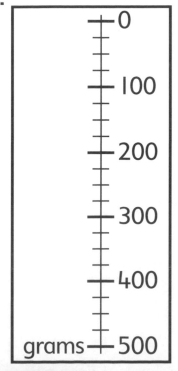

5.

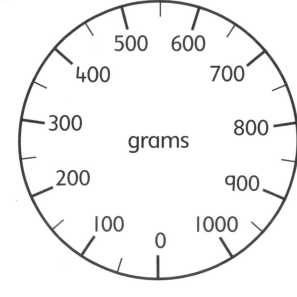

■S C H O L A S T I C PHOTOCOPIABLE

BLOCK C

Handling data and measures

Handling data and measures

Speaking and listening objectives
● Participate in whole-class debate using the conventions and language of debate, including Standard English.

Introduction
Using and applying mathematical knowledge and skills to solve practical problems dominates much of the work in this unit. Children are required to cost out holidays and are encouraged to make their own decisions for much of the time. There is the opportunity to revise the terms 'range' and 'mean' in a holiday setting, and a 'hands-on' probability activity is also included. The use of measuring equipment is featured and, in the last two lessons, children develop calculator skills in the context of organising an end-of-term party.

Use and apply mathematics
● Solve problems by collecting, selecting, processing, presenting and interpreting data, using ICT where appropriate; draw conclusions and identify further questions to ask.

Lesson	Strands	Starter	Main teaching activities
1. Apply	Data	**Use knowledge of place value and multiplication facts to 10 × 10 to derive related multiplication and division facts involving decimals.** (Revision of Blocks A and B)	**Solve problems by collecting, selecting, processing, presenting and interpreting data, using ICT where appropriate; draw conclusions and identify further questions to ask.**
2. Apply	Data	As for Lesson 1	As for Lesson 1
3. Apply	Data	Use decimal notation for tenths, hundredths and thousandths; partition, round and order decimals with up to three places, and position them on the number line. (Revision of Block A)	As for Lesson 1
4. Apply	Data	Construct and interpret frequency tables, bar charts with grouped discrete data, and line graphs; interpret pie charts.	As for Lesson 1
5. Practise	Data	As for Lesson 4	Describe and interpret results and solutions to problems using the mode, range, median and mean.
6. Practise	Data	**Use knowledge of place value and multiplication facts to 10 × 10 to derive related multiplication and division facts involving decimals.** (Revision of Blocks A and B)	Describe and predict outcomes from data using the language of chance or likelihood.
7. Teach	Measure	Use approximations, inverse operations and tests of divisibility to estimate and check results. (Revision of Blocks A and B)	Read and interpret scales on a range of measuring instruments, recognising that the measurement made is approximate and recording results to a required degree of accuracy; compare readings on different scales, for example when using different instruments.
8. Apply	Measure	**Select and use standard metric units of measure and convert between units using decimals to two places (eg change 2.75 litres to 2750ml, or vice versa).**	**Select and use standard metric units of measure and convert between units using decimals to two places (eg change 2.75 litres to 2750ml, or vice versa).**
9. Review and apply	Calculate	As for Lesson 8	Use a calculator to solve problems involving multi-step calculations.
10. Review, apply and evaluate	Calculate	As for Lesson 8	As for Lesson 9

Lessons 1-6

Preparation
Lesson 1: Prepare the 'Beauty Villas' activity sheet for display.
Lesson 2: Collect travel brochures and copy extracts if needed.
Lesson 3: Prepare the 'Ferry crossings and mileage information' general resource sheet for display.
Lesson 5: On squared paper, draw the bar chart for use in the Starter activity. Prepare list of internet sites for children to visit to find prices of flights, hotels, car hire, etc. Decide how children are going to gather data for activities.
Lesson 6: For each group prepare a bag containing five red counters, two blue counters and one red counter.

You will need
Photocopiable pages
'Best buy holidays' (page 129), 'Which ferry?' (page 130) and 'How far is it?' (page 131), one per child or pair.
CD resources
'Beauty Villas'; support and extension versions of 'Best buy holidays' and 'Which ferry?'; support, extension and template versions of 'How far is it?'. General resource sheet: 'Ferry crossings and mileage information'.
Equipment
Holiday brochures (or copies of details from brochures) for each child; atlases; computers with access to the internet; materials for making posters; squared paper; counters and bags.

Learning objectives

Starter
● Use knowledge of place value and multiplication facts to 10 × 10 to derive related multiplication and division facts involving decimals. (Revision of Blocks A and B)
● Use decimal notation for tenths, hundredths and thousandths; partition, round and order decimals with up to three places and position them on the number line. (Revision of Block A)
● Construct and interpret frequency tables, bar charts with grouped discrete data, and line graphs; interpret pie charts.

Main teaching activities
2006
● Solve problems by collecting, selecting, processing, presenting and interpreting data, using ICT where appropriate; draw conclusions and identify further questions to ask.
● Describe and interpret results and solutions to problems using the mode, range, median and mean.
● Describe and predict outcomes from data using the language of chance or likelihood.
1999
● Solve a problem by representing, extracting and interpreting data in tables, graphs, charts and diagrams including those generated by a computer.
● Find the mode and range of a set of data; begin to find the median and mean of a set of data.
● Use the language associated with probability to discuss events, including those with equally likely outcomes.

Vocabulary
discount, price, cost, costs more, more/most expensive, cheap, costs less, less/least expensive, how much, how many, total, amount, value, problem, solution, calculate, calculation, method, explain, reasoning, reason, predict, represent, analyse, interpret, fair, unfair, risk, doubt, likely, unlikely, equally likely, likelihood, certain, uncertain, probably, possible, impossible, chance, good chance, poor chance, no chance, equal chance, even chance, outcome, biased, random, estimate, approximate, data, information, graph, chart, table, scale, interval, division, horizontal axis, vertical axis, axes, label, title, pictogram, bar chart, bar line chart, line graph, pie chart, range, mean, average

Lesson 1 (Apply)

Starter
Reason: Give the children a target number such as 353. The aim is to find a product of two numbers that is as close as possible to the target number. You may allow some children to use a calculator. Let the children compare their suggestions to see which is the closest and explain the mental calculations they used. Repeat.

Main teaching activities
Whole class: Explain to the children that they are going to be looking at holiday brochures and working out how to cost a holiday. Display the 'Beauty Villas' activity sheet, showing the first page of the two extracts from the holiday brochure. Ask the children to look carefully at the first extract, showing prices for 'Beauty Villas'. Point out that in this brochure the dates are written across the top of the table, and information for one bedroom

accommodation (four adults sharing, then for the first child and the second child) is given on the left-hand side, with prices for seven nights and 14 nights. Point out that it is important to read the 'small print' to find conditions for child discounts and any supplements that may be payable.

Ask: *Who can give me the price for two adults staying seven nights with a departure between 13 December and 14 December?* The answer £259 per person will probably be given, but point out that this is in an apartment for four people, so if only two people stay there they will have to pay an under-occupancy supplement. There are three rates for supplements, depending upon whether it is high, medium or low season; this holiday is low season, so the supplement is £2 per person per night. Ask: *How much extra is that for each person for a week?* (£14) *So, this increases the cost per person to £273.*

Explain that there are often reductions for children, with the first child usually being the cheapest. Ask: *Who can give me the price that this family would have to pay to take their two children with them for that week?* (First child £99, second child £99 = £198.)

Independent work: Give each child a copy of the 'Best buy holidays' activity sheet. Remind them to read the information carefully and to make sure they calculate and include any supplements that are payable. The children's answers will vary, depending on their choices of dates, locations, types of board required and sleeping arrangements. They will need to show you their workings out as there will be many permutations.

Review

Go through the answers for each version of the activity sheet and discuss any difficulties. Display the whole of the 'Beauty Villas' activity sheet (ie both pages) and ask the children what differences they notice with the way the information is presented in the second table from the first. (Dates are down the side and there are different accommodation options and different holiday length options.)

Differentiation

Less confident learners: Give this group the support version of 'Best buy holidays', where they are directed towards a particular holiday and have fewer decisions to make and simpler calculations.
More confident learners: Give this group the extension version of 'Best buy holidays', where they have to calculate different alternatives in order to find the most economical, and which also includes an extension activity.

Lesson 2 (Apply)

Starter

Reason: Repeat the Starter from Lesson 1, but stipulate that the answer must be the product of two two-digit numbers.

Main teaching activities

Whole class: Hand out details from holiday brochures to each child. Tell them that today they will choose a holiday and cost it from the brochures they have. The holiday must be for a family of two adults and two children and they must be sure to include all the necessary extras such as insurance and any flight supplements. Remind them to read the information carefully, especially the 'small print'. Point out that they may have to look in different places in the brochure for information such as the cost of insurance and the flights.

Independent work: Explain to the children that when they have identified 'their holiday' they should make a leaflet giving as much information as possible about their chosen holiday destination. Tell them that their leaflets should include the cost for their family holiday and show how this is made up.

Review

Look at the different holiday brochures that the children have used and compare the way in which information is presented. Discuss different holiday destinations that have been chosen and other ways of travelling to these destinations.

Differentiation

Less confident learners: Limit the choice of destination for this group and provide them with data for that particular area.
More confident learners: The task for this group should be more open-ended. Encourage them to consider a range of possibilities and to justify their choices.

Lesson 3 (Apply)

Starter
Revisit: Write a set of mixed numbers on the board, such as: 4.37, 14.2, 6.97, 6.9. Ask the children to order these largest to smallest. Repeat for another set, including up to three decimal places, such as 6.665, 6.656, 6.566, 6.576. This time, ask the children to order these smallest to largest. Repeat for other sets of numbers.

Main teaching activities
Whole class: Explain to the children that they have looked at costing package holidays, but many people prefer to travel independently. In this lesson they will be looking at costing ferry crossings. Ask the children about any channel crossings they know about (eg Dover-Calais, Portsmouth-Le Havre). Discuss which are the shortest and the longest, and reasons why people may choose a longer route rather than the quickest. Consider where the starting points are in the UK.

Show the first part of the 'Ferry crossings and mileage information' general resource sheet, with costs for Dover-Calais and Poole-Cherbourg. Talk about the way the information is presented, reminding the children that they need to read everything, as the overall price is usually made up of several different parts, such as the cost for a vehicle, adult and child passengers. Discuss the reasons why the prices vary at different times of the year. You may work through some examples of costs if you feel the children need support.

Independent/paired work: Give the children the 'Which ferry?' activity sheet and a copy of 'Ferry crossings and mileage information'. Tell them they will need to refer to the latter for the prices for the activity. Point out that they must read the 'small print'. The children may work independently or in pairs to complete the activity.

Differentiation
Less confident learners: Give this group the support version of 'Which ferry?', which guides them through the task.
More confident learners: This group should work from the extension version of 'Which ferry?', which asks them for two different routes and to cost alternative routes.

Review
Go through the answers to the activity sheet and ask children to explain their calculations. Make sure that they have included all parts of the costing and used the correct prices. Ask them to explain how they built up the cost of the ferry. Work through one example, asking the children to contribute at each stage. Ask questions such as: *How many passengers are there? How many are children under 15? Is the driver included in the cost for the car? Is the cost of the return leg the same as the outward leg? Would there be any savings if the family travelled back in September?*

Lesson 4 (Apply)

Starter
Revisit: Display an example of a pie chart to revise with the children how they should be interpreted. An example might be how children travel to school. Invent your own data. Use the following questions: *Which way of travelling is used by most children? Which way of travelling is used by fewest children?* Put the ways of travelling in order, fewest first. Then use True or False statements, for example: *More children walk than cycle. More children come by bus than travel by car. More than half the class travel by car.* Also check that children can convert the 'pieces of the pie' into approximate fractions and/or percentages.

Main teaching activities
Whole class: Continuing from Lesson 3, display the 'Ferry crossings and mileage information' general resource sheet, focusing on the mileage charts at the end of the sheet. Discuss the different ferry routes and identify them on a map. Point out that, when deciding which ferry route to take, people usually consider the mileage involved on either side of the ferry journey. Some people may like to drive longer distances and have a shorter ferry

journey, and the mileage costs will vary depending upon the vehicle.

Consider a trip for a family from Bristol to Faro in Portugal. Tell the children they are going to calculate how many miles driving there would be if the family used the Dover–Calais route. Ask: *How many miles is it from Bristol to Dover?* (206)... *and then from Calais to Faro?* (1293) *So the total mileage is 1499 miles.* Ask the children how much the overland cost would be if the average costs per mile is 20p for their car. Invite a child to explain how to work this out (1499 × 20p = £299.80). Remind the children to think about the method for calculation and to choose the most suitable – in this example it is easiest to say 1500 × 20p = £300 and then take away 20p.

Independent/paired work: Give the children the 'How far is it?' activity sheet and a copy of 'Ferry crossings and mileage information' general resource sheet. The children may work independently or in pairs to complete the activity.

Review

Discuss the costs of the various routes and make sure that children understand that the mileage costs given are based on average fuel consumption for the vehicle. Discuss what other costs would have to be taken into account, for example overnight accommodation on the longer routes.

Lesson 5 (Practise)

Starter

Revisit: Make a bar chart on squared paper for display on the OHP or whiteboard showing the length of some children's feet. Show number of children on the vertical scale (1 square = 2 children) and length of foot in centimetres on the horizontal scale. Record the following data:

    19cm, 2 children
    20cm, 4 children
    21cm, 9 children
    22cm, 12 children
    23cm, 16 children
    24cm, 10 children
    25cm, 6 children
    26cm, 1 child

Ask the following questions:

- *How many children have a foot length of (a) 22cm, (b) 26cm?*
- *Which foot length is most common?*
- *Which foot length is least common?*
- *How many children have a foot length greater than 24cm?*
- *How many children have a foot length of less than 21cm?*

Discuss the general shape of the graph and what this implies. (Few short and long foot lengths. Most come in the middle range.)

Main teaching activities

Whole class: Explain that for this lesson you want the children to research a holiday destination of their own choice. They will need access to weather data. This may be information they have collected for homework, or they could access data on a computer during the lesson.

Paired/group work: Working in ability pairs or small groups, ask the children to identify a holiday destination and look at the weather data that is available. Write the following instructions on the board:

- Choose a holiday destination and look at the weather information that you have available.
- Produce a poster giving as much weather information about your destination as you can.
- Include the range of temperatures that holidaymakers should expect for both daytime and night-time, as well as the expected mean temperatures.

Encourage children to present their information in the best way they can – this may involve graphs or charts.

Differentiation

Less confident learners: Give this group the support version of 'How far is it?', where the cost per mile is given as 20p, making an easier calculation. They may need help identifying the distances when using the mileage chart.

More confident learners: This group should work from the extension version of 'How far is it?', where calculations are more difficult and they are asked to calculate additional alternative routes.

Differentiation

Less confident learners: Provide adult support for these children.

More confident learners: Encourage these children to use more complex graphs and charts to present their data.

▷ **Review**
Invite the children to present their group's information to the rest of the class.

Lesson 6 (Practise)

Starter
Revisit: The children should revise multiplying and dividing an integer by 1000. For example, 527 × 1000 = 527,000 and 435,000 ÷ 1000 = 435.

Main teaching activities
Whole class: Provide mixed-ability groups of children with eight counters and a small bag. Five of the counters should be coloured red, two blue and one green. Encourage them first to think about possible outcomes in terms of fractions, and then using the language of chance or likelihood. They should predict the chances of pulling out each different colour and then test out their ideas. Remind them to replace the counter each time it has been taken out and to record their results fully.

Review
Check the children's findings. Pool the results of all the groups together. Help the children to appreciate that the larger the number of results collected, the more likelihood there is of getting closer to the ratio 5:2:1.

Lessons 7-10

Preparation
Lesson 7: Prepare an OHT of the 'Reading from scales' activity sheet. Prepare the various types of equipment needed for the two versions of the ' How good are your estimates?' activity sheets.
Lesson 9: Prepare the 'Fruit punch recipe' general resouce sheet for display.
Lesson 10: Children need to research costs so will either need to access this information online or be supplied with catalogue or price lists.

You will need
Photocopiable pages
'Party hotdogs' (page 132), one per child or pair.
CD resources
'Reading from scales'; core and support versions of 'How good are your estimates?'; support, extension and template versions of 'Party hotdogs'. General resource sheet: 'Fruit punch recipe'.
Equipment
Metre sticks; tape measures (cm/mm); 30cm rulers; trundle wheel; weighing scales; containers filled with water or beads; calculators; computer with access to internet or catalogues and price lists for food and other party supplies.

Learning objectives

Starter
● Use approximations, inverse operations and tests of divisibility to estimate and check results. (Revision of Blocks A and B)
● Select and use standard metric units of measure and convert between units using decimals to two places (eg change 2.75 litres to 2750ml, or vice versa).

Main teaching activities
2006
● Read and interpret scales on a range of measuring instruments, recognising that the measurement made is approximate and recording results to a required degree of accuracy; compare readings on different scales, for example when using different instruments.
● Select and use standard metric units of measure and convert between units using decimals to two places (eg change 2.75 litres to 2750ml, or vice versa).
● Use a calculator to solve problems involving multi-step calculations.
1999
● Record estimates and readings from scales to a suitable degree of accuracy.
● Use, read and write standard metric units (km, m, cm, mm, kg, g, l, ml, cl) including their abbreviations and relationships between them. Convert smaller to larger units (eg m to km, g to kg, ml to l) and vice versa.
● Develop calculator skills and use a calculator effectively.

Vocabulary
problem, solution, calculate, calculation, method, explain, reasoning, reason, predict, pattern, relationships, classify, represent, analyse, interpret, estimate, approximate, measure, millimetre (mm), centimetre (cm), metre (m), kilometre (km), gram (g), kilogram (kg), tonne (t), millilitre (ml), centilitre (cl), litre (l), scale

Lesson 7 (Teach)

Starter

Revisit: Ask: *How can we tell if a number is divisible by 2, 5 or 10?* Recap on the meaning of the term 'factor', then write the following numbers on the board: 30, 48, 96, 16, 40, 25, 50, 81. Ask the children, working in pairs, to list the factors for each number using a diagram as shown below. Check the answers. Ask: *What do you notice about the number of factors for 16, 25 and 81?* (Square numbers have an odd number of factors.) Try another square number to check this statement.

```
5,6           1,30
    \        /
     ( 30 )
    /        \
3,10          2,15
```

Main teaching activities

Whole class: Discuss the importance of estimating when calculating or solving problems. Explain that it helps to check whether final answers are reasonable. Ask the children to study carefully a 30cm ruler and to fix in their mind set distances like 1cm, 10cm and 30cm. Now ask them to put the rulers out of sight and to estimate the length of a thumb, an exercise book, the height of the table, the length of their arm and so on. Ask them to write down the estimated measurement each time. Then, with a partner, they should check their answers, seeing how close to the estimates they were. Discuss strategies that can be used, such as visualising the ruler or using a 'span' to help them. Tell the children that once estimations have been made they need to measure objects accurately to find the true amount. Display the OHT of the 'Reading from scales' activity sheet, which illustrates some measuring apparatus. Using an OHT pen, mark on the different scales to show different amounts, asking the children to read the scales accurately. When displaying the OHT, explain how scales are marked in divisions that are labelled. Explain that the label 25g would mean divisions of 25g.
Independent/paired work: Provide the children with the 'How good are your estimates?' activity sheet. This is in two sections: the first gives practice in estimating; the second involves reading from scales.

Review

Return to the 'Reading from scales' OHT. Ask children to come to the board and mark on given measurements. Mark positions on the equipment and pose questions such as: *If I add 75g more flour to the scales, what amount will the dial show now?*

Differentiation

Less confident learners: This group will require support for section 2 of the support version of the worksheet. Alternatively, you may wish to set up practical reinforcement tasks involving estimating and reading from scales using various containers filled with water and/or jars filled with beads.
More confident learners: Once the activity sheet has been completed, challenge this group, working in pairs, to set up practical tasks and to make up their own scale, reading questions for a partner to solve.

Lesson 8 (Apply)

Starter

Recall: First check that children remember there are 10mm to every centimetre. Then revise the following conversions: *How many millimetres are there in (a) 3½cm; (b) 5cm 7mm; (c) 6cm 4mm; (d) 4cm 3mm; (e) 7.2cm; (f) 9cm 8mm; (g) 12cm 1mm; (h) 5.3cm; (i) 9.6cm; (j) 20cm?* Check also that the children can write mm measures in two other ways, for example 36mm = 3cm 6mm = 3.6cm.

Main teaching activities

Whole class: Tell the children they are going to use their knowledge of metric length measurements to complete some tasks involving scale drawing where actual sizes are reduced in proportion so comparisons can be made. Write on the whiteboard the true size of some mammals, for example: blue whale, length 30m; killer whale, length 10m; giraffe, height 5m; human,

Unit 3 ▸ 2 weeks

Differentiation

Less confident learners: Explain how the scale conversions have been done. It may be necessary to provide them with a chart to help them eg 50cm = 1cm, 100cm = 2cm, 150cm = 3cm, 200cm = 4cm and so on.
More confident learners: Set this group some scale-drawing problems based on model aircraft: *A drawing of a space shuttle has a wingspan of 4½cm. What would the actual size be using a scale of 1cm = 5m?* (22½m.) *A drawing of a Boeing 747 has a wingspan of 6cm. What would the real-life wingspan be using a scale of 1cm = 10m?* (60m.)

height 1.8m. Ask the children to calculate the scaled measurements of each mammal using the scale 1cm = 2m. They should draw straight lines to do this and label them. Check that correct lines have been drawn, ie blue whale (15cm), killer whale (5cm), giraffe (2½cm) and human (0.9cm).
Paired work: Provide pairs of children with the true lengths of some snakes and ask them to draw straight lines to represent scale drawings of them. This time use the scale 1cm = 50cm. Use the following: grass snake 1m (2cm), rattlesnake 1.5m (3cm), cobra 2m (4cm), boa constrictor 5m (10cm), anaconda 7m (14cm) and python 8.5m (17cm).

Review

Look at the work produced by the children. Discuss strategies used for calculation. Clarify problems and check the correct units have been used in the conversions. How easy were the calculations? Did they need to use a calculator? Discuss other activities where scale drawing is important, such as map reading and making. Try to bring in model cars and aeroplanes that have actually been made to scale to check out their dimensions.

Lesson 9 (Review and apply)

Starter

Recall: Revise the units of metric capacity with the children by giving them ten quick-fire questions:
1. *What is 2020ml in litres and millilitres?*
2. *What is 4.4l in ml?*
3. *How many ml are there in 1¾l?*
4. *How many 5ml doses of medicine are there in a ¼l bottle?*
5. *Write 0.023l in ml.*
6. *Write 1250ml in l.*
7. *Write 600ml in l.*
8. *How many 300ml bottles can be filled from a 6l container?*
9. *Write 2.007l in ml.*
10. *Write 6006ml as a decimal number.*

Invite the children to make up similar questions for the rest of the class to answer.

Main teaching activities

Whole class: Explain to the class that over the next two lessons they will be planning and costing an end-of-term party. Discuss what tasks will need to be undertaken, such as working out how much food is required, the costs of the food, a disco or group, hire of a hall and leaving presents. Say: *In this lesson we will be working out quantities of food and drink and the costs of these.* Ask: *If we know that one bottle of coke will serve six people, how many bottles will we need to buy for 40 people?* (7) If there are any children who do not give the correct answer, ask another child to explain the reasoning. Point out that we divide 40 by 6 to give 6.66, but this must be rounded up to 7, so we will buy seven bottles.
Independent/paired work: Let the children work individually or in pairs on the 'Party hotdogs' activity sheet. Explain that they should first work out the quantities needed for the disco and then calculate the costs. They may use a calculator. Encourage them to estimate their answers first and to check their calculations with an equivalent calculation.

Differentiation

Less confident learners: Provide these children with the support version of 'Party hotdogs'.
More confident learners: Provide this group with the extension version of the activity sheet.
▷

Review

Discuss any difficulties that have been encountered during the lesson. Display the 'Fruit punch recipe' general resource sheet. Ask: *How much orange juice would be needed for 20 people?* (2½ litres.) Discuss how this is calculated, asking the children to explain their method. Ask: *How many oranges would be needed for 20 people?* (10)

If further assessment is needed, ask the children to calculate other quantities, such as how much blackcurrant cordial is needed (⅚ of a litre).

Lesson 10 (Review, apply and evaluate)

Starter

Recall: Make sure the children are aware that really heavy weights like lorries, buses, railway locomotives, aircraft etc are measured in metric tonnes. Check they recall that 1 tonne (t) = 1000 kilogram (kg). Then use these quick-fire questions:

1. *Write in t and kg: (a) 7030kg; (b) 4250kg; (c) 3100kg.*
2. *Write in tonnes using a decimal point: (a) 2605kg; (b) 478kg.*
3. *Write the following in kg: (a) 9t 700kg; (b) 3t 60kg; (c) 7t 9kg; (d) 4.75t; (e) 6.957t.*

Invite the children to make up similar questions for the rest of the class to answer.

Main teaching activities

Group work: Working in small groups, ask the children to decide what food they would like for their party – they might prefer a barbecue. They need to consider how many people will be at their party. Is it just their year group, or are others invited? They should decide how much food they will need, make a shopping list and cost it for the amounts required. They will need price lists, or they could use the internet to visit online supermarkets to find out prices and delivery costs. You may decide to set a budget for them or a cost per head.

Review

Invite the children to compare their shopping lists and discuss what would be a reasonable cost per head.

Ask the children to write an evaluation of what they have learned in this unit and to state what they still find difficult.

Name _____   Date _____

Best buy holidays

The Smith family have three children, but as Gemma is 16 they have to pay the adult rate for her. They would like to spend a week at either the Rialto or Paradise, but only have £1500 to spend, on accommodation. What is the cheapest holiday that you can find for them at each resort?

Remember to show your working out.

Resort **Rialto** _____

Date _____

_____ Adults _____

1st child _____

2nd child _____

Supplement @ £_____ per adult per night _____

Total _____

Resort **Paradise** _____

Date _____

_____ Adults _____

_____ Children _____

Total _____

Name _____   Date _____

Which ferry?

You will need a copy of 'Ferry crossings and mileage information'.

- The Patel family live in London and are planning a summer holiday in Spain. They will be staying near Barcelona for three weeks in August and can choose between several different routes.
- Mr Patel enjoys driving and is happy to use the cheapest route, but Mrs Patel would prefer the quickest journey.
- The children, Sita aged 16, Raj aged 8, and Sami aged 5, would all like to drive through France.

1. How much will it cost to travel using the Dover to Calais route?

_____

2. Which route would you choose and why?

_____

3. How much would your route cost the family?

_____

Name _____ Date _____

How far is it?

You will need a copy of 'Ferry crossings and mileage information'.

The Hopkins family are taking their car on holiday and are trying to decide which route they should use. They live in Birmingham and are going to drive to a villa near to Alicante in Spain. They have calculated that the average cost per mile for their car is 35p.

- The shortest route for driving is to take the ferry from Portsmouth to Santander. How many miles will they have to travel if they use this route?

Show your workings:

- What will the overall driving costs be?

Show your workings:

- Mum says it will be cheaper to use the Dover to Calais route. How much will the driving costs be using this route?

Show your workings:

- Although Poole is closer than Portsmouth, the Portsmouth to St Malo route will involve less driving than the Poole to Cherbourg route. How much more will the driving costs be if they take the Poole to Cherbourg route rather than the Portsmouth to St Malo route?

Show your workings:

BLOCK C Handling data and measures

Name _____   Date _____

Party hotdogs

For each hotdog, we need one roll, one sausage, spread, onions and sauce. We will also need a serviette to serve it in.

We have calculated that:

● one tub of spread is enough for 30 rolls

● one kilogram of onions is enough for 25 hotdogs

● one large bottle of tomato sauce is enough for 50 hotdogs.

There will be 75 people at the barbecue who would like two hotdogs each.

1. Calculate the quantities of each ingredient that we have to buy and then work out the total cost based on the prices below.

	Price	Quantity	Cost
Sausages (pack of 24)	£2.50		
Rolls (pack of 36)	98p		
Spread per tub	46p		
Onions per kilogram	75p		
Tomato sauce	£1.25		
Serviettes (pack of 200)	£1.45		
Total cost			

2. At least 50% of the selling price of the hotdogs must be profit. What would be a good price for the hotdogs?

Calculating, measuring and understanding shape

Key aspects of learning
- Enquiry
- Information processing
- Problem solving
- Evaluation

Expected prior learning
Check that children can already:
- solve one- and two-step problems involving whole numbers and decimals, explaining their methods, and using a calculator where appropriate
- multiply and divide whole numbers and decimals by 10, 100 or 1000
- mentally multiply a two-digit by a one-digit number (eg 12 × 9) and multiply by 25 (eg 16 × 25)
- use efficient written methods to multiply and divide HTU × U, TU × TU, U.t × U and HTU ÷ U
- apply their knowledge of multiplication and division facts to estimate and check results
- use standard metric units to estimate and measure length, weight and capacity
- convert larger to smaller units using decimals to one place (eg change 2.6kg to 2600g)
- measure and calculate the perimeter of regular and irregular polygons; use the formula for the area of a rectangle to calculate its area
- read and plot coordinates in the first quadrant
- identify lines of symmetry in 2D shapes; draw the position of a shape after a reflection or translation
- estimate, draw and measure acute and obtuse angles using an angle measurer or protractor
- calculate angles on a straight line.

Objectives overview
The text in this diagram identifies the focus of mathematics learning within the block.

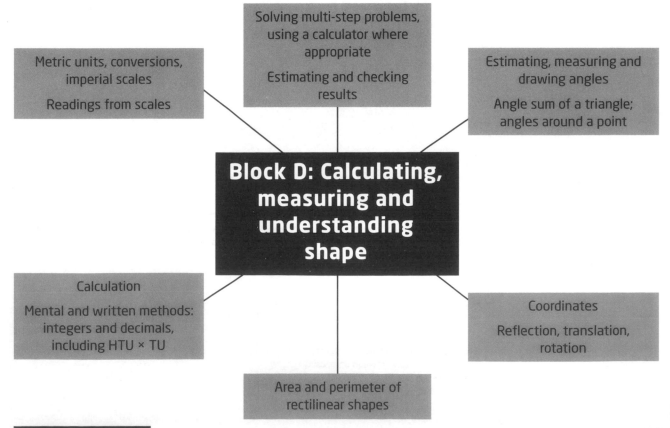

Solving multi-step problems, using a calculator where appropriate

Estimating and checking results

Metric units, conversions, imperial scales

Readings from scales

Estimating, measuring and drawing angles

Angle sum of a triangle; angles around a point

Block D: Calculating, measuring and understanding shape

Calculation

Mental and written methods: integers and decimals, including HTU × TU

Coordinates

Reflection, translation, rotation

Area and perimeter of rectilinear shapes

BLOCK D

Unit 1 ▢ 2 weeks

Calculating, measuring and understanding shape

Speaking and listening objectives
- Use a range of oral techniques to present a persuasive argument.

Introduction

This ten-lesson unit opens with more practice of using and applying mathematics to solve word problems in practical settings. Children then revise addition and subtraction strategies, in some cases dealing with money problems or those involving metric measures. There are also lessons that practise multiplication methods with decimal numbers and division activities that produce remainders. Division using money is also considered, and children are shown how answers sometimes need to be rounded up or down. The unit ends with two lessons dealing with finding the perimeter and area of compound shapes.

Use and apply mathematics

- Solve multi-step problems, and problems involving fractions, decimals and percentages; choose and use appropriate calculation strategies at each stage, including calculator use.

Lesson	Strands	Starter	Main teaching activities
1. Teach	Use/apply	Use approximations, inverse operations and tests of divisibility to estimate and check results.	Solve multi-step problems, and problems involving fractions, decimals and percentages; choose and use appropriate calculation strategies at each stage, including calculator use.
2. Apply	Use/apply	Calculate mentally with integers and decimals: U.t ± U.t, TU × U, TU ÷ U, U.t × U, U.t ÷ U.	As for Lesson 1
3. Review	Calculate	Solve problems by measuring, estimating and calculating; measure and calculate using imperial units still in everyday use; know their approximate metric values. (Progression to Y7)	**Use efficient written methods to add and subtract integers and decimals, to multiply and divide integers and decimals by a one-digit integer, and to multiply two-digit and three-digit integers by a two-digit integer.**
4. Review	Calculate	Calculate mentally with integers and decimals: U.t ± U.t, TU × U, TU ÷ U, U.t × U, U.t ÷ U.	As for Lesson 3
5. Review	Calculate	As for Lesson 4	As for Lesson 3
6. Teach	Calculate	As for Lesson 4	As for Lesson 3
7. Teach	Calculate	As for Lesson 4	As for Lesson 3
8. Teach	Calculate	Read and interpret scales on a range of measuring instruments, recognising that the measurement made is approximate and recording results to a required degree of accuracy; compare readings on different scales, for example when using different instruments.	• **Use efficient written methods to add and subtract integers and decimals, to multiply and divide integers and decimals by a one-digit integer, and to multiply two-digit and three-digit integers by a two-digit integer.** • Use a calculator to solve problems involving multi-step calculations.
9. Practise	Measure	Use approximations, inverse operations and tests of divisibility to estimate and check results.	Calculate the perimeter and area of rectilinear shapes; estimate the area of an irregular shape by counting squares.
10. Practise and evaluate	Measure	**Select and use standard metric units of measure and convert between units using decimals to two places (eg change 2.75 litres to 2750ml, or vice versa).**	As for Lesson 9

Lessons 1-8

Preparation

Lesson 1: It would be useful to have the questions for the main teaching activity written on the board, OHP or interactive whiteboard.
Lesson 2: Display the questions and menu for the main teaching activities.
Lesson 4: Display the questions for the main teaching activities.
Lesson 5: Prepare the 'Random times and Share machines' general resource sheet for display.
Lesson 8: Display the questions for the main teaching activities.

You will need

Photocopiable pages
'Solve these 1' (page 145), one per child.
CD resources
Support, extension and template versions of 'Solve these 1'; core, support, extension and template versions of 'Solve these 2', 'Addition and subtraction', 'Decimal numbers' and 'Eating out'; core, support and extension versions of 'Speed check'. General resource sheets: 'Five steps to successful problem solving' and 'Random times and Share machines'. Interactive resource: 'Number sentence builder'.
Equipment
Calculators; stopwatch or class clock; individual whiteboards and pens.

Learning objectives

Starter

- Use approximations, inverse operations and tests of divisibility to estimate and check results.
- Calculate mentally with integers and decimals: U.t ± U.t, TU × U, TU ÷ U, U.t × U, U.t ÷ U.
- Solve problems by measuring, estimating and calculating; measure and calculate using imperial units still in everyday use; know their approximate metric values. (Progression to Y7)
- Read and interpret scales on a range of measuring instruments, recognising that the measurement made is approximate and recording results to a required degree of accuracy; compare readings on different scales, for example when using different instruments.

Main teaching activities

2006
- Solve multi-step problems, and problems involving fractions, decimals and percentages; choose and use appropriate calculation strategies at each stage, including calculator use.
- Use efficient written methods to add and subtract integers and decimals, to multiply and divide integers and decimals by a one-digit integer, and to multiply two-digit and three-digit integers by a two-digit integer.
- Use a calculator to solve problems involving multi-step calculations.

1999
- Identify and use appropriate operations to solve word problems involving numbers and quantities based on 'real life' money or measures (including time) using one or more steps; explain methods and reasoning.
- Extend written methods to column addition and subtraction of numbers involving decimals.
- Extend written methods to short multiplication of numbers involving decimals; short division of numbers involving decimals.
- Express a quotient as a fraction or as a decimal rounded to one decimal place.
- Develop calculator skills and use a calculator effectively.

Vocabulary

problem, solution, answer, method, strategy, operation, calculation, calculate, decimal, decimal point, decimal place, add, subtract, multiply, divide, sum, total, difference, plus, minus, product, quotient, remainder, calculator, memory, display, key, enter, clear, divisible by, multiple, factor

Lesson 1 (Teach)

Starter

Recall: Investigate the strategy of rounding numbers to help find the approximate answer to multiplication problems. For example, 19 × 9 (171), approximate answer 20 × 10 = 200; 48 × 11 (528), approximate answer 50 ×10 = 500; 197 × 18 (3546), approximate answer 200 × 20 = 4000. Try also with decimal numbers, such as 1.9 × 9 (17.1), approximate answer 2 × 9 = 18; 28.9 × 5.8 (167.62), approximate answer 30 × 6 = 180.

Main teaching activities

Whole class: Write this problem on the board: *A garden centre is situated on a busy main road. It is open every day until 7.00pm. It sells a variety of rose bushes that are kept in five plots of land measuring 7 metres by 12 metres each. The owner wants to enclose the plots with new fencing wire. How* *much fencing must he buy?* Tell the children to look carefully at the question, then ask what information is needed to solve it. Establish that they need first to find the perimeter of each plot of land and then multiply this answer by 5. Discuss the information given. Ask: *Is there any information that does not help to solve the problem?* (Yes, the location of the garden centre and its opening times.) Establish that when solving problems they need to:

1. Read the question carefully to identify key words and numbers (these can be underlined).
2. Decide what operation(s) will need to be done.
3. Estimate the answer.
4. Decide which method of calculation is required.
5. Check to see that the answer is correct and makes sense.

Ask the children to complete the calculation of the question. Discuss the answer and the strategies used.

Then write up the next problem: *The roses at the garden centre cost £5.95 each. Jayne buys five of them: three pink and two yellow. How much change does she get from £30?* Ask the children to complete the calculation and discuss the methods used. Some children will need to use a pencil and paper method, whereas more confident children might calculate mentally. Check answers. Some children will have worked out the cost of the plants and given that as the answer, forgetting that the question asked for the change. Discuss the importance of re-reading the question to check what answer is required.

Write up another question: *I buy 2000 pencil cases and pack them into boxes of eight. How many full boxes can I make? Each box costs £7.50. How much money do I make?* Discuss the best way to solve this. Can it be done mentally? Should pencil and paper be used, or a calculator? Elicit that the figures involved would necessitate a calculator, although the children would still need to understand the operations required to work out the question. Ask them to work out the answers on their calculators. Recap on the sequence of tasks needed to solve written problems.

Group work: Provide the children with the 'Solve these 1' activity sheet, which gives practice in solving real-life problems. Encourage them to recognise and explain any patterns and relationships. Tell them to be prepared to generalise on their findings and predict outcomes.

Review

Choose a question from each of the activity sheets to solve together. For each question, work through the strategies that the children used. Recap on the list of instructions for solving problems (you might like to display the 'Five steps to successful problem solving' general resource sheet).

Differentiation

Less confident learners: This group should work from the support version of the activity sheet.
More confident learners: This group should work from the extension version of the activity sheet, where the problems are more complex and include some items from the Year 7 framework.

Lesson 2 (Apply)

Starter

Revisit: Recap on the term 'factor'. Tell the children that factors can help when multiplying and dividing large numbers. Show the following: 42 × 24. Ask for factors of 24 (1 and 24, 2 and 12, 3 and 8, 4 and 6). Using 3 and 8, the calculation could be done as follows: 42 × 24 → 42 × 8 = 336 and 336 × 3 = 1008. By breaking 24 into its factors, the calculation can be carried out mentally. Ask the children to try 27 × 18 and 36 × 16. Discuss answers.

Write on the board 756 ÷ 27. Show that the same method can be used when dividing, for example: 756 ÷ 3 = 252; 252 ÷ 9 = 28. Ask the children to try 800 ÷ 32 and/or 768 ÷ 24. Again, collect and discuss answers.

Main teaching activities

Whole class: Write the following question on the board: *Grant is planning his eleventh birthday party. He has to make his food choices from this menu* (see right). *What is the difference in price between the cheapest and dearest item?*

Party menu for 24	
Pizzas	£54.40
Burgers	£40.88
Sandwiches	£43.92
Chicken pieces	£58.56
Spaghetti	£47.76

▷ *Grant decides to buy chicken pieces and spaghetti. How much does it cost? What change does he get from £110?* Ask the children, working in pairs, to calculate the answers on their whiteboards. Discuss their answers. Ask: *Were there any questions that could be done mentally?* For instance, the last question required the children to subtract £106.32 from £110. This can be done mentally by counting up. Choose one part of the question and ask a child to work it out on the class board. Ask the rest of the class to check the answer by using the inverse operation.

Then ask the next question: *Grant's mum decides to add one more item to his choice. The food now costs £147.20. Which extra item did she buy?* Ask the children, again in pairs, to complete the calculation and feed back on the method used. Tell them they are now going to work on similar problems themselves. They will need to decide the most efficient method to use (mental or pencil and paper) for each calculation.

Group work: Provide the children with the 'Solve these 2' activity sheet to work through.

Review

Choose one of the problems from the 'Solve these 2' activity sheet. Discuss the strategies used to solve it. Recap on what the children have learned from this unit of work. They should appreciate the following: when to choose suitable methods of calculation (mental or pencil and paper); how to use the inverse operation, especially for checking; the importance of setting out calculations accurately, especially with regard to the positioning of the decimal point.

Differentiation

Less confident learners: Let this group work from the support version of the activity sheet. Provide adult assistance to help them convert the word problems into numerical calculations.
More confident learners: Give this group the extension version of the resource sheet, which has more complex problems.

Lesson 3 (Review)

Starter
Revisit: Remind the children that the imperial measure of capacity, the gallon, is equal to approximately 4½ litres. Ask them to make approximate conversions to gallons for the fuel tanks of the following vehicles:

1 9 litres (2)   **2** 18 litres (4)
3 36 litres (8)   **4** 27 litres (6)
5 45 litres (10)   **6** 13.5 litres (3)
7 22.5 litres (5)   **8** 40.5 litres (9)
9 49.5 litres (11)   **10** 31.5 litres (7)

Main teaching activities
Whole class: Explain to children that they are going to revise addition and subtraction strategies from Year 5 in preparation for extending these to standard written methods. Discuss informal pencil and paper methods the children might use. Write 9742 + 6381 on the board. Ask the children to estimate the answer first to help check its reasonableness at the end of the calculation. Record on the board as you work out the answer with the children. Check with the original estimate. Is the answer reasonable? Remind the children that it is important that the units line up under the units, that tens line up under tens and so on. Set another calculation for the children to work out on their whiteboards. Share the answer and discuss the calculation.

```
  9742
+ 6381
 15000
  1000
   120
     3
 16123
```

Write 8419 – 4247 on the board. Ask the children to estimate the answer first. Complete the calculation on the board with the class, using the 'adding on' number line method (see right). Now ask the children to work out 6840 – 2906 using

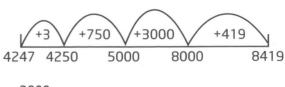

```
  3000
+  750
+  419
+    3
  4172
```

the same method. Share the calculations and discuss the result.

Next, write 7472 – 3661. Remind the children that they could also use a column method to subtract, as shown right. Show the children how they can add on until they reach the next significant number in each stage. Give the children a calculation to try out this method. Collect answers and discuss. Ask: *Which method did you find easier?*

```
   7472
 - 3661
     39  (3700)
 +  300  (4000)
   3000  (7000)
    472  (7472)
   3811
```

Group work: Give the children copies of the 'Addition and subtraction' activity sheet, which provides practice using the methods outlined above.

Differentiation

Less confident learners: This group should work on the support version of the activity sheet.
More confident learners: This group should work from the extension version of the activity sheet, with two sections. Then challenge them to prepare word-based problems that will test out the different methods. For example: *If a crowd of 8642 is watching a football match and 2037 leave early, how many are left?*

Review

Pose the following question: *Last year 10,482 people visited Anytown Zoo during the months of July and August. During September and October only 6973 people visited. What was the difference in visitors during the two periods?* (3509) Ask the children to use the method they feel most comfortable with to calculate the answer. Discuss strategies and why some may consider one method easier than another.

Lesson 4 (Review)

Starter

Reason: Use addition sentences such as 3.2 + ☐ + 3.9 = 9.8; 4.1 + 1.9 + 3.4 = ☐. Display these using the 'Number sentence builder' interactive resource. Invite the children to explain the strategies that they used, such as starting with the largest number, and looking for pairs that make whole numbers and doing these first.

Main teaching activities

Whole class: Write the following problem on the board: *In a sports shop I spend £43.50 on trainers, £8.25 on a pair of shorts and £3.79 on a whistle. How much do I spend altogether?* Establish that column addition would be an efficient method to use. Ask the children to work out the answer, reminding them that units should be under units, tens under tens and that the decimal points should line up (see (a) below). Check what the children have written.

a
```
   £43.50
 +   8.25
 +   3.79
 ─────────
   £55.54
```

b
```
      7 11 1
   £8.25
 -  3.79
 ─────────
   £4.46
```

Now ask: *What is the difference in price between the shorts and the whistle?* Ask the children to use an efficient column subtraction method to work this out, as shown in (b) above. Again, check the position of the decimal points when setting out the column and also when calculating the answer.

Move on to the following question: *A builder has a 12.5kg sack of sand. He uses 3250g to make cement. How much sand is left?* Establish that the calculation requires subtraction and ask the children how they would set it out. Elicit that the units of measurement need to be the same and that either 12.5kg needs to be converted to grams or 3250g needs to be converted to kilograms. Both methods are acceptable. Ask the children to make the conversion and write as column subtraction. Demonstrate on the board (see (c) and (d) below).

c
```
      4 1
   12.500
 -  3.250
 ─────────
    9.250  9kg 250g
```

d
```
      4 1
   12500
 -  3250
 ─────────
   9250  9250g
```

Unit 1 ▭ 2 weeks

Check place value and the position of the decimal point. Remind the children to place the decimal point in the answer box before undertaking any calculation. Work out the problem and discuss the answers. Elicit from the children that (c) will give an answer in kg and g and that (d) will provide an answer in g only. If necessary, give the children another example to try.
Group work: Provide children with copies of the 'Decimal numbers' activity sheet. This provides practice in adding and subtracting decimal numbers.

Review
Write on the board 4.6kg – 780g. Ask the children the following questions to ensure understanding: *What do you need to remember when setting this out as a column subtraction?* Elicit converting to the same unit, lining up units, tens, and so on, lining up decimal points. *How can we check the answer?* Elicit using the inverse operation.

Lesson 5 (Review)

Starter
Recall: Use the 7- and 9-times tables grids on the 'Random times and Share machines' general resource sheet.

Main teaching activities
Whole class: Review multiplication methods taught previously. Remind the children about the effect of multiplying decimal numbers by 10 or 100, and the use of doubling and halving strategies when multiplying, for example 24.2 × 2 = 48.4 (double) 24.2 × 4 = 96.8 (double again). Repeat for × 6 (trebling strategy). Also, remind the children about the work done previously on short multiplication of decimal numbers. Go through an example on the whiteboard, such as 2.34 × 3. Encourage estimation first and then suggest that the children partition the numbers as follows:

$$2 \times 3 = 6.0$$
$$0.3 \times 3 = 0.9$$
$$0.04 \times 3 = \underline{0.12}$$
$$\underline{7.02}$$

Stress that the decimal points should be lined up underneath each other before addition takes place. Work through other examples, such as 5.17 × 5 (25.85) and 4.83 × 6 (28.98). Move on to show a larger decimal number using the same method, such as 13.72 × 4:

$$13.00 \times 4 = 52.0$$
$$0.70 \times 4 = 2.8$$
$$0.02 \times 4 = \underline{0.08}$$
$$= \underline{54.88}$$

Independent work: Provide copies of the 'Speed check' activity sheet. Tell the children to try this activity against the clock.

Review
Check through the answers on the activity sheets. Play a 'hit the target' type activity as follows: Provide the answer to a decimal number multiplication calculation and ask children to provide you with the question. For example, if you say 0.6 they could answer 0.6 × 1 or 0.3 × 2; if you say 1.8 they could answer 0.6 × 3 or 0.9 × 2.

Lesson 6 (Teach)

Starter
Recall: Revise multiplying decimal numbers by 10 and 100. Work through some examples to show the movement of the digits to the left relative to the decimal point, for example 0.5 × 10 = 5 and 0.5 × 100 = 50. Try other

Differentiation
Less confident learners: Provide this group with the support version of the activity sheet, which has just one section.
More confident learners: Provide this group with the extension version and ask them to work through all sections.

Differentiation
Less confident learners: Ensure that children understand how the grid system works on the support version of the 'Speed check' activity sheet, and that they appreciate the value of the numbers in the tenths column, to the right of the decimal point.
More confident learners: This group should work through the extension version of the 'Speed check' activity sheet, which has more difficult calculations. Then ask them to check the inverse operation of the multiplication facts they have calculated on the activity sheet.

Calculating, measuring and understanding shape

BLOCK D

⊪SCHOLASTIC

100 MATHS FRAMEWORK LESSONS · YEAR 6   139

examples: 0.8, 2.3, 6.8. Then introduce numbers written to two decimal places, for example 0.42 × 10 = 4.2 and 0.42 × 100 = 42. Use other examples: 0.73, 1.27 and 13.59. Extend to multiplying integers by 1000.

Main teaching activities

Whole class: On the whiteboard write an example of division that produces a remainder, for example 31 divided by 5. Establish that this is 6 remainder 1. Write up 31 ÷ 5 = 6 r1 and demonstrate this on a number line if necessary. Tell the children that 1 ÷ 5 is $\frac{1}{5}$ and that 31 ÷ 5 = 6 and $\frac{1}{5}$. Repeat the same process with other numbers in the 5-times table, such as: 26 ÷ 5 = 5 r1 or 5 and $\frac{1}{5}$; 43 ÷ 5 = 8 r3, or 8 and $\frac{3}{5}$. Revise how we can write $\frac{1}{5}$ as a decimal (0.2), and that 5 and $\frac{1}{5}$ would be 5.2 and 8 and $\frac{3}{5}$ would be 8.6. Now write 36 ÷ 10 on the board and ask for alternative answers. The children should provide 3 r6 or 3 and $\frac{6}{10}$. Point out that $\frac{1}{10}$ is written as 0.1, so the answer could be written as 3.6. Finally, write 19 ÷ 2. Answers provided should be 9 r1 or 9$\frac{1}{2}$. Point out that when dividing by 2 the only remainder can be 1. We write a half as 0.5, so 19 ÷ 2 = 9.5.

Paired work: In pairs, children choose numbers to divide by 2, 5 and 10 and give their answers in fraction and decimal form. Pairs of ten-sided dice can be used to generate numbers. Draw up the following table and do the first two rows together:

Digits chosen	÷ 2	÷ 5	÷ 10
32	16	6 r2	3.2
47	23$\frac{1}{2}$	9 r2	4.7

Review

Again use a 'hit the target' type game. Ask the children to provide division calculations that will give a whole number and a remainder equivalent to 0.3, 0.7 (divide by 10, eg 23 ÷ 10 = 2.3; 57 ÷ 10 = 5.7), 0.5 (divide by 2, eg 17 ÷ 2 = 8.5) 0.2, 0.4, 0.6 and 0.8 (divide by 5, eg 16 ÷ 5 = 3.2; 32 ÷ 5 = 6.4; 43 ÷ 5 = 8.6; 69 ÷ 5 = 13.8). Check with the more confident group to see how they divided by 4 and converted remainders into decimal numbers.

Differentiation

Less confident learners: It may be better to begin with dividing by 10, where the remainder automatically becomes a decimal number. Fifths and halves can then be introduced later.
More confident learners: Work with this group and extend the activity to include dividing by 4. Revise with the children that $\frac{1}{4}$ is 0.25 as a decimal, $\frac{2}{4}$ or $\frac{1}{2}$ is 0.5 and $\frac{3}{4}$ is $\frac{1}{2}$ + $\frac{1}{4}$, ie 0.5 + 0.25 = 0.75. So 17 ÷ 4 = 4 r1, or 4.25; 22 ÷ 4 = 5 r2, or 5.5; 27 ÷ 4 = 6 r3 or 6.75. Then try the same method with three-digit numbers.

Lesson 7 (Teach)

Starter

Recall: Revise dividing decimal numbers by 10 and 100. Work through some examples to show the movement of digits to the right relative to the decimal point (3.8 ÷ 10 = 0.38 and 3.8 ÷ 100 = 0.038). Stress that the 0 is included as a place holder. Try other examples before introducing numbers to two decimal places, such as 16.57 ÷ 10 = 1.657 and 16.57 ÷ 100 = 0.1657. Use other examples: 9.34, 12.72, 37.54. Extend to dividing integers by 1000.

Main teaching activities

Whole class: Briefly revise the work done in the previous lesson on dividing numbers by 5, 10, 2 and 4 and giving answers in fraction and decimal form. Then go on to look at what happens when the divisor is different from these numbers. Write 75 ÷ 9 on the whiteboard. Ask the children to provide the answer with a remainder and then show the remainder as a fraction. They should reply with 8 r3 or 8 and $\frac{3}{9}$. Ask them how the $\frac{3}{9}$ can be written in decimal terms. Ask them to work out 3 ÷ 9 = 0.333333333 using a calculator. Tell them this is called a recurring decimal number because the same digit is repeated or recurs throughout. Then check the solution to the whole calculation on the calculator: 75 ÷ 9 = 8.333333333. Ask: *What is the answer to the nearest whole number?* The answer is 8 because 8.3 is nearer to 8 than it is to 9. Say: *If we rounded to one decimal place the answer would be 8.3. The 3 in the hundredths column is less than 5, so it would not be big enough to round up the 3 in the tenths column.* Try other examples, such as 65 ÷ 6 (11 and 10.8), 123 ÷ 8 (15 and 15.4).

Next, move on to calculations where the divisor is a two-digit number. Write 274 ÷ 14 on the whiteboard. Demonstrate a method of long division to get the answer 19 r8, or 19 and $^8/_{14}$. Then go through the method on the calculator to find $^8/_{14}$ as a decimal, ie 8 ÷ 14 = 0.571428571. Check the solution to the whole calculation on the calculator 274 ÷ 14 = 19.57142857. Ask: *What would this be to the nearest whole number? And rounded to one decimal place?* It would be 20 to the nearest whole number because 19.57 is more than a half, and 19.6 rounded to one decimal place because the 7 in the hundredths column is more than 5, so the 5 is rounded up to a 6. Try other examples, such as 356 ÷ 24 (15 and 14.8) and 475 ÷ 36 (13 and 13.1).

Independent work: Put other examples on the whiteboard for the children to calculate. Start with the divisor as a single digit, for example: 32 ÷ 9, 74 ÷ 7, 56 ÷ 5, 98 ÷ 8; then move on to two-digit numbers, such as 46 ÷ 11, 64 ÷ 12 and 97 ÷ 15. Each time, the children should show the remainder, the remainder as a fraction, the answer to the nearest whole number and then the answer rounded to one decimal place.

Review

Mark the work the children have produced and clarify any points that have arisen. They should be able to give a quotient as a decimal rounded to at least one decimal place. Remind them that the quotient is the answer to a division calculation. Ask: *How many different ways do you know of showing the remainder in a division calculation? When rounding remainders to one decimal place, what rules govern changes to digits in the tenths column?*

Lesson 8 (Teach)

Starter

Recall: Check that children can work out quickly and mentally the value of sub-divisions on a set of weighing scales when they are given the main markings. Use these examples: scale 0–100g, nine divisions (10g); scale 0–500g, four divisions (100g); scale 0–1kg, three divisions (250g); scale 0–100g, one division (50g); scale 0–1kg, nine divisions (100g); 0–5kg, nine divisions (500g).

Main teaching activities

Whole class: Explain to the children that in this lesson they will learn how to divide pounds and pence by a two-digit number to get £ and p. Give them this problem: *Twelve people went out for a meal in a restaurant. The bill came to £110.40. How much did they need to pay each?* Working in pairs with a calculator, children find the answer: 110.40 ÷ 12 = 9.2. Point out that as it is a money calculation the .2 has to be written in money terms, so it becomes 20p. Each person has to pay £9.20. Tell the children to check the answer using the inverse operation (ie £9.20 × 12 = £110.40). Try another example, such as 16 people sharing a food bill of £135.68. Tell the children they will return to some of these questions later.

Move to 'real-life' division calculations that require rounding up or rounding down. Write this problem on the whiteboard: *The football club organiser has £100. Tickets for the match are £7 each. How many children can she take?* Do the calculation £100 ÷ 7 = 14 remainder 2. Point out that you cannot buy two-sevenths of a ticket, so the answer is rounded down. Only 14 tickets can be bought and £2 will be left over. Ask: *How many more tickets could be bought if the price was reduced to £5.50 at the last moment?* £100 ÷ £5.50 = 18.18. This would be 18 tickets. (4 tickets more.) Fans would save £1.50 each. The 18 tickets would cost a total of £99 and £1 would be saved. Write up a second problem: *There are 127 adults going on a trip. Only 20-seater minibuses can be hired. How many minibuses are needed?* (127 ÷ 20 = 6 remainder 7.) Seven people cannot be left behind, so the answer has to be rounded up. Seven minibuses will be needed, even though one of them will not be full. If the minibuses cost £58 each to hire,

Differentiation

Less confident learners: Restrict the divisor to a single-digit number until the children are able to work out these calculations confidently.

More confident learners: Continue to encourage children to use the inverse operation (in this case multiplication) to check the answers to division calculations, for example: if 426 ÷16 = 26 r10, then 26 × 16 + 10 = 426.

Differentiation

Less confident learners:
Provide the support version of 'Eating out'. Make sure these children are able to interpret the calculator display correctly (eg £15.2 being read as £15.20).
More confident learners:
Provide the extension version of 'Eating out'. Calculators can be used to check answers.

how much would this cost? £58 × 7 = £406. *How much each would it cost the 127 adults?* £406 ÷ 127 = £3.196. This would be £3.20 each.
Independent work: Return to the division tasks carried out in the first part of the lesson. Continue the 'eating-out' theme with groups of children working in ability pairs from the differentiated 'Eating out' activity sheets.

Review

Ask quick-fire questions in which 'read outs' from the calculator have to be converted into £ and p. For example, 14.3 becomes £14.30, 27.5 becomes £27.50 and 49.9 becomes £49.90. Check the individual work carried out in the lesson on restaurant bills.

Lessons 9-10

Preparation

Lesson 9: Display the shapes shown in Lesson 9 below on the board, OHP or interactive whiteboard.
Lesson 10: Display the shapes shown for Lesson 10 below on the board, OHP or interactive whiteboard.

You will need

CD resources
Core and support versions of 'All the way round'; core, support and extension versions of 'Calculating area'.

Learning objectives

Starter

● Use approximations, inverse operations and tests of divisibility to estimate and check results.
● Select and use standard metric units of measure and convert between units using decimals to two places (eg change 2.75 litres to 2750ml, or vice versa).

Main teaching activities

2006
● Calculate the perimeter and area of rectilinear shapes; estimate the area of an irregular shape by counting squares.
1999
● Calculate the perimeter and area of simple compound shapes that can be split into rectangles.

Vocabulary

measure, estimate, approximately, metric unit, standard unit, length, distance, perimeter, area, surface area, units of measurement and their abbreviations, pound (£), penny/pence (p)

Lesson 9 (Practise)

Starter

Revisit: Organise the children into pairs and provide each pair with a calculator.

Put the following calculations on the whiteboard and ask children to check their accuracy by using the inverse operation. Remind them before starting that + and – are inverse operations, as are × and ÷, but that they cannot be mixed. Use the following examples: 725 + 394 = 1119, 5276 – 856 = 4420, 16,422 ÷ 23 = 714 and 254 × 36 = 9144.

Main teaching activities

Whole class: Remind the children of the meaning of the word 'perimeter'. Ask them how they can find quickly the perimeter of the rectangle (a) below:

a   14cm

4cm

Elicit one of these two methods: either (14 + 4) × 2 or (14 × 2) + (4 × 2).
Now draw some simple rectangles on the board and ask the children to calculate the perimeter. Then draw shape (b) on the board, explaining that it is not to scale:

BLOCK D

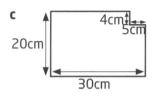

Ask the children to find the perimeter. Ask: *What information is missing?* (the length of two of the sides.) *What can be done to find these two lengths?* Establish that length a can be found by subtracting side e from side c (12cm – 10cm = 2cm). Also, side b can be found by subtracting side f from side d (14cm - 6cm = 8cm). Now the perimeter can be found.

Ask the children to draw the shape shown in (c) below on their whiteboards and work in pairs to establish the perimeter. Discuss answers

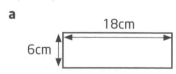

Differentiation

Less confident learners: Give this group the support version of 'All the way round', which consolidates finding the perimeter of rectangles before moving on to compound shapes.
More confident learners: Once this group has completed the core activity sheet, challenge them, in pairs, to make up word problems involving perimeter. For example: *A farmer owns a rectangular field measuring 270m by 450m. He sells a 60m by 60m square of land in one of the corners for house building. What is the perimeter of his field now?*

and correct any misunderstandings. If necessary, work during independent work time with any children who are finding it difficult to calculate the missing measurements.
Independent work: Hand out the 'All the way round' activity sheet for the children to work on individually.

Review

Ask: *If Sasha has three tiles measuring 9cm by 5cm, how can she arrange them to give the following perimeters: 48cm and 64cm?* (Two different answers.) Discuss the solutions, ensuring children understand that only the outside of the shape is counted, not the individual perimeters of each shape.

Lesson 10 (Practise and evaluate)

Starter

Recall: Tell the children they are going to convert centimetres to metres, metres to kilometres, millilitres to litres and grams to kilograms. Remind them to be careful with place value and the position of the zero as a place-holder. Answers can be displayed on whiteboards or written as a list to be checked at the end. Change to km: 360m, 2401m, 18m, 4km 25m. Change to litres: 8643ml, 290ml, 15ml, 2l,109ml. Change to kg: 1kg 302g, 19g, 400g, 9736g. Discuss the answers and check that the decimal points and/or zeros are correctly positioned.

Main teaching activities

Whole class: Draw shape (a) below on the board. Ask the children to find the perimeter (48cm).

a

```
      18cm
   ┌──────────┐
6cm│          │
   └──────────┘
```

Tell them that you now want to find out how much surface area the rectangle covers. Explain that area is not the space inside a shape but the amount of surface the shape covers. Ask the children for suggestions as to how they could find the surface area, reminding them of work covered in Year 5. Elicit the method of multiplying length by width or breadth. Remind them that this is written as area = length × width or a = l × w. Stress that the

BLOCK D

answer will always be in square centimetres or whatever unit is being used (square metres, square kilometres and so on).
Now draw the following compound shape:

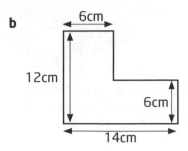

b

6cm

12cm

6cm

14cm

Ask for suggestions as to how the area might be calculated. Establish that the shape will need to be divided into two smaller rectangles that can be labelled *a* and *b* (see (c) below).

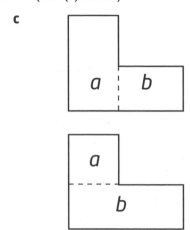

c

a ⋮ *b*

a

b

Explain that there is more than one way to divide the shape, as shown, and that both ways are acceptable. Establish that the area of *a* is found by multiplying 12 by 6 = 72 in the top diagram of (c). The area of *b* will be 6 × 8 = 48. So the total area will be 72 + 48 = 120 square centimetres, or 120cm².
Try another shape together as a class (see (d) below). This time, divide the shape into three sections and then find the area.

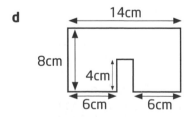

d

14cm

8cm

4cm

6cm   6cm

Independent work: Distribute copies of the 'Calculating area' activity sheet. The children have to find the area of compound shapes, and there are also real-life problems to solve.

Review
Ask the following question: *A gardener creates a vegetable plot with a perimeter of 36m. The plot is rectangular. Of all the possible rectangles, which would give the greatest surface area for his vegetables?* Ask the children for strategies they could use to solve this problem. Then ask them to work in pairs to solve it. Ask: *What do you discover about the best possible length × width to use?* (9 × 9.) *Do you recognise what type of number the size of the area is?* (It is a square number.)
Ask the children to write an evaluation of their learning from this unit, identifying strengths and areas for improvement.

Differentiation
Less confident learners:
Provide this group with the support version of 'Calculating area', on which the shapes are more straightforward.
More confident learners:
Provide this group with the extension version of the activity sheet. You may need to work with this group, as one set of questions involves finding the surface area of a box.

Name _____   Date _____

Solve these 1

Solve the following word problems.

1. A sales person drives an average of 4560 kilometres each month.

How far will she drive in a year? _____

2. The Sales Manager drives 3000 kilometres a month.

What is this in miles? **(Remember: 1km = 0.62 miles)** _____

3. A class of 32 children take part in a Maths Challenge. I want to give each of them a prize. Would it be cheaper for me to buy pencils at 65p each or novelty rubbers at £3.00 for a box of 5?

_____

Sid's Snacks

BURGER ------ £1·50

BURGER WITH CHEESE ---- £1·75

MUSHROOM PIZZA ...£2·75

HOT DOG .... £1·60

BACON ROLL .... £2·25

VEGGIE BURGER ... £1·90

CHICKEN BITES ... £2·45

4. **Use the above menu to answer the following questions.**

a) Which two snacks could I buy for exactly £4.65? _____

b) A family buys two pizzas, a veggie burger and chicken bites.

How much change do they get from £10? _____

c) I have £5. Can I buy two cheeseburgers and a hot dog? _____

d) Is it possible to buy three different snacks without spending more than £5? If so, what can I buy?

_____

5. A theatre presented five performances of the play 'The Magic Wand'. A total of 1860 people attended during the week. What was the average size of the audience each night?

_____

Calculating, measuring and understanding shape

Speaking and listening objectives
● Participate in a whole-class debate using the conventions and language of debate.

Introduction
There are further opportunities to use and apply mathematical skills to solve word problems at the start of this unit. Then children practise their ability to use written methods of calculation involving multiplying three-digit by two-digit integers and dividing a three-digit integer by a two-digit integer. Three lessons on angles follow, providing the chance to use protractors and calculate the internal angles of a triangle. Two lessons are also provided on the use of coordinates, and the unit finishes with tasks about reflecting shapes.

Use and apply mathematics
● Solve multi-step problems, and problems involving fractions, decimals and percentages; choose and use appropriate calculation strategies at each stage, including calculator use.

Lesson	Strands	Starter	Main teaching activities
1. Review	Use/apply Calculate	Use decimal notation for tenths, hundredths and thousandths; partition, round and order decimals with up to three places, and position them on the number line. (Revision of Block A)	• Solve multi-step problems, and problems involving fractions, decimals and percentages; choose and use appropriate calculation strategies at each stage, including calculator use. • Use a calculator to solve problems involving multi-step calculations.
2. Review	Use/apply Calculate	As for Lesson 1	As for Lesson 1
3. Teach	Calculate	Calculate mentally with integers and decimals: U.t ± U.t, TU × U, TU ÷ U, U.t × U, U.t ÷ U.	**Use efficient written methods to add and subtract integers and decimals, to multiply and divide integers and decimals by a one-digit integer, and to multiply two-digit and three-digit integers by a two-digit integer.**
4. Teach	Calculate Knowledge	As for Lesson 3	**• Use efficient written methods to add and subtract integers and decimals, to multiply and divide integers and decimals by a one-digit integer, and to multiply two-digit and three-digit integers by a two-digit integer.** • Use approximations, inverse operations and tests of divisibility to estimate and check results.
5. Teach	Shape	Estimate angles, and use a protractor to measure and draw them, on their own and in shapes; calculate angles in a triangle or around a point.	Estimate angles, and use a protractor to measure and draw them, on their own and in shapes; calculate angles in a triangle or around a point.
6. Teach	Shape	As for Lesson 5	As for Lesson 5
7. Practise	Shape	As for Lesson 5	Use coordinates in the first quadrant to draw, locate and complete shapes that meet given properties.
8. Review	Shape	**Select and use standard metric units of measure and convert between units using decimals to two places (eg change 2.75 litres to 2750ml, or vice versa).**	As for Lesson 7
9. Practise	Shape	Use coordinates in the first quadrant to draw, locate and complete shapes that meet given properties.	**Visualise and draw on grids of different types where a shape will be after reflection, after translations, or after rotation through 90° or 180° about its centre or one of its vertices.**
10. Teach and evaluate	Shape	**Select and use standard metric units of measure and convert between units using decimals to two places (eg change 2.75 litres to 2750ml, or vice versa).**	As for Lesson 9

Lessons 1-4

Preparation

Lesson 1: Prepare the 'Five steps to successful problem solving' and 'Football factsheets questions' general resource sheets for display.
Lesson 4: If necessary, prepare your own versions of the 'Division problems' activity sheet from the template.

You will need

Photocopiable pages
'Football factsheets questions' (page 155), one per child.
CD resources
Core, support, extension and template versions of 'Division problems'. General resource sheets: 'Five steps to successful problem solving' and 'Football factsheets'.
Equipment
Table squares or charts.

Learning objectives

Starter

● Use decimal notation for tenths, hundredths and thousandths; partition, round and order decimals with up to three places, and position them on the number line. (Revision of Block A)
● Calculate mentally with integers and decimals: U.t ± U.t, TU × U, TU ÷ U, U.t × U, U.t ÷ U.

Main teaching activities
2006
● Solve multi-step problems, and problems involving fractions, decimals and percentages; choose and use appropriate calculation strategies at each stage, including calculator use.
● Use a calculator to solve problems involving multi-step calculations.
● Use efficient written methods to add and subtract integers and decimals, to multiply and divide integers and decimals by a one-digit integer, and to multiply two-digit and three-digit integers by a two-digit integer.
● Use approximations, inverse operations and tests of divisibility to estimate and check results.
1999
● Identify and use appropriate operations, including combinations of operations, to solve word problems involving numbers and quantities based on 'real life' money or measures, using one or more steps; explain methods and reasoning.
● Develop calculator skills and use a calculator effectively.
● Extend written methods to column addition and subtraction of numbers involving decimals. Extend written methods to short multiplication of numbers involving decimals; short division of numbers involving decimals. Express a quotient as a fraction or as a decimal rounded to one decimal place.
● Check results of calculations.
● Know and apply simple tests of divisibility.

Vocabulary
problem, solution, answer, method, strategy, operation, calculation, calculate, decimal, decimal point, decimal place, add, subtract, multiply, divide, sum, total, difference, plus, minus, product, quotient, remainder, multiple, factor

Lesson 1 (Review)

Starter
Revisit: Write 2.5 on the board and ask: *What does the 2 represent? What does the 5 represent?* Now write a number with two decimal places, such as 4.56. Ask what each digit represents. Repeat for other similar numbers. Extend this to numbers with three decimal places, such as 6.254. Invite the children to re-order the digits to make a new number and say what each digit is now worth.

Main teaching activities
Whole class: Tell the children that during the next two lessons they are going to work on choosing and using appropriate number operations to solve problems. Explain that they will also need to choose appropriate ways of calculating, such as mental, mental with jottings, written and calculator. Revise these terms to make sure the children understand what they mean. Explain that calculators will not be an option on this occasion. Tell the children that the problems will involve football matches played

Calculating, measuring and understanding shape

BLOCK D

Differentiation

Less confident learners: Ensure that these children receive support in their groups, especially with place value and ordering attendance figures. Tell them to focus particularly on one-step questions. Stress that they should follow the guide provided in 'Five steps to successful problem solving'.

More confident learners: Encourage this group to focus on the multi-step questions. They can then make up their own questions using the information provided.

in the Premiership. Point out that they will be working in this lesson on attendance figures (shown on the first sheet) and ground capacities (shown on the second sheet). Remind them of the step-by-step approach to problem solving. Some children may benefit from using the 'Five steps to successful problem solving' general resource sheet. Stress that they should use this method, estimating answers first, showing their working out and checking their answers. Say that they will be asked to explain their methods and reasoning. Split the class into mixed-ability pairs or groups of three for these activities.

Group work: Distribute copies of 'Football factsheets' to each group. These contain the information that the children will need. Then display the 'Football factsheets questions' activity sheet as an OHT or on the whiteboard. Ask the children to work through the 'Attendance figures' questions.

Review

Review the problems the groups of children have been working on. Discuss which parts of solving problems they found most difficult and which they found easiest. Assess how helpful the five-step guide was.

Lesson 2 (Review)

Starter

Revisit: Write on the board a list of numbers such as 4.25, 18.7, 6.39, 8.25, 5.3. Invite the children to order the numbers from smallest to largest. Repeat with a set such as 4.25, 9.72, 4.52, 9.27. Repeat, extending the number range to include some numbers with three places of decimals.

Main teaching activities

Whole class: Review the work on attendance figures from the previous lesson. Tell the children that in this lesson they will be looking at the number of goals scored in a particular week and the time in which they were scored (shown on the first sheet beside the name of the scorer). They will also look at the difference between goals scored and conceded (shown in bold on the first sheet) by each side. Check that the children understand the naming of the column letters and the points system on the second sheet. Remind them that, although mathematically a difference cannot be negative, in football terms 17 goals for and 23 goals against would give a 'difference' of -6. Work through an example of each type of question.

Group work: Again, split the class into mixed-ability pairs or groups of three. Distribute copies of the 'Football factsheets' general resource sheet to the children and a set of 'Football factsheets questions' (or display them on OHT). They should now work through the second and third sets of questions.

Differentiation

Less confident learners: Provide support in the mixed-ability groups. If necessary, work with these children on similar examples, particularly related to the 'Goal difference and points' questions. For example: *A team that has played 14 games, won 7, drawn 5 and lost 2, has 26 points.* Demonstrate that the 3-times table could be used to calculate the points scored from wins: 7 × 3 + 5 = 26.

More confident learners: Once this group has answered all the questions encourage them to make up their own questions using the information provided on 'Football factsheets'.

Review

Examine the methods children have used to find solutions. Try out further examples: *What is the time difference between goals scored at 16 minutes and 83 minutes? Did you find it easier to add on or subtract in these examples?* Review the use of negative numbers for goal difference (for example, 26 goals scored, 31 conceded gives a goal difference of -5 or 5 fewer goals scored than conceded) and checking total points (for example, P20, W14, D4, L2 = 14 × 3 + 4 = 46). Allow additional time for the children to complete all the factsheet questions and set as homework if necessary.

Lesson 3 (Teach)

Starter

Recall: Revise with the children what a factor is (a number that divides into another number exactly without leaving a remainder). Then write numbers on the whiteboard and ask the children to give you a pair of factors for each number. For example, 12 would produce 6 and 2, 4 and 3, 12 and 1; 18 would produce 1 and 18, 2 and 9, 3 and 6; 20 would produce 2 and 10, 1 and 20, 5 and 4. Include some square numbers such as 16, which produces 2 and 8, 1 and 16 and 4 and 4.

Main teaching activities

Whole class: Write the calculation 16 × 12 on the whiteboard. Ask: *How can factors be used to help make this multiplication easier?* Start with the 12 first. It could be broken down into 16 × 2 × 6 or 16 × 3 × 4. Ask the children to work out the answers and then suggest which way they found most straightforward. Then look at ways of factorising 16 as well. Try 8 × 2 × 3 × 4 or 4 × 4 × 2 × 6. Discuss the most efficient method. Then show the children how factors can be used in the division process. For example, 288 ÷ 18; since 2 × 9 = 18, this division can be calculated as 288 ÷ 2 = 144, then 144 ÷ 9 = 16.

Independent work: On the whiteboard write ten examples showing the use of factors in multiplication and division calculations. Ask the children to work these out individually. Tell them they should use the factors they feel are most suitable. Examples might include: 16 × 8, 19 × 12, 20 × 24, 28 × 14, 36 × 18, 45 × 30, 112 ÷ 14, 324 ÷ 36, 432 ÷ 18, 456 ÷ 24.

Review

Play a game in which the children have to spot the odd one out in a list of factors. For example, if the factors of 21 were given as 1, 3, 4, 7 and 21, then 4 would be the odd one out because 21 does not come in the 4-times table. Or leave out a factor and ask children to tell you what is missing. For example, if the factors of 24 were given as 1, 2, 3, 4, 6, 12 and 24, then 8 would be the missing number. Ensure that the children understand the difference between the terms 'multiple' and 'factor'. The multiples of 9 are 9, 18, 27, 36..., while the factors of 9 are 1, 3 and 9.

Differentiation

Less confident learners: Work with this group to ensure numbers are being factorised correctly. Table squares or charts showing factors of numbers may be needed by some children for reference purposes.
More confident learners: Invite children to make their own factor trees - that is, splitting up numbers into multiplication facts. A factor tree of 20, for example, would include the branches 1 × 20, 2 × 10 and 4 × 5.

20

1 × 20   2 × 10   4 × 5

Lesson 4 (Teach)

Starter

Refine: Ask: *What is 20 multiplied by 5? So what is 20 multiplied by 50? How could we calculate 20 multiplied by 49... 51?* Elicit the response that you can multiply by 50 and adjust by subtracting or adding 20. Repeat for other examples, such as 30 × 51, 30 × 41.

Main teaching activities

Whole class: Review previous work on division. Then consider division where HTU is divided by TU. Look at the example 980 ÷ 28. Approximate first (990 ÷ 30 = 33), then explain orally (see workings). The answer would be 35. Compare this with the estimate.

```
        35                      12.3
  28)980                  8)98.4
  -   560   20 × 28       -   80.0   10 × 8
      420                     18.4
  -   280   10 × 28       -   16.0   2 × 8
      140                      2.4
  -   140   5 × 28        -    2.4   0.3 × 8
      000                      0.0
```

Finally, demonstrate an example of the short division method involving the use of decimal numbers. Remind the children that when setting this down it is important that the decimal points are lined up underneath each other. Use the example 98.4 ÷ 8. Approximate first (96 ÷ 8 = 12), then explain orally (see workings). The answer is 12.3.

Independent work: Children practise examples of these calculations individually, using the 'Division problems' activity sheet. Stress the importance of estimating first and showing each stage of the working-out.

Differentiation

Less confident learners: Provide this group with the support version of 'Division problems', where children are asked to divide three-digit numbers by a single digit first. A template version of the resource sheet is also provided for you to fill in with suitable smaller numbers if necessary.
More confident learners: Provide these children with the

extension version of the activity sheet. They should also show evidence in their calculations that they are checking answers by using the inverse operation (multiplication in this case).

Review

Invite the children to demonstrate each of the three types of division covered in this lesson and in Block A, Unit 2, Lesson 9. Look at some examples of division calculations that have been checked by using the inverse operation. What do the methods demonstrate about the relationship between multiplication and division?

Lessons 5-10

Preparation

Lesson 5: Display the angles for the Starter activity and prepare examples of angles on large flashcards for the Review.
Lesson 6: Display the angles for the Starter activity.
Lesson 7: Prepare an OHT of the 'Grids' general resource sheet (this will be used in the next few lessons).
Lesson 9: Prepare a 10 × 10 grid for the Starter. Prepare a template of the parallelogram from the 'Shape translation' sheet.
Lesson 10: Prepare a shape and grid to show reflection on the OHP.

You will need
Photocopiable pages
'Hit out' (page 156) and 'Best of three' (page 157), one per child.
CD resources
Core, support, extension and template versions of 'Shape maker'; core, support and extension versions of 'Map reading'; core, support and template versions of 'Shape translation'; core and template versions of 'On reflection'. General resource sheet: 'Grids'.
Equipment
OHP protractor; thick paper or thin card; squared grid paper; mirrors; tracing paper.

Learning objectives

Starter
● Estimate angles, and use a protractor to measure and draw them, on their own and in shapes; calculate angles in a triangle or around a point.
● Select and use standard metric units of measure and convert between units using decimals to two places (eg change 2.75 litres to 2750ml, or vice versa).
● Use coordinates in the first quadrant to draw, locate and complete shapes that meet given properties.

Main teaching activities
2006
● Estimate angles, and use a protractor to measure and draw them, on their own and in shapes; calculate angles in a triangle or around a point.
● Use coordinates in the first quadrant to draw, locate and complete shapes that meet given properties.
● Visualise and draw on grids of different types where a shape will be after reflection, after translations, or after rotation through 90° or 180° about its centre or one of its vertices.
1999
● Estimate angles; use a protractor to measure and draw acute and obtuse angles to the nearest degree.
● Check that the sum of the angles of a triangle is 180°: eg by measuring or paper folding.
● Calculate angles in a triangle or around a point.
● Read and plot coordinates.
● Recognise where a shape will be after reflection, or after two translations. Recognise where a shape will be after a rotation through 90° about one of its vertices.

Vocabulary
angle, degree (°), angle measurer, protractor, acute, right angle, reflex, obtuse, position, direction, reflection, reflective symmetry, line of symmetry, mirror line, translation, origin, coordinates, x-coordinate, y-coordinate, x-axis, y-axis, axes, quadrant, congruent

Lesson 5 (Teach)

Starter
Revisit: Draw a selection of angles on the whiteboard at random and ask the children to name them. Include selections of acute angles (0°–90°), right angles (90°), obtuse angles (90°–180°) and straight angles (180°).

Main teaching activities
Whole class: Explain to the children that you will be showing them how to draw and measure angles using a protractor or angle measurer. Revise work done previously on angles by seeing how much the children remember. Ask: *What is an angle? How are angles measured? What types of angles do you know?* Check the children's understanding of the terms 'acute angle' (less

than 90°), 'right angle' (90°), 'obtuse angle' (between 90° and 180°) and 'straight angle' (180°). Also introduce the term 'reflex' (an angle 'between 180° and 360°), and remind the children that 360° is a complete turn. On the OHP, show them some large examples of angles. Ask them to name each angle and to estimate its size. They should explain their reasoning, for example: *The angle is about half way between a right angle and a straight angle, so it is roughly 140°–150°.*

Then demonstrate how to measure an angle using the OHP protractor (or use a large board protractor on the whiteboard). Stress the importance of placing the protractor on the correct line and reading the correct scale. Make sure that not all lines are horizontal. Ask: *How accurate was the estimated answer?* Also demonstrate how angles can be drawn using a protractor. Include a selection of acute and obtuse angles. Show how lines should be turned into the horizontal position to make the angle-drawing task easier. Point out that at this level, angles should be accurate to within one degree.

Paired work: Provide the children with copies of the 'Hit out' activity sheet, which provides practice in measuring and naming angles. For practice in drawing angles write the following on the whiteboard: 55°, 140°, 25°, 84°, 127°, 14°, 108°, 182°. Then say: *Using a protractor, draw these angles carefully. Name and label them. Remember, they will be checked for their accuracy and should be within one degree of the number given.* Let the children work in mixed-ability pairs, taking it in turns to check their partner's measurements.

Review

Revise the names of angles, including 'reflex', by showing the children a series of angles on flashcards. Check and discuss the results produced on the activity sheets. List the steps used to measure and/or draw angles with a protractor.

Lesson 6 (Teach)

Starter

Revisit: Display the angles given below on the whiteboard (or interactive whiteboard) and ask the children to estimate how big they are – perhaps to the nearest 10° or nearest 5°. Once completed, use a board protractor to show them how accurate they were. Try the following angles: 10°, 30°, 50°, 70°, 120°, 160°, 40°, 140°, 90°, 110°.

Main teaching activities

Whole class: Tell the children that in this lesson they are going to focus on the angles in a triangle. Remind them that a straight line is made up of two right angles, ie 180°. Show them a large triangle made from sugar paper or thin card. Demonstrate how the three angles can be cut or torn off and arranged into a straight line to show that the angles in a triangle add up to 180°. Also provide examples of calculations to find the angles in a triangle. For example: *If two angles in a triangle are known to be 120° and 40°, the third angle will be 180° – 160° = 20°.* Also show examples of calculating angles involving a straight line and angles around a point.

Paired work: Ask the pairs to make their own large triangles from thick paper or card and carry out the experiment showing how the three angles produce a straight line (180°). Then give out copies of 'Best of three' to provide practice in measuring the angles in a triangle and calculating angles in a triangle (total 180°), on a straight line (180°) and around a point (360°).

Review

Ask the children some quick-fire calculation questions involving the angles in a triangle. Provide them with two angles and they calculate the third. For example, 40° and 75° (65°), 115° and 30° (35°). Also work with the more confident group on quadrilaterals. Give three angles and ask them to calculate the fourth – for example, 70°, 45° and 90° (155°).

Differentiation

Less confident learners: Work with this group as much as possible and provide extra practice with the protractor, both drawing and measuring angles. Pay particular attention to inaccurate use of the inner and outer scales. Encourage double-checking of measurements. For example, if an angle is acute it cannot have a measurement of 150°.

More confident learners: Challenge this group to draw pairs of intersecting lines and to measure the angles they form. What do they notice?

Differentiation

Less confident learners: Again, provide plenty of practice and support with the use of a protractor in measuring activities. Check that angle calculation tasks are carried out accurately.

More confident learners: Encourage these children to experiment with several different triangles to prove that the same result is always produced. Challenge them to carry out an investigation of the four angles in a quadrilateral to prove that they always total 360°.

Lesson 7 (Practise)

Starter
Recall: Check that the children remember the internal angles of a triangle always add up to two right angles or 180 degrees. Provide them with two of the angles from triangles and ask them to calculate the third angle. Here are some examples: 90 and 40 (50); 100 and 60 (20); 50 and 40 (90); 60 and 60 (60); 70 and 30 (80); 40 and 40 (100). Then try multiples of 5 eg 45 and 45 (90); 55 and 60 (65); 75 and 45 (60).

Main teaching activities
Whole class: Display the 'Grids' general resource sheet, which contains two coordinate grids. Work with Grid A, which shows the first quadrant. Recap important vocabulary from Year 5, ensuring that the children are conversant with 'x-axis', 'y-axis', 'quadrant' and 'origin'.

Point to point A on the grid and ask the children for the coordinates (2,1). Remind them how to write down pairs of coordinates. Also point out that the numbers are enclosed in brackets. Plot points B, C and D, joining them to make a parallelogram. Ask for the coordinates of each point.

Now look at Grid B, which illustrates all four quadrants. Explain the numbering of each quadrant (first is top right, second is top left, third is bottom left and fourth is bottom right). Label the x- and y-axes, explaining that the x-axis in the second and third quadrants and the y-axis in the third and fourth quadrants are negative numbers. Fill in the axes labels. Draw a parallelogram in the second quadrant. Ask for the coordinates. Check that the children understand that the x-coordinates will be negative. Repeat for the third and fourth quadrants, drawing attention to the negative coordinates.
Independent work: Give out copies of the 'Shape maker' activity sheet. Invite the children to complete each shape, writing the coordinates of each vertex.

Review
Return to the 'Grids' OHT. Label a point A at (3, 2) and a point B at (−1, 2) on Grid B. Ask: *Where could points C and D be marked to draw a trapezium?* There will be a number of possible answers. Encourage answers that use all four quadrants.

Differentiation
Less confident learners: This group should work from the support version of 'Shape maker', which contains completed shapes. Children are asked to write the coordinates.
More confident learners: Give this group the extension version of 'Shape maker', where just two vertices have been plotted and they have not been joined.

Lesson 8 (Review)

Starter
Recall: Write a list of measurements on the whiteboard and ask children to convert them to larger units. For example, convert 2356m to km, 9124mm to m, 15,325g to kg and 69,540ml to l. Write another list and ask children to convert these from larger to the smaller units, such as 8.456km to m, 7.403kg to g and 4.103l to ml.

Main teaching activities
Whole class: Explain to the children that in this lesson they are going to revise their knowledge and understanding of coordinates by accurately reading and plotting the position of places on a map. Use the diagram shown here to illustrate important teaching points. Point out that spaces are being used as the coordinates now, rather than the points where lines cross. Explain that position × would be given as (45,30) because it is in square 45 going across and square 30 going up. Remind the children about putting references inside brackets to keep them separate, and the use of a comma between the two numbers. Go on to show that even more accurate positions can be given using six-figure references. The black dot would have a reference of (458,292).

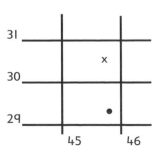

It is in position 45 and 8/10 going across and position 29 and 2/10 going up. Show other examples if necessary.

Individual/group work: The children can either work individually or in small mixed-ability groups. Provide copies of the 'Map reading' activity sheet. Ask the children to answer all the questions given on the sheet.

Review
Put up some large blank grids on the whiteboard. Ask pairs of children to come and work with them. One should use a cross to make a point within the grid system while the other should give its reference, using four figures at first and then six figures. Repeat this process several times. Ask: *Why is the six-figure reference much more accurate than the four-figure one?*

Lesson 9 (Practise)

Starter
Recall: Provide the children with some quick-fire coordinates revision. Put up a 10 × 10 square on the whiteboard (or interactive whiteboard). Use letters on the horizontal axis and numbers on the vertical axis. Ensure that the children remember that across references (letters) are given before vertical references (numbers). Place crosses or dots in a selection of squares and ask the children to give you the grid references. Then name some simple 2D shapes and ask the children to give you the grid references needed to construct them on the large square. Use shapes such as square, triangle, rectangle, pentagon and hexagon. Draw these shapes to check that they are accurate.

Main teaching activities
Whole class: Show the 'Grids' OHT. Provide the children with their own copies, as well as the 'Shape translation' activity sheet. This shows a parallelogram drawn in the first quadrant. Ask the children to write down the coordinates of the parallelogram in the space provided on the sheet. Put the parallelogram template onto the OHT and explain that you are going to slide it into a new position within the first quadrant. Its orientation will remain the same. Explain that this is called translation. Describe the translation: for example, three units up, two units right and so on. Ask for the coordinates of the new position. Continue to translate the parallelogram, ensuring that it moves into all four quadrants.

Independent work: Ask the children to complete the translation of the parallelogram into all four quadrants themselves on the 'Shape translation' activity sheet. It may be necessary for the children to trace the template and use it to translate the shape until they feel confident.

Review
Show the 'Grids' OHT again. Place the card parallelogram in quadrant four. Ask the children to describe the translation from the parallelogram in quadrant one to quadrant four. Repeat to different quadrants.

Lesson 10 (Teach and evaluate)

Starter
Recall: Ask the children to write 7.45 kg in grams and 10.6kg in grams. Repeat this for capacity, such as l, ml and cl. Invite the children to write 1.36l in ml, and so on.

Main teaching activities
Whole class: Explain to the children that in this lesson they are going to reflect shapes in a mirror line but without the use of a grid. Go through some important rules. Stress that the reflected shape must be identical to the original, and that the distance of the shape from the mirror line stays the same. Discuss the meaning of the word 'congruent' (plane figures that

---

Differentiation
Less confident learners: Remind this group that horizontal references should be read first and then vertical references. The support version of the activity sheet includes four-figure references only.

More confident learners: The extension version of the sheet includes six-figure references only. Encourage these children to make up their own maps and to devise games like battleships using six-figure grid references.

Differentiation
Less confident learners: Let this group use the support version of 'Shape translation', which asks them to translate fully into each quadrant without the shape lying astride any axis.

More confident learners: Encourage this group to use the standard method of recording a translation, for example A, B, C, D to A¹, B¹, C¹, D¹ is

$$\begin{pmatrix} -3 \\ 1 \end{pmatrix}$$

153

are identical in shape and size). Then use a prepared shape on the OHP and demonstrate how it is reflected, asking the children to offer advice and assistance. Ask them to explain step by step how the process is carried out. Go on to demonstrate reflection in two mirror lines. Provide an example (as shown below):

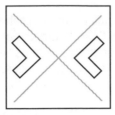

Differentiation

Less confident learners: This group will receive support by working in mixed-ability pairs. Provide mirrors, tracing paper and card templates when needed. Focus on single mirror line activities. Discuss the sketches produced by the children.

More confident learners: Encourage this group to move on to the examples with two mirror lines as soon as they can.

Group work: Provide the children with copies of the 'On reflection' activity sheet.

Review

Discuss a selection of reflections the children have produced. What strategies were used? Which proved to be the most successful? Ask: *How can you be sure that the reflection you have drawn is correct?* Discuss checking with mirrors and tracing paper.

Invite the children to evaluate their learning from this unit by writing about the aspects of learning where they feel confident. Now ask them to write down those aspects where they need more support in order to feel confident.

Name _____   Date _____

Football factsheets questions

Attendance figures

1. Which game had the smallest crowd? _____

2. Which game had the largest crowd? _____

3. Put the games in order of crowd size, smallest first. _____

_____

4. How many people saw the games at Aston Villa, Fulham and Sunderland altogether? _____

5. What is the difference in crowd size between Manchester United and Charlton?   _____

6. What is the difference in crowd size between Everton and Middlesborough?   _____

7. If Chelsea took 15,300 supporters to Aston Villa, how many in the crowd were home fans?

_____

8. How short of ground capacity were the games at Manchester United, Southampton,

Middlesborough and Everton?   _____

Goal scorers

1. What was the total number of goals scored by the home teams?   _____

2. What was the total number of goals scored by the away teams?   _____

3. How many goals were scored in the games altogether?   _____

4. Who scored the earliest goal? What time was it? What team does he play for?

_____

5. Who scored the latest goal? What time was it? What team does he play for?

_____

6. Which players scored doubles (two goals)? Which teams do they play for? Give the time

difference between the two goals they scored.

_____

Goal difference and points

1. What is the goal difference between

a) Arsenal and Tottenham,   _____

b) Leeds and West Brom?   _____

2. Which team has scored most goals at home?   _____

3. Which team has scored most goals away?   _____

4. How many points has Everton collected at home?   _____

5. How many points has Newcastle collected away from home?   _____

6. Manchester City has a total of 45 points. How many games have been won,

drawn and lost?   _____

Name _____   Date _____

Hit out

These are the angles made by some shots played by a batsman during a cricket match.

● Identify the type of angle first.

● Estimate what you think it will be in degrees.

● Then measure each angle from 0° on the base line using a protractor to see how close you were.

Remember to use the outer scale of the protractor.

Record your three answers for each angle on a different sheet of paper.

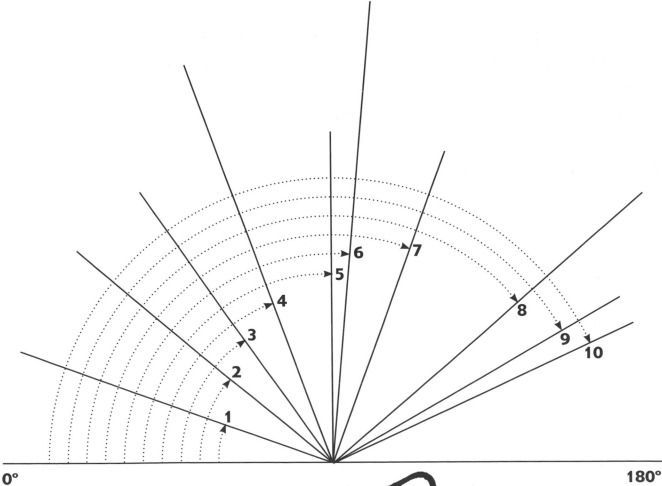

0°   180°

Name _____   Date _____

Best of three

Using a protractor, measure the three angles in each of these triangles and then find their total.

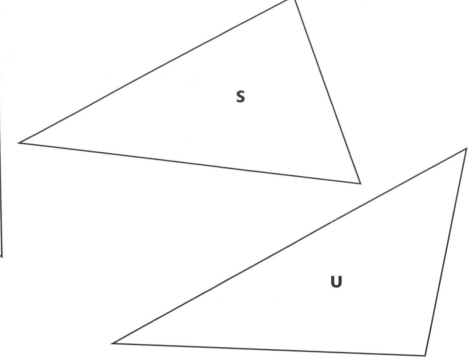

DO NOT measure but calculate each angle marked x in these diagrams.

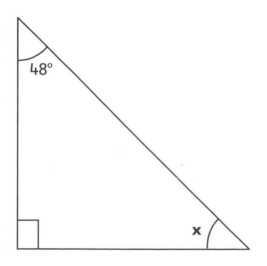

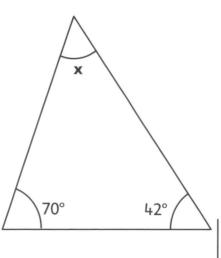

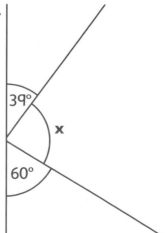

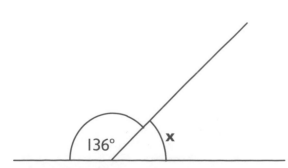

Calculating, measuring and understanding shape

BLOCK D

Unit 3 🔲 2 weeks

Calculating, measuring and understanding shape

Speaking and listening objectives
- Analyse and evaluate how speakers present points effectively through use of language, gesture, models and images.

Introduction
Using and applying mathematics in practical problem-solving situations forms the basis of much of this unit. Children have the chance, for example, to redesign their school play area and also to use metric measures to plan a new bedroom at home. Methods of checking calculations, using decimal numbers and working with imperial units are revised. The unit concludes with work on the perimeter and area of compound shapes.

Use and apply mathematics
- Solve multi-step problems, and problems involving fractions, decimals and percentages; choose and use appropriate calculation strategies at each stage, including calculator use.

Lesson	Strands	Starter	Main teaching activities
1. Apply	Use/apply	**Use efficient written methods to add and subtract integers and decimals, to multiply and divide integers and decimals by a one-digit integer, and to multiply two-digit and three-digit integers by a two-digit integer.**	Solve multi-step problems, and problems involving fractions, decimals and percentages; choose and use appropriate calculation strategies at each stage, including calculator use.
2. Apply	Use/apply	As for Lesson 1	As for Lesson 1
3. Apply	Use/apply	Read and interpret scales on a range of measuring instruments, recognising that the measurement made is approximate and recording results to a required degree of accuracy; compare readings on different scales, for example when using different instruments.	As for Lesson 1
4. Practise	Knowledge	Use a calculator to solve problems involving multi-step calculations.	Use approximations, inverse operations and tests of divisibility to estimate and check results.
5. Review	Calculate	Use approximations, inverse operations and tests of divisibility to estimate and check results.	Calculate mentally with integers and decimals: U.t ± U.t, TU × U, TU ÷ U, U.t × U, U.t ÷ U.
6. Apply	Measure	As for Lesson 5	**Select and use standard metric units of measure and convert between units using decimals to two places (eg change 2.75 litres to 2750ml, or vice versa).**
7. Apply	Measure	**Select and use standard metric units of measure and convert between units using decimals to two places (eg change 2.75 litres to 2750ml, or vice versa).**	As for Lesson 6
8. Review	Measure	Use approximations, inverse operations and tests of divisibility to estimate and check results.	Solve problems by measuring, estimating and calculating; measure and calculate using imperial units still in everyday use; know their approximate metric values. (Progression to Y7)
9. Review	Measure	Solve problems by measuring, estimating and calculating; measure and calculate using imperial units still in everyday use; know their approximate metric values. (Progression to Y7)	Calculate the perimeter and area of rectilinear shapes; estimate the area of an irregular shape by counting squares.
10. Practise and evaluate	Measure	**Visualise and draw on grids of different types where a shape will be after reflection, after translations, or after rotation through 90° or 180° about its centre or one of its vertices.** (Revision of Block D, Unit 2)	• Calculate the perimeter and area of rectilinear shapes; estimate the area of an irregular shape by counting squares. • Solve problems by measuring, estimating and calculating; measure and calculate using imperial units still in everyday use; know their approximate metric values. (Progression to Y7)

Lessons 1–5

Preparation
Lessons 1, 2 and 3: Collect price lists of garden/play materials. Measure the playground or site to be re-designed. Prepare list of internet sites for children to visit to find prices for materials, plants, and so on.
Lesson 4: Prepare the 'Check it out' activity sheet for display.

You will need
Photocopiable pages
'Multiplying and dividing decimals' (page 166), one per child.
CD resources
'The ideal playground' and 'Check it out'; support, extension and template versions of 'Multiplying and dividing decimals'.
Equipment
Squared paper; colouring pens/pencils.

Learning objectives

Starter
● Use efficient written methods to add and subtract integers and decimals, to multiply and divide integers and decimals by a one-digit integer, and to multiply two-digit and three-digit integers by a two-digit integer.
● Read and interpret scales on a range of measuring instruments, recognising that the measurement made is approximate and recording results to a required degree of accuracy; compare readings on different scales, for example when using different instruments.
● Use a calculator to solve problems involving multi-step calculations.
● Use approximations, inverse operations and tests of divisibility to estimate and check results.

Main teaching activities
2006
● Solve multi-step problems, and problems involving fractions, decimals and percentages; choose and use appropriate calculation strategies at each stage, including calculator use.
● Use approximations, inverse operations and tests of divisibility to estimate and check results.
● Calculate mentally with integers and decimals: U.t ± U.t, TU × U, TU ÷ U, U.t × U, U.t ÷ U.
1999
● Identify and use appropriate operations (including combinations of operations), to solve word problems involving numbers and quantities based on 'real life', money or measures (including time), using one or more steps; explain methods and reasoning.
● Check results of calculations. Know and apply simple tests of divisibility.
● Use known number facts to consolidate mental addition/subtraction and multiplication and division.

Vocabulary
problem, solution, answer, method, strategy, explain, operation, calculation, calculate, decimal, decimal point, decimal place, add, subtract, multiply, divide, sum, total, difference, plus, minus, product, quotient, remainder, measure, estimate, approximately, metric unit, standard unit, length, distance, perimeter, area, surface area, square metre (m^2)

Lesson 1 (Apply)

Starter
Reason: Ask children to come to the whiteboard to show the class examples of addition and subtraction calculations involving decimals that could be done (a) mentally and (b) in written form on paper. Discuss reasons for the choice of methods. Provide the children with addition and subtraction calculations and ask for volunteers to show the others an efficient written method to solve it. Here is an example: *A packet contains 1.6kg of rabbit food. Alan feeds his rabbit 75g on Monday, Tuesday and Wednesday, 80g on Thursday and Friday and 100g on Saturday and Sunday. How much rabbit feed did he use?* (585g) *How much feed is left in the bag at the end of a week?* (1.015kg or 1015g)

Main teaching activities
Whole class: Explain to the children that the next three lessons will be spent on redesigning your own school playground or an area of the school grounds (or, alternatively, working on their dream playground). Using the

activity sheet 'The ideal playground', let the children work in mixed-ability groups to agree a design and draw an accurate scale plan showing all the relevant dimensions, taking into account existing features. Discuss the kinds of issues that need to be considered in relation to your own setting. Is there an area for outdoor apparatus? Is this something to be considered for your school? Is there a shaded area? Talk about the kinds of materials that would be appropriate for your school and encourage the children to share information they have on prices.

You may prefer to work on the whole design as a class and then give each group a different part of the plan to work on. If it is not appropriate to use your own grounds for this exercise, let the children work on their 'dream playground'. Tell them that by the end of the first lesson they should have agreed and drawn their scale plan. The next two lessons should be spent identifying materials and costing the project.

Group work: Agree with the children some ground rules for group working, to ensure that all members of the group participate. They should use 'The ideal playground' activity sheet to plan and cost their designs; however, they may prefer to work on squared paper for their plan.

Differentiation

Children should agree to undertake different tasks within the group, thus enabling tasks to be allocated to children of all abilities. Check that task allocation has been organised in a way that will benefit the less confident and more confident learners.

Review

At the end of each lesson, ask one group to give an update on their progress and share their ideas with the class. Discuss any general difficulties. Each group should have the opportunity to show their ideas. For the final lesson, each group should make a presentation to the rest of the class showing their designs and the costs.

Lesson 2 (Apply)

Starter

Reason: This time provide examples of multiplication and division calculations that can be done (a) mentally and (b) written down on paper. Discuss reasons for the choice of methods. Provide the children with multiplication and division calculations and ask for volunteers to show the others an efficient written method to solve it. Here is an example: *Tickets for a concert cost £18.50. How much would it cost to buy tickets for 26 people?* (£481) Check the calculation by using the inverse operation.

Main teaching activities
See Lesson 1.

Lesson 3 (Apply)

Starter

Read: Draw up on the whiteboard two scales on instruments for measuring mass or weight so that children can make comparisons between the two. On the first scale show 0–4kg with 100g divisions between each kg and on the second show 0–4kg with 200g divisions between each kg. Ask for two volunteers. One child should show a measurement on the first scale while the other locates its equivalent on the other. (Note: Some will need to be approximate positions only on the second scale.) Try these examples. 1kg 400g; 200g; 1kg 800g; 3kg 600g; 2½ kg (scale two approximation here).

Main teaching activities
See Lesson 1.

Lesson 4 (Practise)

Starter

Reason: Provide the children with calculators. Ask them to show you the calculator keys they would press to solve a problem. Ask them to write down the calculations they did. Discuss how they used the calculator to find the answer. Could they do the calculation with fewer key operations? Try this problem first: *Ali is 96cm tall and Nina is 1.38m tall. Darren's height is half way between Ali's height and Nina's height. Calculate Darren's height.* (1.17m)

Main teaching activities
Whole class: Explain that in this lesson the class will look at two ways of checking calculations (adding lists of numbers in reverse order and using an equivalent calculation). On the whiteboard, work through the examples shown below, explaining each step of the process. Estimate answers first. Focus particularly on +, - and × calculations and include some decimal numbers.

Examples
Reverse order:
652 + 198 + 354 = 1204 and 354 + 198 + 652 = 1204.
Equivalent calculations:
1900 + 4725 = 5000 + 1625 or 2625 + 4000 = 6625
36.5 - 9.25 = 27 + 0.5 - 0.25 or 36.5 - 9.5 + 0.25 = 27.25
536 × 9 = 536 × 10 - 536 or 536 × 5 + 536 × 4 = 4824

Paired work: Display the calculations given on the activity sheet 'Check it out'. Ask the children, working in pairs, to estimate each answer. They should then calculate answers, first using the usual written methods and then checking solutions using strategies outlined above. Stress that they should show clearly their working out. Questions 1–4 are easiest to check by adding in another order, questions 5–8 by using an equivalent calculation.

Review
Ask for volunteers to show the rest of the class how they checked solutions for each of the given questions. Ask: *What rule can you apply to adding numbers?* (Numbers can be added in any order and will always produce the same answer.) *What other operation does this apply to?* (Multiplication). *For which operation did you find the 'equivalent calculation' method most suitable: addition, subtraction or multiplication?*

Differentiation
Less confident learners:
Encourage this group to focus on the reverse order (questions 1-4) particularly. It may be necessary to simplify the numbers used in the later questions and limit them to finding one equivalent calculation only. Assist with methods of recording.
More confident learners:
Expect this group to be able to explain to other children in the class the exact method they are using. Children can generate their own calculations using larger numbers.

Lesson 5 (Review)

Starter
Recall: Revise with children the tests of divisibility for multiples of 3, 6 and 9.
   3: A number is divisible by 3 if the sum of its digits is divisible by 3.
   6: A number is divisible by 6 if it is even and also divisible by 3.
   9: A number is divisible by 9 if the sum of its digits is divisible by 9.
Ask questions such as:
● *Are these numbers divisible by 3: 53, 108 and 247?*
● *Are these numbers divisible by 6: 87, 144 and 372?*
● *Are these numbers divisible by 9: 109, 441 and 609?*

Main teaching activities
Whole class: Write the following place value headings on the board: Th H T U . t h th. Write 4.5 on the chart. Check that everyone understands that this means four units and five tenths, or $4^5/_{10}$ (if necessary, recap that $^1/_{10}$ = 0.1 and $^5/_{100}$ = 0.01). Multiply the 4.5 by 10 and discuss the effect. Multiply the resulting 45 by 100. Discuss the effect. Repeat for division by writing 62 on the chart and dividing by 10 then by 10 again. Ensure that the children understand the movement left or right and the use of zeros as place holders. Reinforce that the decimal point does not move.
   Write £250,000 on the board. Explain that a TV contestant has won $^1/_4$ million pounds. Ask: *If it is given to him in £100 notes, how many notes will he get?* Explain that the question is the same as dividing 250,000 by 100 (2500). Ask: *How many £10 notes would he get?* (25,000) Set the following

challenge, which can be solved in pairs: *How many 10p coins will he get?* (250,000 × 10, as each £1 has ten 10p coins: 2,500,000). *How many 1p coins will he get?* (25,000,000)

Independent work: Hand out the 'Multiplying and dividing decimals' activity sheet for the children to complete individually.

Differentiation

Less confident learners: The support version of the activity sheet asks children to divide and multiply only by 10 and 100.
More confident learners: The extension version of the sheet asks children to multiply and divide by 100 and 1000.

Review

Pose the following questions, asking children to explain how they solved each one.

- *£28 was shared between 10 people. How much did each receive?*
- *There are 10 people in Group A and 100 people in Group B. Group A shares £3500 between them. Group B shares £350,000. Which group would you rather be in? Why?*
- *Nathan cycles in a 1.5 kilometre race. Jordan's race is 100 times longer. How far is his race?*

Lessons 6-10

Preparation

Lesson 7: Collect brochures, catalogues and newspaper advertisements with prices of carpets, wallpapers, soft furnishings, etc.
Lesson 9: Draw examples of compound shapes on the whiteboard or OHT.

You will need
Photocopiable pages
'Fully carpeted' (page 167) and 'Ideal bedroom' (page 168), one per child.
CD resources
Support, extension and template versions of 'Fully carpeted'; 'Inch by inch', 'Country gardens'; core, support and extension versions of 'How many tiles?'. General resource sheet: '2cm squared paper'.
Equipment
Calculators; 30cm rulers; metre ruler.

Learning objectives

Starter

- Use approximations, inverse operations and tests of divisibility to estimate and check results.
- Select and use standard metric units of measure and convert between units using decimals to two places (eg change 2.75 litres to 2750ml, or vice versa).
- Solve problems by measuring, estimating and calculating; measure and calculate using imperial units still in everyday use; know their approximate metric values.
- Visualise and draw on grids of different types where a shape will be after reflection, after translations, or after rotation through 90° or 180° about its centre or one of its vertices. (Revision of Block D, Unit 2)

Main teaching activities
2006
- Select and use standard metric units of measure and convert between units using decimals to two places (eg change 2.75 litres to 2750ml, or vice versa).
- Solve problems by measuring, estimating and calculating; measure and calculate using imperial units still in everyday use; know their approximate metric values.
- Calculate the perimeter and area of rectilinear shapes; estimate the area of an irregular shape by counting squares.
1999
- Use, read and write standard metric units including their abbreviations and relationships between them. Convert smaller to larger units and vice versa.
- Know imperial units (mile, pint, gallon, lb, oz); know rough equivalents of lb and kg, oz and g, miles and km, litres and pints/gallons. (Year 6 progression to Year 7)
- Calculate the perimeter and area of simple compound shapes that can be split into rectangles.

Vocabulary
multiple, factor, measure, estimate, approximately, metric unit, standard unit, Imperial, length, distance, perimeter, area, surface area, mass, weight, capacity, units of measurement and their abbreviations, mile, inch, foot, yard, square centimetre (cm²), square millimetre (mm²), pound (£), formula, base, height, penny/pence (p), position, direction, reflection, rotation

Lesson 6 (Apply)

Starter
Reason: Pose the following word problems to the children:
1. *I added the weight of three parcels together. The weights were all odd numbers and the answer came to 480g. Explain why the statement cannot be true.* (Three odd numbers always add up to an odd number. To get an even number answer, one of the weights would need to be an even number or all three.)
2. *Mary says that every multiple of 5 ends in 5. Is she correct?* (No, alternate multiples of 5 end in 0.)
3. *A square number always has an odd number of factors. Is this statement correct?* (Yes, factors of 9 are 1, 3, 9; factors of 16 are 1, 2, 4, 8, 16; factors of 25 are 1, 5, 25, and so on.)

Main teaching activities
Whole class: Tell the children that in this lesson they will be looking at how to calculate the amount of carpet needed and the cost of different carpets. Draw a diagram on the board of a rectangular room roughly 2.8m × 3.9m, showing a door and window on opposite walls. Ask the children how they would calculate the area of carpet that is needed for this room. Explain that this is not just about calculating the area - the carpet will come in particular widths, so the task is to choose the most economical width to avoid too much wastage. Point out that sometimes the carpet fitter will join a carpet, but for the purpose of this activity you want a carpet without any joins.

Tell the children that the carpet chosen for this room comes in widths of 3m or 4m. Ask them to discuss with their partner which width they should choose and then to decide what length of carpet is required (3m width × 3.9m or 4m length × 2.8m). Explain that there may be some wasted carpet, but it is sold in lengths so still has to be paid for. Point out that the cost of carpets is usually calculated by the square metre, so they should calculate which of these two options will be the cheaper. (3m width is 11.7m², 4m width is 11.2 m², so 4m width is more economical.) Finally, ask how they would calculate the cost if the carpet is £10.50 a square metre.
Paired work: Give pairs the 'Fully carpeted' activity sheet. Explain that when completing this activity, they must think about the most economical way to choose the carpet. Point out that often there are additional charges, such as for fitting and carpet gripper. Let them use a calculator to check their results.

Review
Tell the children to think about a room that is 4.2m × 6m. The carpet available only comes in widths of 3m or 4m. Ask them for suggestions about where they would join a carpet. They may suggest using two 3m widths with a join in the middle, or a 4m width with 0.2m 'fill in'. Point out that the decision may be different depending upon whether the carpet is plain or patterned, and how well the type of carpet will join.

Differentiation
Less confident learners: Provide this group with the support version of 'Fully carpeted', with simpler calculations.
More confident learners: This group should work on the extension version of the activity sheet, where they are also asked to include the cost of VAT.

Lesson 7 (Apply)

Starter
Refine: Invite the children to put up their hands to say metric units of length. Invite the child who responds to write the unit as a word, and to write its abbreviated form. Ask: *How many ___ in a ___?* Repeat this for mass and capacity metric units.

Main teaching activities
Whole class: Explain to the children that in this lesson they will have the opportunity to plan and design their own bedroom. Discuss with them what features they would like in their ideal bedroom. They should work individually to plan their own room using the 'Ideal bedroom' activity sheet. Ask them to calculate the amount of wallpaper and carpet that would be

Unit 3 ◻ 2 weeks

needed. They will need catalogues and price lists for soft furnishings, wallpaper etc which they should use to gather information on prices of carpets, curtains and wallpaper to cost their ideal room. They may also include fitted bedroom furniture. By the end of the lesson, they should have made a complete costing for their room.

Review

Ask the children to compare their plans with their partner's, discuss improvements and consider each other's suggestions. Allow them to show their designs and costings to the class and discuss.

Lesson 8 (Review)

Starter

Reason: Invite the children to suggest how to find out if a number can be divided by 9. (A number is divisible by 9 if the sum of its digits is divisible by 9.) Put some numbers on the board (such as 549, 289, 369, 108) for the children to investigate if this method is accurate.

Main teaching activities

Whole class: Recap on imperial measurements (inch, foot, yard, etc). Explain that many years ago people measured length by pacing with their feet. Unfortunately, feet are different sizes, so the length had to be standardised (12 inches = 1 foot). Tailors measured cloth by holding it between the tip of the nose and the tips of the fingers. This also created different lengths, so again this length was standardised (3 feet = 1 yard). Ask: *If 1 yard = 3 feet and 1 foot = 12 inches, how many inches are there in a yard?* (36) Make sure that the children understand the abbreviations ft, yd and ".

Write down metric equivalents for imperial units: 1 inch = approximately 2.5cm and 1 metre = 39 inches (3ft 3"). Rehearse these equivalents. Ask the children how they can convert between these units. Elicit that if 1 inch = 2.5cm, multiply the number of inches by 2.5. Say: *Try converting the following: 6 inches, 9 inches, 15 inches. Use calculators if necessary. When converting centimetres to inches, divide by 2.5. Try converting the following: 24cm, 14cm, 30cm.*

Ask the children to work in pairs to measure two or three objects in either centimetres or inches and convert to the metric/imperial equivalent. Share outcomes with the rest of the class.
Group work: Provide the children with copies of the 'Inch by inch' activity sheet. This provides practice in using centimetres and inches and converting between the two.

Review

Review the work that the children have carried out in their groups. Recap on some of the conversions they have made. Ask questions such as: *How many inches in 10cm?* (4) *How many centimetres in 16 inches?* (40)

Lesson 9 (Review)

Starter

Reason: Provide children with a 30cm ruler each and ask them to examine it carefully. Then ask them to estimate the length of suitable small objects in the room (estimating to the nearest centimetre or nearest half centimetre). Use objects like a pencil, a sheet of paper, a calculator, an exercise book, a reading book, etc. Then repeat the process after showing them a metre stick. This time use items like the length and width of a table, the height of a chair, the length of a bookcase, the width and height of the door. Make accurate measurements of the items afterwards to see how close the estimates were.

Main teaching activities

Whole class: Revise work done previously on area and perimeter. Discuss

Unit 3 ▬ 2 weeks

Differentiation

Less confident learners: Provide support with splitting shapes into convenient shapes for calculation purposes, finding missing measurements and multiplying numbers to calculate area.

More confident learners: Ask these children to investigate whether different rectangles with the same area will all have the same perimeter, or whether they can draw rectangles with different areas that all have the same perimeter. Introduce the formula for finding the area of a triangle ($\frac{1}{2}$ base × height or base × height ÷ 2). Include some triangular shapes when finding the area of more complicated compound shapes.

with the children the difference between area, a measurement of surface calculated in square units, and perimeter, a measurement of distance calculated in length units. Write on the OHP or whiteboard some simple examples of finding area and perimeter using squares and rectangles. Show how the perimeter of a square will be side × 4 and that the perimeter of a rectangle will be length × 2 + width × 2. Revise that the area of a square or a rectangle can be calculated using the formula length × width. Now show the children some examples of simple compound shapes. Demonstrate how the measurement of these shapes, both area and perimeter, can be found by splitting them into convenient squares or rectangles. Point out that often additional measurements have to be calculated first.

Group work: Provide the children with copies of 'Country gardens' to work through. The calculations become progressively more difficult and some of the later ones also involve things like working out the area of ponds and flowerbeds. Talk through some of the earlier examples with the children before letting them work on their own.

Review

Check that definitions of both area and perimeter are accurate, and that the correct units have been used in answers. Mark the answers with the children. Discuss methods, especially how all the necessary dimensions were calculated and where lines were drawn to split up the compound shapes.

Lesson 10 (Practise and evaluate)

Starter

Revisit: The children will need 2cm squared paper. Tell them they have one minute to draw as many different shapes as they can using four squares, with the stipulations that all squares must have at least one side in common with another, and each arrangement must be different and cannot be a reflection or a rotation of another. (There are five possible different shapes.) Ask children to come out and draw their different arrangements on the board.

Main teaching activities

Whole class: Ask the children where they are most likely to see tiles. (Floors, walls, kitchens.) Tell them that they will be looking at how to calculate how many tiles are needed. For the first activity they will be using square tiles. Say: *Imagine you want to tile a floor that is 3m × 2m, and the tiles you have chosen are 25cm × 25cm. How could you calculate the number of tiles needed?* Invite the children to discuss this with their partner and then ask for their ideas. They may suggest finding the total area of the floor ($6m^2$) and then dividing by the area of the tile ($625cm^2$ or $0.0625m^2$), which makes 96 tiles. Also ask them how many tiles will be needed for $1m^2$ (16). They may need to draw this on squared paper. If they know that there are 16 tiles for each square metre, then the total required is 16 × 6 = 96.

Now ask the children to think about a border tile to go all around the edge of the floor. These tiles are 25cm long. How many tiles will they need? Ask them to discuss this with a partner. Remind them that they will need to to calculate the perimeter of the floor and then decide how many tiles are needed. Ask a pair to come out and show how they calculated the perimeter (2 × (3 + 2) = 10m) and then the number of border tiles required. (Tiles are 25cm long, divide 10m by 0.25m = 40 tiles.)

Independent work: Give the children the 'How many tiles?' activity sheet. Explain that they have to calculate the number of tiles needed and the cost of the tiles. Remind them to read the information carefully and to check the sizes of the tiles.

Differentiation

Less confident learners: Give this group the support version of the activity sheet, plus some squared paper so that they can draw the plan for the wall tiles.

More confident learners: Give this group the extension version of the activity sheet with the more complex wall plan. Remind them to think carefully about the different methods that they will use to calculate how many tiles are needed for the main part of the wall and how many for the border.

Review

Ask the children to calculate the number of tiles needed for $1m^2$ when the tiles are 20cm × 25cm. (20) Discuss any difficulties with this. Ask them to evaluate their strengths and weaknesses in their learning from this unit.

Name _____   Date _____

Multiplying and dividing decimals

1. Divide and multiply each money bag by 10 and 100.

£46.00

× 10 _____

÷ 10 _____

× 100 _____

÷ 100 _____

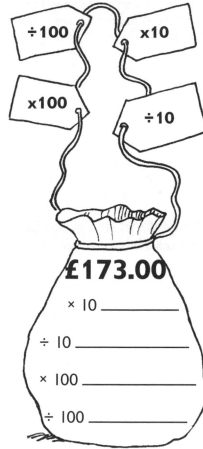

£173.00

× 10 _____

÷ 10 _____

× 100 _____

÷ 100 _____

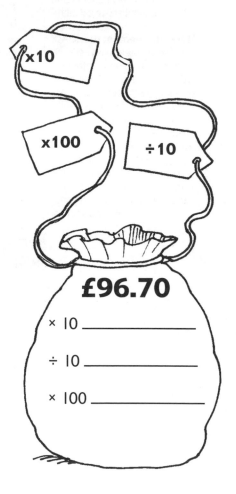

£96.70

× 10 _____

÷ 10 _____

× 100 _____

2. Complete the following sums:

a) $9.6 \div 10 = \boxed{}$

b) $\boxed{} \div 100 = 0.24$

c) $4.2 \boxed{} 100 = 420$

d) $17.2 \times \boxed{} = 172$

e) $206 \div \boxed{} = 2.06$

f) $3.6 \div 100 = \boxed{}$

g) $0.24 \times 100 = \boxed{}$

h) $41.6 \boxed{} 100 = 0.416$

i) $0.3 \div 10 = \boxed{}$

j) $9 \div \boxed{} = 0.09$

3. Write true or false beside each statement:

a) $262 \times 10 \times 10 = 26.2 \times 100$ _____

b) $345 \times 100 = 3.45 \times 10$ _____

c) $76.1 \times 100 = 7610 \div 100$ _____

d) $304.1 \div 100 = 30.41 \times 10$ _____

e) $96.3 \div 10 = 0.963 \times 10$ _____

Name _____   Date _____

Fully carpeted

Jenna would like a new carpet in her room, shown below.

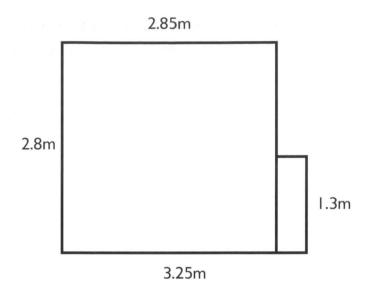

The carpet she has chosen comes in two different widths, 3m or 4m.

The price of the carpet is £9.50 per square metre.

Jenna would prefer not to have a join in the carpet.

● Calculate the cost of the carpet for the bedroom.

_____

The carpet fitter charges an extra £1.50 a square metre to fit the carpet, but this includes grippers and door rod.

● Look at the plan of the bedroom and calculate the cost for the carpet and fitting.

_____

_____

Calculating, measuring and understanding shape

BLOCK D

Name _____ Date _____

Ideal bedroom

How would you like to design your ideal bedroom? Think about the colour scheme you would like to have and any special features.

Draw a plan of your ideal bedroom – you may like to measure your own room and draw a plan of that. Think about the shape of your room and where the door and windows are. How will you arrange furniture in your room?

Use the chart below to calculate the number of rolls of wallpaper you will need.

Height of walls in metres	Length of walls in metres, including doors and windows						
	8.53	9.75	10.97	12.19	13.41	14.63	15.85
2.13–2.29	4	4	5	5	6	6	7
2.30–2.44	4	4	5	5	6	6	7
2.45–2.55	4	5	5	6	6	7	7
2.56–2.74	4	5	5	6	6	7	7
2.75–2.90	4	5	6	6	7	7	8

Carpet comes in 3m or 4m widths. Calculate the length of carpet you will need, choosing the most economical width.

Securing number facts, relationships and calculating

Key aspects of learning
- Problem solving
- Communication
- Reasoning

Expected prior learning
Check that children can already:
- solve one- and two-step problems involving whole numbers and decimals
- use understanding of place value to multiply and divide whole numbers and decimals by 10, 100 or 1000
- use efficient written methods to add and subtract whole numbers and decimals with up to two decimal places, to multiply HTU × U and TU × TU, and to divide TU ÷ U
- find equivalent fractions
- understand percentage as the number of parts in every 100, and express tenths and hundredths as percentages
- use sequences to scale numbers up or down
- find simple fractions of percentages of quantities.

Objectives overview
The text in this diagram identifies the focus of mathematics learning within the block.

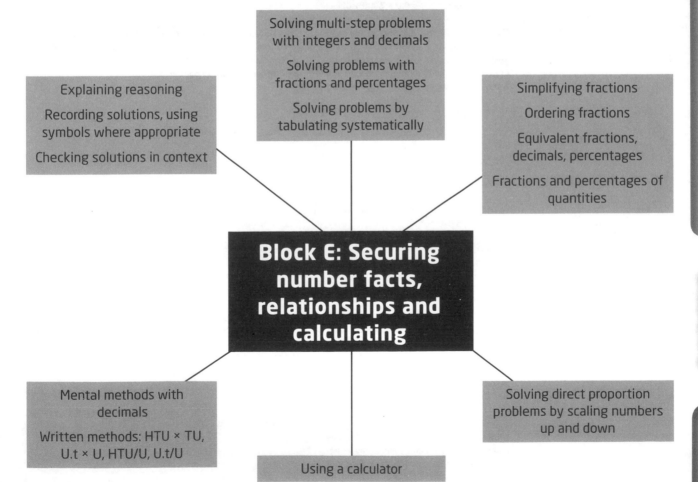

Solving multi-step problems with integers and decimals

Solving problems with fractions and percentages

Solving problems by tabulating systematically

Explaining reasoning

Recording solutions, using symbols where appropriate

Checking solutions in context

Simplifying fractions

Ordering fractions

Equivalent fractions, decimals, percentages

Fractions and percentages of quantities

Block E: Securing number facts, relationships and calculating

Mental methods with decimals

Written methods: HTU × TU, U.t × U, HTU/U, U.t/U

Using a calculator

Solving direct proportion problems by scaling numbers up and down

Securing number facts, relationships and calculating

Lesson	Strands	Starter	Main teaching activities
1. Teach and practise	Use/apply	Tabulate systematically the information in a problem or puzzle; identify and record the steps or calculations needed to solve it, using symbols where appropriate; interpret solutions in the original context and check their accuracy.	Tabulate systematically the information in a problem or puzzle; identify and record the steps or calculations needed to solve it, using symbols where appropriate; interpret solutions in the original context and check their accuracy.
2. Practise and apply	Use/apply	As for Lesson 1	As for Lesson 1
3. Teach and apply	Use/apply	As for Lesson 1	Explain reasoning and conclusions, using words, symbols or diagrams as appropriate.
4. Apply	Use/apply	Solve multi-step problems, and problems involving fractions, decimals and percentages; choose and use appropriate calculation strategies at each stage, including calculator use.	Solve multi-step problems, and problems involving fractions, decimals and percentages; choose and use appropriate calculation strategies at each stage, including calculator use.
5. Apply	Use/apply	As for Lesson 4	As for Lesson 4
6. Review	Knowledge	**Use knowledge of place value and multiplication facts to 10 ×10 to derive related multiplication and division facts involving decimals (eg 0.8 × 7, 4.8 ÷ 6).**	**Use knowledge of place value and multiplication facts to 10 ×10 to derive related multiplication and division facts involving decimals (eg 0.8 × 7, 4.8 ÷ 6).**
7. Practise and apply	Calculate	**Use efficient written methods to add and subtract integers and decimals, to multiply and divide integers and decimals by a one-digit integer, and to multiply two-digit and three-digit integers by a two-digit integer.**	**Use efficient written methods to add and subtract integers and decimals, to multiply and divide integers and decimals by a one-digit integer, and to multiply two-digit and three-digit integers by a two-digit integer.**
8. Apply	Calculate	As for Lesson 7	As for Lesson 7
9. Practise and apply	Calculate	As for Lesson 7	As for Lesson 7
10. Apply	Calculate	As for Lesson 7	As for Lesson 7
11. Review	Calculate	Use a calculator to solve problems involving multi-step calculations.	Use a calculator to solve problems involving multi-step calculations.
12. Teach	Counting	As for Lesson 11	Express a larger whole number as a fraction of a smaller one (eg recognise that 8 slices of a 5-slice pizza represents $^8/_5$ or $1^3/_5$ pizzas); simplify fractions by cancelling common factors; order a set of fractions by converting them to fractions with a common denominator.
13. Practise and apply	Calculate	Express a larger whole number as a fraction of a smaller one (eg recognise that 8 slices of a 5-slice pizza represents $^8/_5$ or $1^3/_5$ pizzas); simplify fractions by cancelling common factors; order a set of fractions by converting them to fractions with a common denominator.	Relate fractions to multiplication and division (eg $6 ÷ 2 = ^1/_2$ of $6 = \quad ^1/_2$); express a quotient as a fraction or decimal (eg $67 ÷ 5 = 13.4$ or $13^2/_5$); find fractions and percentages of whole-number quantities (eg $^5/_8$ of 96, 65% of £260).
14. Teach	Counting	**Use efficient written methods to add and subtract integers and decimals, to multiply and divide integers and decimals by a one-digit integer, and to multiply two-digit and three-digit integers by a two-digit integer.**	Solve simple problems involving direct proportion by scaling quantities up or down.
15. Practise and evaluate	Counting	As for Lesson 14	As for Lesson 14

Securing number facts, relationships and calculating

BLOCK E

Unit 1 ▢ 3 weeks

Speaking and listening objectives

● Participate in a whole-class debate using the conventions and language of debate, including Standard English.

Introduction

Using and applying mathematics is more specifically dealt with in the first four lessons, where the children think about how to solve problems systematically and record and explain their reasoning, as well as applying calculation strategies. Other lessons reinforce children's knowledge and use of number facts and secure their ability to use efficient written methods to calculate and apply relationships. They work with fractions, relating these to multiplication and division and also use scaling of numbers to solve direct proportion problems. The speaking and listening objective is considered throughout the unit, but specifically in Lesson 8, where children debate the merits of different subtraction methods.

Use and apply mathematics

● Tabulate systematically the information in a problem or puzzle; identify and record the steps or calculations needed to solve it, using symbols where appropriate; interpret solutions in the original context and check their accuracy.
● Explain reasoning and conclusions, using words, symbols or diagrams as appropriate.
● Solve multi-step problems, and problems involving fractions, decimals and percentages; choose and use appropriate calculation strategies at each stage, including calculator use.

Lessons 1–5

Preparation

Lesson 1: Prepare a display copy of 'The farmer and his cows'.
Lesson 2: Prepare a display copy of 'Happy and sad numbers'.
Lesson 3: Prepare a display copy of 'Five steps to successful problem solving'.
Lesson 4: Prepare a display copy of 'Wallpaper dimensions'.

You will need
Photocopiable pages
'How many rolls?' (page 183) and 'Shelf fit' (page 184), one per child.
CD resources
Core, support and extension versions of 'The farmer and his cows' and 'Happy and sad numbers'; core, support, extension and template versions of 'Step by step; support, extension and template versions of 'How many rolls?'; 'Wallpaper dimensions'; support and extension versions of 'Shelf fit'. General resource sheets: 'Five steps to successful problem solving' and 'Hundred square'.
Equipment
Counters or other 'counting' objects; individual whiteboards and pens.

Learning objectives

Starter
● Tabulate systematically the information in a problem or puzzle; identify and record the steps or calculations needed to solve it, using symbols where appropriate; interpret solutions in the original context and check their accuracy.
● Solve multi-step problems, and problems involving fractions, decimals and percentages; choose and use appropriate calculation strategies at each stage, including calculator use.

Main teaching activities
2006
● Tabulate systematically the information in a problem or puzzle; identify and record the steps or calculations needed to solve it, using symbols where appropriate; interpret solutions in the original context and check their accuracy.
● Explain reasoning and conclusions, using words, symbols or diagrams as appropriate.
● Solve multi-step problems, and problems involving fractions, decimals and percentages; choose and use appropriate calculation strategies at each stage, including calculator use.
1999
● Explain methods and reasoning, orally and in writing.
● Identify and use appropriate operations (including combinations of operations) to solve word problems involving numbers and quantities based on 'real life', money or measures (including time), using one or more steps; explain methods and reasoning.

Vocabulary
problem, solution, calculator, calculate, calculation, jotting, equation, operation, symbol, inverse, answer, method, strategy, explain, predict, reason, reasoning, pattern, relationship

Lesson 1 (Teach and practise)

Starter

Rehearse: Write five digits on the board, such as 2, 4, 5, 6 and 7. Ask the children to write down the highest number they can make using the five digits (76542) and then the lowest (24567). Then tell them that you want them to list all the numbers that they can make using four of the five digits. Explain that you would like them to think about how they could find the numbers systematically and how they could tabulate their results. You may like to suggest that they start by listing all the numbers starting with 2.

Main teaching activities

Whole class: Explain to the children that in this lesson they will be investigating a problem. Point out to the children that when they are carrying out an investigation there is often more than one answer and there may be different ways to take the investigation forward. They should be asking the question 'What if?' Remind them that with an investigation they can stop at the stage where they feel they have found out something, or they may like to investigate other possibilities.

Display the activity sheet 'The farmer and his cows'. Explain to the children that they may use models or symbols to help them investigate the problem. Encourage them to pose questions and look for alternatives, such as 'What if there were more fields?' Encourage them to think about how they could tabulate their results systematically in order to find 'a rule'. Will diagrams help them?

Individual work: Ask the children to work through the activity sheet 'The farmer and his cows', tabulating their results in a way that helps them most.

Review

Discuss the children's solutions. Can they think of any variations to the problem? (For example, more cows in each field.) Ask them to suggest a variation and work through it as a class. Ask questions such as: *For the farmer to see the largest number of sheep from each window, which fields need to have the most sheep?* (The corner fields.) *What about if he wants to see the fewest sheep?* (Corner fields should have fewest sheep.) *Why do you think the number of sheep in the corner fields is the most important?* (The corner fields are seen from two windows.) Ask: *How did it help to put your results into a table? What kind of diagrams did you use to help to you? How does your diagram compare with others in your group?*

Differentiation

Less confident learners: Provide the support version of the activity sheet. It is also helpful to provide some apparatus, such as counters, for the children to work with so that they can physically move the 'cows' from field to field.
More confident learners: The extension version of the activity sheet includes suggestions for children to extend this investigation. There are a number of 'open' questions which enable them to investigate a wide range of possibilities.

Lesson 2 (Practise and apply)

Starter

Refine and rehearse: Repeat the Starter from Lesson 1, using a different set of digits – but tell the children that this time you would like them to start to set up a table to list all the numbers that they could make using the digits. Suggest that they work in pairs and discuss the best way to tabulate their numbers.

Main teaching activities

Whole class: Give each child a copy of 'Happy and sad numbers'. Explain that this is another investigation and that in order to do the activity they will be investigating different numbers to find out whether they are happy or sad. Display the activity sheet and go through the example with the class: *Starting with 32, we need to square each of the digits: 3 (to get 9) and 2 (to get 4). We then add together 9 and 4 to get 13. Then, continuing from 13, the squares of 1 and 3 are 1 and 9, added together give 10. Continuing from 10, the sum of the squares of 1 and 0 is 1. As we have reached 1 this is the end of the chain, so 32 is a happy number. Some numbers seem to go round in circles. These are called sad numbers.*

Work through the process for 14, asking the children to work out each

step: *14 gives 1 + 16 = 17, then 1 + 49 = 50, 25 + 0 = 25, 4 + 25 gives 29, 4 + 81 = 85, 64 + 25 = 89, 64 + 81= 145, 1 + 16 + 25 = 42, 16 + 4 = 20, 4 + 0 = 4, 16, 1 + 36 = 37, 9 + 49 = 58, 25 + 64 = 89, which 'loops back' into the chain. Hence, 14 is a sad number.*

Ask: *From these two chains, can you tell me any other numbers that you know will be either happy or sad?* The children may suggest that all numbers in the chain will be happy if the starting number is happy, and all the numbers will be sad if the starting number is sad. If they do not notice this, draw it to their attention, hence: 32, 13 and 10 are all happy; 14, 17, 50, 25, 29, 85, 89, 145, 42, 20, 4, 16, 37 and 58 are all sad. Ask the children to think about ways they could tabulate their 'chains'.

Individual work: Ask the children to continue with the investigation using their own copies of 'Happy and sad numbers' (and a 'Hundred square' as necessary). Some children may wish to extend the investigation further.

Review

Discuss the strategies that the children used. Did they notice that there were pairs of numbers? For example, if 32 is happy then 23 must also be happy, and if 14 is sad then 41 must also be sad. Did they notice any patterns in the investigation? Ask: *What investigative techniques did you use? How have you recorded the solutions? Explain how you have tabulated all your solutions. How has this helped with the development of the investigation?* Remind them that an investigation can be ongoing.

Lesson 3 (Teach and apply)

Starter

Rehearse: Tell the children that you are going to give them a problem and they must write down on their whiteboards the calculation(s) that are needed in order to solve it. Tell them not to solve the problem, you just want them to identify the calculations. For example, say: *Jenna has £5. She buys four books that cost 85p each. How much change does she have?* The children should write 500 - (4 × 85) or 5 - (4 × 0.85) or in two steps, 4 × 85p = T, and £5 - T. Encourage them to discuss with partners the different ways the calculation can be recorded. Check that they are confident with using a symbol for an unknown quantity (in this case T). Give other questions.

Main teaching activities

Whole class: Write two simple word problems on the whiteboard - the first involving a one-step process only and the second incorporating at least two steps. Examples might be as follows:
- *Tom, Sanjay and Alison have 72 stickers. They share them out equally. How many do they have each?* (One step.)
- *My reading book has 224 pages. I have read a quarter of it. How many pages are still left to read?* (Two steps.)

Work through the examples with the children using a five-step strategy (display the resource sheet 'Five steps to successful problem solving'). Discuss the different approaches they suggest.

Independent/paired work: Ask the children to work on the 'Step by step' activity sheet. They can either work individually or in pairs. Stress that they should work through the sheet very carefully, because being able to explain their method and reasoning, and showing their working out, are as important on this occasion as producing the correct answer.

Review

Take feedback from each of the groups and discuss with them decisions that were taken about picking out key words and numbers, deciding on operations to use, estimating answers, choosing methods and checking solutions. Sum up with the following questions: *Has the question been answered? Does the answer make sense? Explain how this question helps you to answer similar word problems.*

Differentiation

Less confident learners: Let these children work in pairs, using the support version of the sheet. Start by investigating only the numbers up to 10.
More confident learners: Give these children the extension version of the sheet. Encourage them to look for patterns and to try to predict which numbers will be happy.

Differentiation

Less confident learners: The support version of the 'Step by step' activity sheet uses simpler numbers. Provide verbal support with the use of vocabulary and with the way in which working out is shown and explanations are written down.
More confident learners: Give these children the extension version of the sheet. Ask them to make up their own two-step problems on the back of the sheet, for each of the four main operations.

Lesson 4 (Apply)

Starter

Revisit: Explain that you will write a two-digit number on the board. Ask the children to double it as quickly as they can. Begin with, for example, 36 × 2 and 47 × 2, and extend to decimals such as 7.3 × 2, 0.94 × 2 and 0.78 × 2. Ask for the methods chosen for each example and compare for efficiency and effectiveness.

Main teaching activities

Whole class: Explain that the next two lessons are about redecorating a room. Discuss what might need to be done, such as wallpapering, changing the carpet, installing fitted cupboards and hanging new curtains. Talk to the children about what measurements they would need to take and how they would calculate quantities. Ask them what they would need to consider if they were to use wallpaper. Display the 'Wallpaper dimensions' activity sheet. Explain that the chart will help them to calculate how many rolls of wallpaper would be needed. Remind them how to calculate the perimeter of a rectangular room which measures 2.5m × 3m. (11m) Ask: *If the height of the walls is 2.5m, how many rolls of paper will be needed?* (6) Ask a child to explain how they have used the chart. Point out that they need to go to the next value up on the chart.

Independent work: Ask the children to work individually on the 'How many rolls?' activity sheet to calculate the amount of wallpaper needed. They also have to calculate the cost of the wallpaper. Encourage them to use calculators and to check their answers.

Review

Discuss any difficulties the children had in the lesson. Ask them to think about anything else they would need to consider when wallpapering a room. Explain that the chart is only a rough guide. Ask: *Why might you need more rolls of some paper than another?* Discuss the facts that pattern matching may result in wasted paper, and that paper will be saved if there are big windows and doorways. Ask: *Can you explain how you solved the problem? Did you need to use a calculator?*

Differentiation

Less confident learners: Ask this group to work in pairs on the support version of the activity sheet.
More confident learners: Give this group the extension version of the activity sheet.

Lesson 5 (Apply)

Starter

Refine: The children will need whiteboards and markers. Give quick-fire questions involving doubling and halving decimal fractions. For example, say: *Halve 1.26* (0.63)... *3.90* (1.95)... *8.06* (4.03)... *0.15* (0.075). *Double 0.85* (1.7)... *1.23* (2.46)... *1.8* (3.6) *and double again* (7.2). Discuss any difficulties. Remind the children that this can be an effective strategy for mentally multiplying and dividing (for example, by 2, 4, 8, and so on).

Main teaching activities

Group work: Continuing from Lesson 4, discuss with the children what fitted furniture they may want in the bedroom, such as fitted wardrobes or built-in cupboards and shelves. Tell them that for this lesson they will be thinking about putting some shelves into the room. Explain that timber comes in various lengths and qualities. Sometimes it is easier to buy several shorter lengths and cut off any surplus, or it may be possible to buy fewer longer lengths and cut them to size.

Independent work: Explain that you want the children to calculate the cost of shelves using the 'Shelf fit' activity sheet. When they have completed the activity sheet, they should design their own shelf unit for a bedroom and list the timber they need.

Review

Ask the children to show their designs for shelves. Discuss what other

Differentiation

Less confident learners: Give this group the support version of the activity sheet. Ensure that they understand that the timber is priced per metre, but comes in 2m lengths.
More confident learners: Give this group the extension version of the sheet. Point out that often VAT is not included in the price of materials when they are bought from a wholesale outlet, so the cost has to be added.

Unit 1 ▷ 3 weeks

timber may be needed if the shelves are not going to be fitted in an alcove – they may need side panels or a back panel, for example. Ask the children to explain how they have calculated their answers.

Lessons 6-10

Preparation
Lesson 7: Prepare a display copy of 'Column addition'.
Lesson 10: Prepare a display copy of 'Division methods'.

You will need

Photocopiable pages
'Choosing decimals' (page 185) and 'Sponsored walk' (page 186), one per child.

CD resources
'Related facts', 'Column addition' and 'Division methods'; support, extension and template versions of 'Choosing decimals' and 'Sponsored walk'. General resource sheet: 'Digit (+ and –) and decimal point cards'. Interactive resource: 'Number sentence builder'.

Equipment
Ten-sided dice for each group; individual whiteboards and pens.

Learning objectives

Starter
● Use knowledge of place value and multiplication facts to 10 ×10 to derive related multiplication and division facts involving decimals (eg 0.8 × 7, 4.8 ÷ 6).
● Use efficient written methods to add and subtract integers and decimals, to multiply and divide integers and decimals by a one-digit integer, and to multiply two-digit and three-digit integers by a two-digit integer.

Main teaching activities
2006
● Use knowledge of place value and multiplication facts to 10 ×10 to derive related multiplication and division facts involving decimals (eg 0.8 × 7, 4.8 ÷ 6).
● Use efficient written methods to add and subtract integers and decimals, to multiply and divide integers and decimals by a one-digit integer, and to multiply two-digit and three-digit integers by a two-digit integer.
1999
● Use known number facts and place value to consolidate mental multiplication and division.
● Extend written methods to column addition and subtraction of numbers involving decimals. Extend written methods to short multiplication of numbers involving decimals; short division of numbers involving decimals.

Vocabulary
add, subtract, multiply, divide, sum, total, difference, plus, minus, product, quotient, remainder, multiple, common multiple, factor, divisor, divisible by

Lesson 6 (Review)

Starter
Recall: Play times-tables bingo. Ask the children to write down six two-digit numbers on their whiteboard, making it a 'bingo card'. Call out different multiplication questions, such as 4 × 9 and 7 × 7. If the answer is one of the numbers on a child's 'bingo card' they can cross it out. The winner is the first to cross out all six numbers.

Main teaching activities
Whole class: Use the 'Number sentence builder' interactive resource to display the calculations during this lesson. (If an interactive whiteboard is not available write the calculations on the board, one under the other.) Ask the children to work out 6 × 78; remind them to approximate first (6 × 80 = 480). Encourage them to use their knowledge of multiplication tables and a multiplication method of their choice to calculate the answer. (468) Next, ask: *What about 60 × 78?* Check that they all understand that this is 10 times more. Then ask: *What about 0.6 × 78?* Remind them that in this example they are dividing by 10. Ask them to suggest other multiplication sums that could be derived from the calculation 6 × 78 = 468. If it is not suggested, demonstrate 6 × 7.8. Remind them that they should always approximate first in order to make sure that they have put the decimal point in the correct place.

Next, ask the children to derive related division facts from 6 × 78 = 468. For example, 468 ÷ 6 = 78, 46.8 ÷ 6 = 7.8, and so on.

Securing number facts, relationships and calculating

BLOCK E

Write another multiplication sum on the 'Number sentence builder' such as 36 × 9 = 324, and ask the children to discuss with their partners the different related multiplication and division facts that they can derive from this.

Independent/paired work: Provide copies of the activity sheet 'Related facts' for children to work on.

Review
Write 0.8 × 7 on the board and ask the children to calculate the answer. Ask them to explain their reasoning. Then give other examples for the children to calculate, such as 56 ÷ 0.4, each time asking them to explain how they have derived the facts.

Lesson 7 (Practise and apply)

Starter
Refine and rehearse: Give a selection of addition sums to be done mentally, such as 24 + 56, 79 + 87, 6 +7 +9 + 7, 230 + 90, 123 + 99. Allow no more than five seconds for the children to answer on their whiteboards.

Main teaching activities
Whole class: Explain that in this lesson the children are going to revisit column addition, looking especially at decimal numbers. Point out that with any calculation the children should first see if they can calculate mentally, then mentally with jottings, before resorting to a standard method.

Write on the board 927.4 + 0.73 + 83.78. Ask a volunteer to come and set this out as a vertical sum and calculate the answer. Demonstrate the different methods, as shown on the 'Column addition' activity sheet, which can be displayed on an OHP or interactive whiteboard.

Stress that care must be taken to ensure that the decimal points are in line and that each digit is written in the correct column. Remind the children to check their work by using an inverse operation or alternative method when using a calculator.

Paired work: Introduce the 'Choosing decimals' activity sheet, on which the children select decimal numbers from boxes, then add them using column addition. Suggest to the children that they could use an approximation and that they should always start off by asking: *Can I do this in my head or with jottings?*

Review
Write these examples on the board and ask the children to tell you which method they would use:
(a) 3899 + 499.5
(b) 54.12 + 267.8 + 3.25
(c) 12.99 + 312.4
(d) 346.2 + 19.93

Remind them that they should look for the method they find quickest and simplest. For example, for (a) mental addition with jottings (3900 + 500 − 1.5 = 4398.5); (b) column addition (325.17); (c) mental addition (13 + 312.4 − 0.01 = 325.39); (d) mental addition with jottings (346.2 + 20 − 0.7 = 366.13). Ask: *Can you suggest ways to check your addition?*

Lesson 8 (Apply)

Starter
Refine and rehearse: Tell the children that they will be practising subtracting numbers in their heads. Give a starting number such as 50 and tell the children to subtract in their head the numbers that you call out from the starting number. For example, 50 minus 8, then 7, then 12. Ask the children to write their answer (23) on their whiteboards and then show their boards when you say *Show me.* Repeat with other sets of numbers.

Differentiation.
Less confident learners: Check that these children are sure of their multiplication tables. Encourage them to check their facts using a calculator.
More confident learners: Encourage these children to derive facts involving more than one decimal point.

Differentiation
Less confident learners: Give this group the support version of 'Choosing decimals', which limits calculations to adding two numbers at a time.
More confident learners: Give this group the extension version of the sheet, on which four or more numbers are added at a time.

Main teaching activities

Whole class: Remind the children about the different subtraction methods that they have been taught in previous lessons. Ask them to give some suggestions such as using a number line and column methods of subtraction. They should also be reminded to think about when it is appropriate to use quick mental methods.

Write 867 – 89 on the board. Ask the children to discuss which would be the best method to use for this calculation and then to calculate the answer. (778) Debate as a class the best method to use for this.

Group work: Ask the children to work in small groups and to consider the following subtraction sums:

876 – 699   305 – 175   1002 – 674

Tell them to discuss the different subtraction methods that they could use for each sum and compare the effectiveness of them. Each group should make a list of the advantages and disadvantages of each method for each calculation. They may then choose some examples of their own.

Review

Tell the children that you want them to debate the different subtraction methods that could be used. Choose a group to give the benefits of one method for the first calculation. Ask for another group to give the benefits of a different method for the same calculation. Repeat with the other calculations, involving different groups.

Differentiation

Children should work in mixed ability groups for this activity. Alternatively, a less confident group may work with an adult or work with simpler calculations using two-digit numbers such as 67 – 19.

Lesson 9 (Practise and apply)

Starter

Recall: Using a set of digit cards (from the 'Digit (+ and –) and decimal point cards' general resource sheet), select pairs of cards for the children to multiply together. Allow five seconds and then select the next pair. They should write their answers on whiteboards and check with their partners after ten pairs of numbers have been shown.

Main teaching activities

Whole class: Write 543 × 38 on the board. Work through the long multiplication as shown below. Remind the children to approximate, and then check the result after completing the long multiplication.

```
              5  4  3
         ×       3  8
            _____
543 × 30  1  6  2  9  0
543 × 8      4  3  4  4
            _____
          2  0  6  3  4
```

Ask the children what the result of multiplying 54.3 × 38 would be. Point out that as 54.3 is ten times smaller than 543, the answer to the calculation 54.3 × 38 will be ten times smaller than 543 × 30 (2063.4) Ask: *What about 5.43?* Point out that in this example the answer will be 100 times smaller than 20,634. (206.34)

Independent work: Encourage the children to work independently through the 'Sponsored walk' activity sheet.

Review

Discuss methods the children used for multiplication. Ask: *Which calculations did you do mentally? What method did you use to check your answers?* One strategy would be to total the amounts per mile and then multiply the total by the number of miles and check that this agrees with the totals.

Differentiation

Less confident learners: Give this group the support version of 'Sponsored walk', with simpler calculations.
More confident learners: This group should work through the extension version of 'Sponsored walk', with more difficult calculations.

Lesson 10 (Apply)

Starter

Reason: Explain that you will write a two-digit number on the board. Ask the children to double it as quickly as they can. Begin with, for example, 36 × 2, 47 × 2 and extend to decimals such as 7.3 × 2, 0.94 × 2, 0.78 × 2. Ask for the methods chosen for each example and compare for efficiency and effectiveness.

Main teaching activities

Whole class: Remind the children how to set out a short division sentence. Write on the board: 274 divide by 6. Ask the children to approximate first (270 ÷ 5 = 54), then work through the example on the board and display the 'Division methods' activity sheet.

Group work: Working in groups of four, the children take turns to roll a ten-sided dice. They record all four digits then have 30 seconds to make up a division sentence, each of which must include a decimal point. First they approximate the answer to their own division sentence, then they calculate the answer. Next, they compare their answers. The winner is the child with the calculation that gives the highest (or lowest) answer (for example, 7, 3, 5 and 6 may give 35.6 ÷ 7 or 6 ÷ 7.35). They repeat this process.

Review

Look at some of the calculations the children have made. Discuss which division methods they used. Ask: *Which methods were the quickest? How did it help you to approximate first?*

Differentiation

Less confident learners: Tell this group not to include a decimal point in their calculations; for example 7, 3, 5 and 6 may give 356 ÷ 7 or 63 ÷ 75.

More confident learners: Allow this group to use five digits and to try with two decimal numbers; for example 2, 7, 3, 5 and 6 may give 32.5 ÷ 7.6 or 6.25 ÷ 7.3.

Lessons 11–15

Preparation

Lesson 12: Prepare a display copy of 'Fraction wall'.
Lesson 13: Prepare several sets of 'Fraction cards' for the Starter.

You will need

Photocopiable pages
'What fraction?' (page 187), one per child.

CD resources
Support, extension and template versions of 'What fraction?'; extension and template versions of 'Ratio and proportion'; core, support, extension and template versions of 'All in proportion'. General resource sheets: 'Fraction cards', 'Fraction muncher' and 'Fraction wall'.

Equipment
Calculators for each child; washing line and pegs; multilink cubes; individual whiteboards and pens.

Learning objectives

Starter

● Use a calculator to solve problems involving multi-step calculations.
● Express a larger whole number as a fraction of a smaller one (eg recognise that 8 slices of a 5-slice pizza represents $^8/_5$ or $1^3/_5$ pizzas); simplify fractions by cancelling common factors; order a set of fractions by converting them to fractions with a common denominator.
● Use efficient written methods to add and subtract integers and decimals, to multiply and divide integers and decimals by a one-digit integer, and to multiply two-digit and three-digit integers by a two-digit integer.

Main teaching activities

2006

● Use a calculator to solve problems involving multi-step calculations.
● Express a larger whole number as a fraction of a smaller one (eg recognise that 8 slices of a 5-slice pizza represents $^8/_5$ or $1^3/_5$ pizzas); simplify fractions by cancelling common factors; order a set of fractions by converting them to fractions with a common denominator.
● Relate fractions to multiplication and division (eg 6 ÷ 2 = $^1/_2$ of 6 = 6 × $^1/_2$); express a quotient as a fraction or decimal (eg 67 ÷ 5 =13.4 or $13^2/_5$); find fractions and percentages of whole-number quantities (eg $^5/_8$ of 96, 65% of £260).
● Solve simple problems involving direct proportion by scaling quantities up or down.

1999

● Develop calculator skills and use a calculator effectively.
● Reduce a fraction to its simplest form by cancelling common factors in the numerator and denominator.
● Order fractions such as $^2/_3$, $^3/_4$ and $^5/_6$ by converting them to fractions with a common denominator, and position them on a number line.

- Find fractions, including tenths and hundredths, of numbers or quantities (eg $5/8$ of 32, $7/10$ of 40, $9/100$ of 400cm). Find simple percentages of small whole-number quantities (eg find 10% of £500, then 20%, 40% and 80% by doubling).
- Solve simple problems involving ratio and proportion.

Vocabulary

decimal fraction, decimal place, decimal point, percentage, per cent (%), fraction, proper fraction, improper fraction, mixed number, numerator, denominator, unit fraction, equivalent, cancel, proportion, ratio, in every, for every, to every

Lesson 11 (Review)

Starter

Rehearse: Tell the children that you want them to use their calculators to work out some quick calculations and to then write their answers on their whiteboards. Remind them to clear the calculator after each process. Give examples such as:

68×35 (2380)
936 divided by 4 (234)
595×23 (13,685)
$60 \times 60 \times 60$ (216,000)

Main teaching activities

Whole class: Ask the children to use the calculator to work out how many seconds there are in a day. Then ask a child to give the calculation and the answer. ($60 \times 60 \times 24 = 86,400$)

Tell the children that in this lesson they will be using a calculator to solve problems with more than one step. Remind them about the five-step strategy (see Lesson 3).

Write the following problem on the board: *There are 265 children in a school. $2/5$ of them have school dinners. School dinners cost £1.75. How much dinner money is collected each week?* Ask the children to discuss the problem with their partners and to decide what calculations should be carried out. They should agree that they need to calculate the number of children who have dinners by dividing 265 by 5 and multiplying the answer by 2. Next they need to calculate how many dinners will be needed in a week – this will be five times the number of children. Finally, they will have to multiply this by £1.75 to find the total amount of dinner money.

Demonstrate to the children how to calculate the answer using a calculator. Tell them not to clear the calculator in between each step; however, they may want to use the equals key at each step.

Paired work: Tell the children that you want them to work in pairs. Each partner should make up a multi-step problem for their partner to solve using a calculator. They should then check each other's calculations. Some suggestions you may give them are:

- *How many hours in February?*
- *How much would 25 tins of sweets cost if they are £2.95 each, but there is a discount of 15% for more than 20?*

Review

Ask some children to share the problems that they made up. The rest of the class should use their calculators to work them out.

Ask questions such as: *What sequence of numbers did you input into the calculator to achieve your answer? Could you have calculated this easily without the calculator?*

Differentiation

More confident learners: These children should try to derive problems involving different operations within each problem.
Less confident learners: Suggest that these children make up problems related to the calendar and time, for example: *How many hours in each month?*

Securing number facts, relationships and calculating

BLOCK E

Lesson 12 (Teach)

Starter
Revisit: Play 'Decimal swap' in pairs. Give the children calculations to do on calculators, which give answers to two decimal places (for example, $26.2 \div 3$). The first child does the calculation and the other child in the pair rounds the answer to the nearest tenth, then the nearest whole number. Swap and repeat for different numbers.

Main teaching activities
Whole class: Give each child a copy of the 'Fraction wall' general resource sheet. Use the walls to compare fractions by asking questions such as: *One-third is equivalent to how many sixths? Six-ninths is equivalent to how many sixths? One-eighth is half of what? One-third is how many times bigger than one-ninth?*

Display a copy of the 'Fraction wall'. Ask the children: *Using the fraction wall, can you write down three equivalent fractions? How can you find a fourth equivalent without using the fraction wall?*

Write on the board $^1/_4 = {}^2/_8 = {}^3/_{12} = {}^4/_{16}$. Identify the pattern of the numerator and the denominator and write the next two fractions in the sequence. Repeat for other fractions such as $^1/_5$ and $^1/_3$.

Paired work: Ask the children to work in pairs to find equivalents of the fractions shown by creating a list and identifying the patterns formed by the numerator and denominator.

Review
Write the following fraction families on the board:

$^1/_4 = {}^2/_8 = {}^4/_{16} = {}^8/_{30} = {}^{16}/_{64}$

$^1/_5 = {}^2/_{10} = {}^3/_{15} = {}^4/_{25} = {}^5/_{30} = {}^6/_{35}$

Can the children identify the mistakes in each family? Ask: *What needs to be done to correct each mistake?*

Differentiation
Less confident learners: This group may require adult support to recognise and generate the number sequences.
More confident learners: This group should be able to find the equivalents without having to write them in a linear format. Alternatively, the 'Fraction muncher' game could be used.

Lesson 13 (Practise and apply)

Starter
Reason: Give each child a card from the 'Fraction cards' set. Select a card from a similar set and hold it up, asking the children to show you a card higher, lower or equal to yours. Children have to show their fraction card if it is appropriate. Repeat. Then select two cards and ask for fractions between these two. Finally, ask children to come up in turns and peg their fraction on a number washing line, in order.

Main teaching activities
Whole class: Write on the board: $^3/_5$ of £625. Point out that the calculation is $^3/_5 \times 625$. Ask the children to approximate the answer. Point out that if we are multiplying by a fraction, the answer will be smaller. This can often confuse children because they see multiplying as 'making bigger'. Tell them that when we multiply by a fraction we first divide by the denominator, so we divide 625 by 5 to get 125. Then we multiply by the numerator '3' to get 375. Hence, $^3/_5$ of £625 is £375.

Work through a similar example, such as $^3/_4$ of 2m. Remind the children that they need to think what units they are going to work in. It is easier to convert 2 metres to 200cm and give the answer in centimetres, but both quantities should be expressed using the same units: $^3/_4 \times 2m = 1.5m$ or $^3/_4 \times 200cm = 150cm$.

Independent work: Introduce the activity sheet 'What fraction?'. Ask the children to complete this independently.

Review
Discuss any difficulties that the children have encountered. Write on the board: *Gemma saved £75. She spent $^3/_5$ on a computer game. How much did*

Differentiation

Less confident learners. The support version of 'What fraction?' is limited to halves, quarters and tenths.

More confident learners: The extension version of the sheet uses a wider range of fractions, including fifths, eighths, hundredths and thousandths.

Differentiation

Less confident learners: This group may need to be supported in this activity in order to access the correct vocabulary.

More confident learners: The 'Ratio and proportion' activity sheet containing written problems can be used for this group. If using this sheet, you will need to work through the following question with the group to prepare them for the level of understanding needed: *There are 32 children in a class, in the ratio of three boys to five girls. How many are girls?* Explain that they need first to add up the parts. (3 boys + 5 girls = 8 parts.) Next, divide the number of children in the class by the number of parts (32 ÷ 8 = 4). Therefore: 3 boys × 4 = 12; 5 girls × 4 = 20, so there are 20 girls. If necessary, work through another question: *Richard, Joss and Sanjay have been given £80 to divide in the ratio 2:3:5. How much does each child get?*

she have left? Ask the children: *What calculations do you need to do to find the answer? Can you solve the problem in your head? Can you do it using jottings?* Ask a child to come out and work through the problem, showing their workings.

Make sure that the children understand that they must first divide by the denominator and then multiply by the numerator. Then re-read the question to decide what the answer should be. Point out that the children are being asked 'How much did she have left?'

Lesson 14 (Teach)

Starter

Revisit: Tell the children that you are going to give them some calculations to do on their whiteboards and they need to think about the best calculation method to use for each one. Give a variety of calculations such as: 14 × 5.99, 1026 + 99 + 387, 1200 - 375, 30 × 7.35. Discuss how children did each calculation, helping them to identify the most efficient methods.

Main teaching activities

Whole class: Explain the term 'ratio' – a comparison of part to part: *I have one toffee **for** every five humbugs.* Explain that this is written as 1:5, and is a total of six items (one toffee and five humbugs). Explain the term 'proportion' – how many in each group: *I have one toffee **in** every five sweets.* Explain that this is written as $^1/_5$ and is a total of five items (one toffee and four other sweets).

On the board, write: Fred the gardener has two roses for every weed in his garden. Then say: *He has eight roses, so how many weeds are there? … six roses, how many weeds?* For some children, it may be necessary to build up a chart so that they can see the relationship (see left). Then ask: *If he has six weeds, how many roses will there be?*

ROSES	WEEDS
2	1
4	2
6	3
8	4

Elicit how they would write down the ratio of roses to weeds. (2:1) Ask: *What proportion of his plants are weeds?* Explain that there are three items in each group – two roses and one weed. Therefore, $^1/_3$ are weeds. Ask: *What proportion are roses?* ($^2/_3$)

Draw on the board, or use multilink to make the following pattern:

Blue	Blue	Green	B	B	G	B	B	G	B	B	G

Elicit that one in every three is green, so the proportion is $^1/_3$ green, $^2/_3$ blue. The ratio is one green for every blue, so is written 1:2. Ask the following questions: *If there were 30 squares, how many would be green? … blue? If there were 300 squares, how many would be green? … blue?* Encourage the children to use their knowledge of finding fractions of quantities to help find the answers.

Independent work: Ask the children to draw strips in their exercise books, colouring them in to match given ratios and proportions. For example, ask them to draw a strip divided into 18 equal parts and say: *Colour this strip red and yellow in the ratio of 2:4.* Ask them to draw a strip divided into 20 equal parts and say: *Colour this strip with three blue sections in every five.*

Review

Ask four boys and three girls to come to the front of the class. Ask for the ratio and proportion of boys and girls. Invite two more girls to come to the front. Ask: *How do the ratio and proportion change?*

Lesson 15 (Practise and evaluate)

Starter

Reason: Explain that you will say a two-digit number. Ask the children to find quickly the number that when added to your number makes a total of 100. Now ask the children to give all the related facts. For example, for 37: 37 + 63 = 100 and 63 + 37 = 100, 100 – 37 = 63 and 100 – 63 = 37.

Main teaching activities

Whole class: Explain that proportion compares a part of something with the whole. For instance, in a packet of five sweets, two sweets are toffees and three are fudge. The toffees can be indicated as two-fifths or two out of five. Then try this question: *Sally has three pens and Josh has three times as many. How many pens are there? What proportion of the pens does each child have?* (Sally has $^3/_{12}$, Josh has $^9/_{12}$.)

Group work: Provide the 'All in proportion' activity sheet and ask the children to solve the problems.

Review

Choose two or three problems from the core 'All in proportion' activity sheet and ask children to explain their reasoning. Ask: *A recipe for five people needs 95g of butter. How much butter do you need for two people? … eight people? Explain how you would solve these problems.*

Ask the children to give feedback about what they have learned from this unit, and of which aspects they are still unsure.

Differentiation

Less confident learners: Use the support version of the activity sheet, on which tiles are coloured in relation to given proportions.

More confident learners: Provide the extension version, with more challenging word-based problems involving proportion.

Name _____   Date _____

How many rolls?

You are going to wallpaper your bedroom.

Your room measures 2.4m × 3.6m.

The height of the walls is 2.35m.

The wallpaper costs £8.25 per roll.

You will also need wallpaper paste, which costs £1.35 for a packet that is sufficient for up to 8 rolls of paper.

- Use the table below to calculate how many rolls of wallpaper you will need. _____
- Calculate the cost for wallpapering this room

Height of walls in metres	Length of walls in metres (including doors and windows)						
	8.53	9.75	10.97	12.19	13.41	14.63	15.85
2.13–2.29	4	4	5	5	6	6	7
2.30–2.44	4	4	5	5	6	6	7
2.45–2.55	4	5	5	6	6	7	7
2.56–2.74	4	5	5	6	6	7	7
2.75–2.90	4	5	6	6	7	7	8

■ SCHOLASTIC PHOTOCOPIABLE

Name _____   Date _____

Shelf fit

1. You want to fit some shelves into the alcove in your bedroom. Each shelf will be 0.85m and you would like four shelves.

The timber comes in three different lengths:
- 1m lengths are £5.75 per metre
- 2m lengths are £5.45 per metre
- 3m lengths are £4.95 per metre.

Work out how much the timber will cost using the most economical sizes.

_____

_____

2. It would be useful to make a moveable bookcase. You could make the same four shelves into a bookcase by adding side pieces. The side panels can be made from the same timber.

Each of the side panels should be 1.5m long.

Work out the cost of the additional timber using the most economical sizes of timber.

_____

Securing number facts, relationships and calculating

BLOCK E

Name _____   Date _____

Choosing decimals

- Choose three numbers from different boxes and add them together. Remember to set the sum out as a column addition.
- Now choose three more numbers to make a sum.
- Make as many different sums as you can, using three numbers from different boxes every time.

Box A

3.2	5.1	9.3	7.8	4.8	4.7	2.9	8.6	6.4	7.7

Box B

12.5	20.5	32.7	40.3	65.2	98.4	12.3	74.8	82.1	56.3

Box C

215.6	330.4	306.8	999.4	868.4	704.3	550.1	199.9	412.2	603.7

Securing number facts, relationships and calculating

BLOCK E

Name _____   Date _____

Sponsored walk

Calculate the answers to these multiplication sums.
Remember to approximate first and then look for the simplest method of multiplication.

1. 32 × 548 _____

2. 3 × 23.7 _____

3. 40 × 735 _____

4. 9 × 567 _____

5. Rosie has completed a sponsored walk of 136 miles.
Work out the total of how much she raised from these four sponsors:

Mum and the family 35p a mile _____

Printo printers £1.36 a mile   _____

Uncle Fred 4.5p a mile   _____

Speedy Sportwear 50p a mile   _____

Total   _____

How can you check your total?

Name _____   Date _____

What fraction?

You may use a calculator to help you answer the following questions.

1. How far is $\frac{3}{5}$ of 2km? _____

2. How many minutes are there in $\frac{1}{3}$ of 4 hours? _____

3. What is $\frac{3}{8}$ of 12kg? _____

4. Rashid had £650 birthday money. He spent $\frac{7}{10}$ on a new bike.

How much did the bike cost? _____

5. Rashid then spent $\frac{1}{5}$ of his remaining birthday money on a game.

How much did he have left? _____

6. Sara entered the long-distance walking race of 24km.

She completed the first $\frac{3}{8}$ in 2 hours. How far did she have left to walk? _____

7. What fraction of £8 is 25p? _____

8. What fraction of 2 weeks is 5 days? _____

Choose a fraction from the first box and use it as an operator on a quantity or measurement from the second box. Repeat.

$\frac{1}{3}$	£240
$\frac{1}{8}$	10km
$\frac{3}{10}$	2kg
$\frac{7}{100}$	

Securing number facts, relationships and calculating

BLOCK E

Securing number facts, relationships and calculating

Lesson	Strands	Starter	Main teaching activities
1. Teach	Use/apply	Tabulate systematically the information in a problem or puzzle; identify and record the steps or calculations needed to solve it, using symbols where appropriate; interpret solutions in the original context and check their accuracy.	Tabulate systematically the information in a problem or puzzle; identify and record the steps or calculations needed to solve it, using symbols where appropriate; interpret solutions in the original context and check their accuracy.
2. Practise	Use/apply	As for Lesson 1	As for Lesson 1
3. Teach and practise	Use/apply	Explain reasoning and conclusions, using words, symbols or diagrams as appropriate.	As for Lesson 1
4. Apply	Use/apply	As for Lesson 3	Explain reasoning and conclusions, using words, symbols or diagrams as appropriate.
5. Practise and apply	Calculate	Use a calculator to solve problems involving multi-step calculations.	Use a calculator to solve problems involving multi-step calculations.
6. Apply	Calculate	As for Lesson 5	As for Lesson 5
7. Teach and practise	Counting	Express a larger whole number as a fraction of a smaller one (eg recognise that 8 slices of a 5-slice pizza represents $^8/_5$ or $1^3/_5$ pizzas); simplify fractions by cancelling common factors; order a set of fractions by converting them to fractions with a common denominator.	Express a larger whole number as a fraction of a smaller one (eg recognise that 8 slices of a 5-slice pizza represents $^8/_5$ or $1^3/_5$ pizzas); simplify fractions by cancelling common factors; order a set of fractions by converting them to fractions with a common denominator.
8. Practise	Counting	As for Lesson 7	As for Lesson 7
9. Practise and apply	Counting	**Express one quantity as a percentage of another (eg express £400 as a percentage of £1000); find equivalent percentages, decimals and fractions.**	**Express one quantity as a percentage of another (eg express £400 as a percentage of £1000); find equivalent percentages, decimals and fractions.**
10. Teach	Counting	As for Lesson 9	As for Lesson 9
11. Teach and practise	Counting	As for Lesson 9	As for Lesson 9
12. Practise and apply	Calculate	As for Lesson 9	Express a larger whole number as a fraction of a smaller one (eg recognise that 8 slices of a 5-slice pizza represents $^8/_5$ or $1^3/_5$ pizzas); simplify fractions by cancelling common factors; order a set of fractions by converting them to fractions with a common denominator.
13. Apply	Calculate	As for Lesson 9	Relate fractions to multiplication and division (eg $6 \div 2 = \frac{1}{2}$ of $6 = 6 \times \frac{1}{2}$); express a quotient as a fraction or decimal (eg $67 \div 5 = 13.4$ or $13^2/_5$); find fractions and percentages of whole-number quantities (eg $^5/_8$ of 96, 65% of £260).
14. Teach	Counting	As for Lesson 9	Solve simple problems involving direct proportion by scaling quantities up or down.
15. Teach, practise and evaluate	Counting	As for Lesson 9	As for Lesson 14

Unit 2 ◻ 3 weeks

Speaking and listening objectives
- Understand a variety of ways to criticise constructively and respond to criticism.

Introduction

Much of the unit is focused upon reinforcing children's knowledge and understanding of fractions and percentages and applying these effectively. The children also relate fractions to multiplying and dividing. Using and applying mathematics is more specifically dealt with in the first four lessons, where the children think about how to solve problems systematically and record and explain their reasoning. Other lessons deal with ratio and proportion. Throughout the unit, opportunities should be taken to teach the speaking and listening objective, which is specifically referred to in Lesson 6.

Use and apply mathematics

- Tabulate systematically the information in a problem or puzzle; identify and record the steps or calculations needed to solve it, using symbols where appropriate; interpret solutions in the original context and check their accuracy.
- Explain reasoning and conclusions, using words, symbols or diagrams as appropriate.

Lessons 1-4

Preparation
Lesson 1: Prepare a display copy of the 'Favourite snacks' activity sheet.
Lesson 4: Draw number lines on the board for the Starter. Prepare examples of formulae to write on the whiteboard.

You will need
Photocopiable pages
'High Street kids' (page 201), one per pair; 'Favourite snacks' (page 202), one per group.
CD resources
Support, extension and template versions of 'High Street kids'; core, support and extension versions of 'Formula 1' and 'Number sequence'.
Equipment
Straws, matchsticks, pegboards and calculators for support; number fans.

Learning objectives

Starter
- Tabulate systematically the information in a problem or puzzle; identify and record the steps or calculations needed to solve it, using symbols where appropriate; interpret solutions in the original context and check their accuracy.
- Explain reasoning and conclusions, using words, symbols or diagrams as appropriate.

Main teaching activities
2006
- Tabulate systematically the information in a problem or puzzle; identify and record the steps or calculations needed to solve it, using symbols where appropriate; interpret solutions in the original context and check their accuracy.
- Explain reasoning and conclusions, using words, symbols or diagrams as appropriate.
1999
- Identify and use appropriate operations (including combinations of operations) to solve word problems involving numbers and quantities based on 'real life', money or measures (including time), using one or more steps; explain methods and reasoning.
- Choose and use appropriate number operations to solve problems, and appropriate ways of calculating: mental, mental with jottings, written methods, calculator.
- Explain methods and reasoning, orally and in writing.

Vocabulary
problem, solution, calculator, calculate, calculation, jotting, equation, operation, symbol, inverse, answer, method, strategy, explain, predict, reason, reasoning, pattern, relationship

---

Lesson 1 (Teach)

Starter
Rehearse: Explain to the children that you want them to arrange the digits 1 to 6 in a triangle, so that each side has three numbers. Tell them to find the sum of the numbers on each side. Ask how can they arrange the

▷ numbers to get the highest/lowest total. Encourage them to tabulate the different results.

Main teaching activities

Whole class: Explain to the children that they are going to be solving problems, but they will be given some information to help them. Display the 'Favourite snacks' problem and ask a child to read out the information. Explain that from the clues it is possible to deduce information in order to solve the problem.

Point out that to the children that It is useful to draw a grid and mark on it the information that they are given and what they can deduce from that information. Go through the problems with the children, ticking and crossing the relevant boxes as you go. Say: *From the first piece of information, we know that one of the boys is called Jon Smith, so we can tick the box for Jon Smith. This means that we can put crosses in some of the other boxes, because if Jon's name is Smith it cannot be Brown or Moore and similarly, neither Ben nor Sam can be Smith. Jon Smith doesn't like crisps, so his snack cannot be crisps, nor does he like football, so his sport cannot be football, so we can put crosses in two more boxes.*

We are next told that Ben's favourite snack is fruit. Ask: *Which box can we tick?* Remind the children that this means that neither Sam's nor Jon's snack is fruit. Ask: *Which other two boxes can we cross?* (Ben – biscuits and crisps.) We now know that Jon Smith's snack can't be fruit or crisps, so it must be biscuits (so we can tick this box), which means that Sam's snack must be crisps (so we can tick this box). We are also told that Brown is the rugby ace, which means he does not play cricket or football, and Moore and Smith do not play rugby.

The final clue is that the first name of Moore is not Sam, which means it must be Ben, hence we have Jon Smith and Ben Moore, so Sam's name must be Brown. We know that Sam (Brown) has crisps for his snack and Jon Smith has biscuits, so Ben Moore must have fruit. We know that Sam Brown is the rugby ace and Jon (Smith) doesn't play football, so he must play cricket, which means that Ben Moore must play football. So we have found out that Ben Moore eats fruit and plays football, Jon Smith eats biscuits and plays cricket and Sam Brown eats crisps and plays rugby.

Paired work: Tell the children that you want them to work together on the 'High Street kids' activity sheet. Point out that sometimes they will be given information that they may not need in order to solve the problem – they have to select the relevant information.

Review

Ask children from the less confident group to demonstrate how they solved their problem. Ask: *How did using the grid help you to solve the problem?* Share the solutions of the other two groups, discussing any difficulties.

Differentiation

Less confident learners: The support version of the activity sheet has fewer criteria, limiting the amount of information needed.

More confident learners: Give this group the extension version of the activity sheet, with five different sets of data and some extra information. The children have to decide which facts are relevant to the task.

Lesson 2 (Practise)

Starter

Rehearse: Play 'Find the fraction'. Write a fraction such as 5¾ on a piece of paper without showing the class. Tell the children that you want them to work out the fraction. Say that it is between 1 and 10 (for example) and write 1 and 10 on the board. They may take it in turns to swap a number. For example they may say 6, you would them swap the 10 for a 6 (leaving 1 and 6). The next number may be 3, then swap to leave 3 and 6. The children keep swapping until they arrive at the required number. They should then play the game with a partner tabulating their line of enquiry.

Main teaching activities

Whole class: Remind the children that in the previous lesson they solved problems from given facts. Today you want them to design their own problem, following the pattern of the one they had been doing. Remind them

▷

Differentiation

Less confident learners: Give this group the blank template version of 'High Street kids' to complete first. If they are able to do this they should then start to design their own problem.

More confident learners: Encourage this group to include superfluous information in order to make their problem more complex. For example, use extra adjectives: *the tall girl; the boy with black hair.*

that the problem should involve having to deduce information. Suggest that they start with the solution and then think of how they can present some of the information.

Group/paired work: Ask the children to work in pairs or small groups to design their problem. When they are happy with their problem they should give it to another pair to solve.

Review

Ask one pair or group to show their problem so far. Let the class discuss how to solve it. Make sure that the children understand how each piece of information 'feeds into' the whole picture. Ask: *How can the grid show that your solution is accurate? Are there other ways the information could be presented?*

Lesson 3 (Teach and practise)

Starter

Revisit: Draw the following number lines on the board:

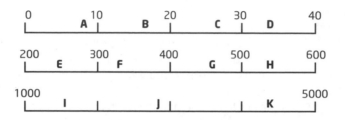

Ask the children what the values of A to K could be. Discuss that when approximating it is best to round to the nearest 10 or 100, whichever is most appropriate. Look at the letters again and decide their values to the nearest 10 or 100. Discuss what might happen if the number ends in a 5 (for example, 385). *Do we round up or down?* Using number fans to show the answers, ask the children to round up the following numbers, to the nearest 10: 81, 276, 455, 79; to the nearest 100: 321, 851, 1672, 450; to the nearest 1000: 4567, 9320, 12,500, 231,761.

Main teaching activities

Whole class: Point out to the children that in mathematics, relationships between numbers can be written using symbols - often letters of the alphabet - and that these are often used in simple formulae to help us with certain rules and calculations. Write up a simple example on the whiteboard or flipchart. Say: *We could denote a packet of sweets by the letter 'p'. The cost of each individual packet could be shown by the letter 'c'. If we wanted to find the total cost (t) of a number of packets of sweets we could use the formula t = p × c or, in full, total cost (t) = numbers of packets (p) × cost of one packet (c).* Use another example. Remind the children that the area of a rectangle or square can be calculated by multiplying the length by the width. In formula terms this could be written as a (area) = l (length) × w (width). Ask the children what other formulae could be developed from this. They should respond that $l = a \div w$ and $w = a \div l$. Then ask if they can give a formula for finding the perimeter of a rectangle or square. They should produce several alternatives. They could use $l + w + l + w$ in various forms, or $(l + w) × 2$ or $2 (w + l)$. From this last example, emphasise that in these types of formulae a letter and a number next to each other with no visible sign always means multiply. So, for example, $2t = 2 × t$ and $5n = 5 × n$.

Group work: Provide the children with copies of the 'Formula 1' activity sheet to work through.

Differentiation

Less confident learners: Provide this group with the support version of 'Formula 1', which deals with using the formula area = length × width only. Support may be needed when the formula is expressed in other ways, such as $w = a \div l$.

More confident learners: The extension version of 'Formula 1' asks children to use other formulae, namely, circumference of a circle = pi × diameter, and converting degrees in Fahrenheit into degrees in Celsius ($F = 9C \div 5 + 32$).

▶

Review

Check through calculations that the children have carried out on the activity sheet and ensure figures have been correctly matched to letters in formulae. Select a formula and ask: *Can you explain what this formula means?*

Lesson 4 (Apply)

Starter
Refine and rehearse: Repeat the Starter from Lesson 2. The children should work in pairs using different mixed numbers

Main teaching activities
Whole class: Explain that during the main part of the lesson, groups will be working on different number puzzles involving number sequences and patterns. Stress that in solving these puzzles it is important to work from the known to the unknown. Emphasise the importance of looking for relationships between numbers that will help to make generalisations about which rules are being applied. Once rules have been established, they should be used to predict what form the pattern or sequence is taking. Point out that the children need to be able to explain their reasoning and conclusions.
Group work: Provide the 'Number sequence' activity sheet. Explain that the children have to work out the patterns involved in making balanced triangles using single-digit numbers.

Review
Ask representatives from each group to report back to the others on the number puzzles they have been working on. Say: *Explain how you have worked this out and what you have concluded.* Put up a display of their work in the classroom. Revise the children's knowledge and understanding of common number patterns covered in previous lessons, like odd and even numbers, square numbers, triangular numbers, Fibonacci numbers and so on.

Differentiation
Less confident learners:
Provide plenty of equipment like straws, matchsticks, pegboards and so on, so that these children can work with patterns and sequences in a concrete way first. This will help them make the link between the spatial and the numerical pattern. They then work on the support version of the activity sheet.
More confident learners:
Encourage this group to extend their own number sequences as far as they can once they have completed the extension version of the activity sheet, which deals with the number sequence associated with Leonardo Fibonacci.

Lessons 5-6

Preparation
Lesson 5: Prepare 'Photo prices' and 'Trendy T-shirts' for display.
Lesson 6: Prepare 'Disco discount' for display.

You will need
CD resources
'Photo prices; core, support and extension versions of 'Trendy T-shirts'; core, support, extension and template versions of 'Disco discount'.
Equipment
Calculators; individual whiteboards and pens.

Learning objectives

Starter
● Use a calculator to solve problems involving multi-step calculations.

Main teaching activities
2006
● Use a calculator to solve problems involving multi-step calculations.
1999
● Develop calculator skills and use a calculator effectively.

Vocabulary
problem, solution, calculator, calculate, calculation

Lesson 5 (Practise and apply)

Starter
Refine and rehearse: Give a starter number and then, as a class, repeatedly halve the number using a calculator – for example: 36, 18, 9, 4.5, 2.25, 1.125. Then give a decimal number as a starter, such as: 5.3, 2.65, 1.325. Ask the children to write their answers on their whiteboards. They can stop at three decimal places. Repeat several times with different numbers.

Main teaching activities
Whole class: Explain to the children that they should imagine that they are holding a leavers' party. Discuss possible ideas for gifts for the leavers, such as T-shirts, autograph books or photos. Point out that, when they are calculating the costs for these, there are a number of things they should consider, such as: Are there bulk discounts or special offers? Do prices include VAT and any other extras? How will they decide between different options?

Unit 2 3 weeks

Display the 'Photo prices' activity sheet. Ask the children: *Which would be the best option if there are likely to be 20 people who want the photos?* Ask them to use their calculators to work out the best option. (Option 1 = £290, option 2 = £300, so option 1 would be better.) *What if 50 people are likely to want photos?* (Option 1 = £650, option 2 = £500, so option 2 would be better.) Point out that they have to estimate how many people they think will want photos.

Group work: Display the core version of 'Trendy T-shirts' and discuss the content. Remind the children that they will need to consider different options before they make their decisions. They should work in pairs or groups and discuss their ideas and responses to the questions. Let them use calculators and encourage them to check their results.

Review

Display the support version of the activity sheet and ask: *How did you use a calculator to help you work this out?* Make sure that the children used all the relevant information. Discuss the different options with the whole group. Do they agree where assumptions have been made? How many people missed out parts of the information, such as the 'set-up' fee? Ask: *Were you surprised by any of your results?*

Lesson 6 (Apply)

Starter

Recall and reason: Ask the children to write the answers to the following questions on their whiteboards: *Divide 4.8 by 6.* (0.8) *How many sevens in 35?* (7) *What is one-twentieth of 380?* (19) *What is 9 multiplied by 0.7 divided by 3?* (2.1) Check the answers and then ask each child to devise a question involving division which can be solved mentally. They should then give it to their partner to solve and check the answer using a calculator.

Main teaching activities

Whole class: Tell the children that in this lesson they will be using their calculators to work out the best price for a disco for the leavers' party. Display the 'Disco discount' activity sheet and explain that these two examples are typical of what may be on offer. Ask the children to identify the most important pieces of information to help them choose between the two. They should suggest working out the price for different group sizes and calculating the cost per individual. The cheapest may not be the best, so if they choose a more expensive option they should be able to justify their decision.

Paired work: Tell the children that you want them to use the information on 'Disco discount' to decide which entertainment they would choose for their party. Point out that they should make sure they include all the costs, and they should be able to justify their choice.

Review

Discuss any difficulties encountered during the lesson. Ask someone from each level to explain the steps they followed to decide which option to go for and how they calculated the costs. Choose one child to talk about how they solved the problem. Ask: *Do you think your method is better/can you explain why it is better?* Encourage the children to criticise constructively and respond to criticism.

Differentiation

Less confident learners: Work with this group, discussing the options on the support version of the activity sheet.

More confident learners: Give these children the extension version of the activity sheet.

Differentiation

Less confident learners: Give this group the support version of the activity sheet.

More confident learners: Give this group the extension version, where they have a choice of three discos and have to include VAT.

Securing number facts, relationships and calculating

BLOCK E

Lesson 7-13

Preparation
Lesson 8: Write the groups of fractions on the board.
Lesson 13: Prepare 'Fraction cards' and 'Percentage cards'.

You will need
Photocopiable pages
'Mark up' (page 203), one per group.
CD resources
Extension and template versions of 'Mark up'; core, support and extension versions of 'Change over'; support version of 'Decimal equivalents'; core, support, extension and template versions of 'Percentage problems'; 'Percentages'; core and support versions of 'All mixed up'. General resource sheets: 'Number lines', 'Fraction cards' and 'Percentage cards'.
Equipment
An OHP calculator; calculators; table squares for support; counting stick; plastic fraction sets for support; ten-sided dice; individual whiteboards and pens.

Learning objectives

Starter
● Express a larger whole number as a fraction of a smaller one (eg recognise that 8 slices of a 5-slice pizza represents $^8/_5$ or $1^3/_5$ pizzas); simplify fractions by cancelling common factors; order a set of fractions by converting them to fractions with a common denominator.
● Express one quantity as a percentage of another (eg express £400 as a percentage of £1000); find equivalent percentages, decimals and fractions.

Main teaching activities
2006
● Express a larger whole number as a fraction of a smaller one (eg recognise that 8 slices of a 5-slice pizza represents $^8/_5$ or $1^3/_5$ pizzas); simplify fractions by cancelling common factors; order a set of fractions by converting them to fractions with a common denominator.
● Express one quantity as a percentage of another (eg express £400 as a percentage of £1000); find equivalent percentages, decimals and fractions.
● Relate fractions to multiplication and division (eg $6 ÷ 2 - ^1/_2$ of $6 = 6 × ^1/_2$); express a quotient as a fraction or decimal (eg $67 ÷ 5 = 13.4$ or $13^2/_5$); find fractions and percentages of whole-number quantities (eg $^5/_8$ of 96, 65% of £260).
1999
● Reduce a fraction to its simplest form by cancelling common factors in the numerator and denominator. Order fractions such as $^2/_3$, $^3/_4$ and $^5/_6$ by converting them to fractions with a common denominator, and position them on a number line.
● Understand percentage as the number of parts in every 100, recognise the equivalence between percentages and fractions and decimals, and find simple percentages of numbers or quantities.

Vocabulary
decimal fraction, decimal place, decimal point, percentage, per cent (%), fraction, proper fraction, improper fraction, mixed number, numerator, denominator, unit fraction, equivalent, cancel

Lesson 7 (Teach and practise)

Starter
Revisit: Write on the board the following fractions: $^1/_4$, $^1/_2$, $^3/_8$, $^7/_8$. Ask: *How can we order these fractions?* Encourage the children to find a common denominator and then to order the fractions. Draw an empty number line labelled 0 at one end and 1 at the other. Invite the children to place each fraction where they estimate it belongs. Repeat this for another family of fractions, such as $^1/_3$, $^4/_5$, $^5/_6$, $^2/_5$.

Main teaching activities
Whole class: Remind the children of the work they have done in previous lessons on equivalence. Demonstrate a further way of finding equivalent fractions by multiplying the numerator and the denominator by the same number. Write up the following fractions as examples:

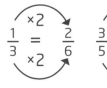

Then ask the children to find equivalents of $^4/_9$, $^7/_{12}$ and $^3/_7$ using the method shown. Explain that this method can be used to help order fractions that have different denominators. Ask the children to order $^{12}/_{15}$, $^{13}/_{15}$ and $^9/_{15}$, smallest to largest. Ask: *Why is it so easy to do?* (They have the same denominator.) Now ask them to try $^3/_5$, $^5/_6$ and $^2/_3$. Ask: *Why is this more difficult?* (The denominators are different.) Explain that the solution lies in finding a denominator that is common to the 5, 6 and 3. Establish that 30 is the common multiple here. Refer to the earlier method as a way to convert $^3/_5$, $^5/_6$ and $^2/_3$ to thirtieths.

As you work through each calculation, give less information, so that the children identify what number they need to use as the multiplier. Repeat for $^1/_8$, $^4/_{12}$, $^9/_{24}$ and $^3/_4$, $^1/_2$, $^4/_8$ and $^4/_5$.

Group work: Give out the 'Mark up' activity sheet. Tell the children they have a set of fractions with each blank number line, which need to be changed to have a common denominator. The converted fractions then need to be placed on the number line.

Review

Ask the children: *Would you rather have $^5/_8$ or $^3/_5$ of a bar of chocolate?* Discuss what they would need to do to find which would be the larger piece. Ask: *Which is the bigger of the two?* ($^5/_8$ is $^{25}/_{40}$, while $^3/_5$ is $^{24}/_{40}$.)

Lesson 8 (Practise)

Starter
Revisit: Write the following sets of fractions on the board:

- $^6/_{12}$, $^3/_4$, $^2/_3$, $^1/_2$, $^1/_3$
- $^2/_5$, $^3/_{20}$, $^6/_{10}$, $^1/_4$, $^3/_4$, $^{17}/_{20}$
- $^{11}/_{16}$, $^1/_4$, $^3/_8$, $^1/_2$, $^7/_8$, $^1/_{16}$
- $^1/_5$, $^2/_3$, $^9/_{15}$, $^4/_5$, $^2/_{15}$

Organise the children into groups of three or four, with one whiteboard per group. Ask the groups to convert the fractions in the first set to have a common denominator and then rewrite in order of size. Allow a time limit. Can the children 'beat the clock'? Repeat for each set. Discuss findings, checking that each group chose the appropriate common denominator.

Main teaching activities
Whole class: Explain that the lesson is about ordering fractions. Write the fractions $^1/_2$, $^1/_4$ and $^1/_3$ on the whiteboard. Ask: *How would you put these fractions into order without using a calculator?* Explain that we need to find the lowest common denominator for each one, ie put them into the same fraction family. Ask the children to find the lowest number common to all three times-tables ($2\times$, $4\times$ and $3\times$). Then show them how to convert $^1/_2$ into $^6/_{12}$, $^1/_4$ into $^3/_{12}$ and $^1/_3$ into $^4/_{12}$. Stress that when converting we must do the same thing to both parts of the fraction – denominator and numerator. Now draw a straight horizontal number line on the whiteboard, divide it into twelve equal sections and ask volunteers to mark the correct position of $^1/_2$ ($^6/_{12}$), $^1/_4$ ($^3/_{12}$) and $^1/_3$ ($^4/_{12}$). Go through the same process with another example (say, $^1/_4$, $^1/_2$ and $^3/_8$) using eighths as the lowest common denominator.

Independent work: Give each child a blank copy of the 'Number lines' general resource sheet, then write the following examples on the whiteboard for them to order in the same way and place in the correct position on a number line. (The lowest common denominator is given in brackets – do not provide these for the children.)

1. $^1/_3$, $^1/_2$, $^5/_6$ (6)

Differentiation
Less confident learners: Prepare a long strip of paper marked with a number line in the same way as the activity sheet. Work with the group to change the fractions, and ask the children to write the positions of the fractions on the line.
More confident learners: Give this group the extension version of the activity sheet, on which they have to draw their own number lines. Without the visual clues they will need to establish the most suitable common denominators.

Differentiation

Less confident learners: Let this group start by ordering fractions that are in the same fraction family (eg $^2/_6$, $^1/_6$ and $^5/_6$) before moving on to pairs of fractions in which the common denominator is easy to find (eg $^1/_6$ and $^1/_4$; $^2/_3$ and $^1/_6$).

More confident learners: Extend the ordering activity from three to four fractions or increase the size of the denominator, eg ordering $^2/_3$, $^1/_2$, $^7/_{10}$ and $^3/_5$ (lowest common denominator 30). Set word problems requiring children to find the common denominator of groups of fractions: *If Rakesh reads $^3/_8$ of his book one day and $^1/_4$ of the book the next day, what fraction does he still have to read?*

2. $^3/_5$, $^1/_2$, $^7/_{10}$ (10)
3. $^1/_3$, $^1/_4$, $^5/_{12}$ (12)
4. $^2/_3$, $^1/_2$, $^7/_{12}$ (12)
5. $^2/_3$, $^5/_6$, $^1/_4$ (12)
6. $^9/_{20}$, $^2/_5$, $^1/_4$ (20)

Review

Go through each of the whiteboard examples with the children and check the fractions have been correctly positioned on each of the number lines. Ensure that the children fully understand each word in the term 'lowest common denominator'. Stress that when converting, both numerator and denominator must be treated in exactly the same way. Ask: *Which three of the following are equal: $^3/_5$, $^2/_3$, $^9/_{15}$, $^{12}/_{20}$, $^5/_9$?*

Lesson 9 (Practise and apply)

Starter

Recall: Label one end of the counting stick 0 and the other end 1. Count in steps of 0.1 along and back on the stick. Point to any point on the stick and ask the children to say what decimal fits there. Repeat, labelling the stick in jumps of 0.2, 0.25, 0.5, 0.6... and so on.

Main teaching activities

Whole class: Refer the children to the work carried out in the previous lesson, where fractions were ordered by finding a common denominator. Ask if they know another approach. Elicit the response that suggests the fractions can be turned into decimal numbers by dividing the denominator into the numerator. Practise with some conversions the children will be familiar with first. For example: order $^1/_4$ (0.25), $^1/_{10}$ (0.1) and $^1/_5$ (0.2) and $^3/_{10}$ (0.3), $^1/_2$ (0.5) and $^4/_5$ (0.8). Then explain that with more difficult divisions it is better to use a calculator. Show some examples on the OHP calculator: $^1/_3$ is 1 ÷ 3 (0.333333333), $^1/_8$ is 1 ÷ 8 (0.125), $^5/_6$ is 5 ÷ 6 (0.833333333) and $^5/_8$ is 5 ÷ 8 (0.625). Use these examples to explain the difference between a terminating decimal number (0.125), an infinite decimal number (0.833333333) and a recurring decimal number, where the same digit comes in every place (0.333333333). Stress that in the last two cases the display on the calculator shows only part of the decimal representation.

Paired work: Let the children work in mixed-ability pairs. Provide each pair with the 'Change over' activity sheet, on which they are required to sort groups of fractions by changing them into decimal numbers. They should convert tenths and fifths mentally, but use calculators to convert the other fractions.

Differentiation

Less confident learners: Support this group in working on the support version of the activity sheet. A copy of 'Decimal equivalents' may be needed by some for reference.

More confident learners: This group should work from the extension version of the activity sheet. Encourage them to make logical steps from some of the solutions they obtain. For example, if one-third is 0.333333333 recurring, then two-thirds is 0.666666666, and if one-eighth is 0.125, then two-eighths is 0.125 × 2 = 0.25.

Review

Mark the ordering activity with the children, checking any calculator calculations that might have caused trouble. Challenge the more confident group to report on any interesting discoveries they have made – for example, $^1/_9$ has a 1 in every place and $^2/_9$ has a 2 in every place. Ask: *What can you predict about the rest of the 'ninths family' from this?*

Lesson 10 (Teach)

Starter

Revisit: Revise the decimal and percentage equivalents of the common fractions half (0.5 and 50%), quarter (0.25 and 25%) and three-quarters (0.75 and 75%). Check that the children remember a tenth (0.1 and 10%), a fifth (0.2 and 20%) and a twentieth (0.05 and 5%).

Write the number 200 on the whiteboard. Ask questions based on this number, such as: *What is half/fifty per cent of 200? What is a quarter/twenty five per cent of 200?* Repeat the same two-part questions for three-quarters, a tenth, a fifth and a twentieth.

Main teaching activities

Whole class: Explain the term 'per cent' (per = for every, cent = 100). Ask: *Can you think of other words with 'cent'?* (Century, centurion, centipede.) Discuss how percentages equate to the number of parts in every 100. Explain that although 100% is the whole amount, there does not have to be 100 in the group. *If there are 32 children in a class, then this is 100%, the whole amount. If we want to find 25% of the class, then the percentage can be converted to a fraction to help us. For example, 25% = ¹/₄, so 25% of 32 = ¹/₄, ¹/₄ of 32 = 8.*

Help the children to convert the following percentages to their equivalent fractions: 50%, 75%, 10%, 20%, 1%. Ask a few simple questions to check understanding, such as:

● *What is 10% of 70?*
● *A pair of jeans costs £20. In the sale they are 20% cheaper. How much do they cost now?*

Independent work: Give each child a copy of the 'Percentage problems' activity sheet, which has a range of written problems to be solved.

Review

Write the following numbers on the board: 10, 25, 7, 40, 70, 63. Ask the children, in pairs, to choose three of the numbers and make up statements which result in the chosen number as the answer. For example:

● *A coat costs £70. It is reduced by 10%. I save £7.*
● *A coat costs £70. It is reduced by 10%. It now costs £63.*

Lesson 11 (Teach and practise)

Starter

Refine: Explain that you will say a number and ask the children to find a given percentage of it. Say, for example: *What is 25% of 40? What is 30% of 90? What is 10% of £400? And 20%?*

Main teaching activities

Whole class: Tell the children that in this lesson you are going to explain how many percentage problems can be calculated without using a calculator. Go through the following examples on the whiteboard or using an OHP:

● *Fifty per cent of 24 would be ¹/₂, so divide by 2: 24 ÷ 2 = 12.*
● *Twenty-five percent of 32 would be ¹/₄, so divide by 4: 32 ÷ 4 = 8.*
● *75% of 40 would be ³/₄, so divide by 4 and multiply by 3: 40 ÷ 4 = 10; 10 × 3 = 30.*
● *Ten per cent of 60 would be 1/10, so divide by 10: 60 ÷ 10 = 6.*

Also explain that finding 20%, 30%, 40% and so on can be done by finding 10% and then multiplying by 2, 3 or 4, and that 5% can be calculated by finding 10% and then halving the answer. For example, 5% of 40 would be 40 ÷ 10 ÷ 2 = 4 ÷ 2. Demonstrate how 15%, 35%, 45%, and so on, can be calculated in the same way.

Group work: Provide the children with the 'Percentages' activity sheet. Invite them to choose a percentage amount from the square and a number from the triangle and work out the answer either in their heads, by using jottings or by using a written method. No calculators should be allowed.

Review

Go through examples worked by each of the ability groups. Revise the general concept of percentage, ie 'out of' or 'parts of' 100. Discuss the % sign with its one and two zeros as a version of writing hundredths. Ask: *What is twenty per cent of seventy pounds?*

Differentiation

Less confident learners: Give this group the support version of 'Percentage problems', with problems using simple percentages.
More confident learners: Give this group the extension version of the activity sheet, with problems extending beyond the percentages used in the main lesson.

Differentiation

Less confident learners: Help make selections for this group so that they focus on the more straightforward percentage numbers, such as 50%, 10% and 20%.
More confident learners: Set this group a time limit to finish ten questions as quickly as they can. Encourage them to find at least two methods of obtaining the same answer.

Lesson 12 (Practise and apply)

Starter
Rehearse: Play equal fractions. Give the children a starter fraction and ask them to write on their whiteboards as many equivalent fractions to this as they can. Repeat with other fractions.

Main teaching activities
Whole class: Check that all the children understand the terms 'numerator' and 'denominator'. Draw three large pizzas on the board, each divided into six equal portions. Ask what fraction of a pizza one slice is ($\frac{1}{6}$). Remind the children that six pieces make one whole one: $\frac{6}{6} = 1$. Now tell them that you have eaten $2\frac{1}{6}$ of the pizzas. Ask: *How many sixths are left?* (5) *How many sixths have been eaten?* (13) Explain that $2\frac{1}{6} = \frac{13}{6}$ and that $2\frac{1}{6}$ is known as a 'mixed number'. Also, that $\frac{13}{6}$ is known as an improper fraction because the numerator is greater than the denominator. Ask: *If I had $\frac{19}{6}$, what would this be as a mixed number?* ($3\frac{1}{6}$) *How many pizzas could I make from $\frac{23}{6}$?*

Try the following questions, asking the children to show the answers on their whiteboards:
- *Change $11\frac{1}{4}$ into an improper fraction.*
- *Change $\frac{11}{8}$ into a mixed number.*
- *If each cake can be cut into 8 pieces, how many cakes do I need to hand out 30 pieces? How many pieces will I have left?*

Group work: Provide the children with copies of the 'All mixed up' activity sheet. This contains practice questions requiring mixed numbers to be changed to improper fractions and vice versa.

Review
Write the following on the board: $4\frac{3}{5} = \frac{24}{5}$; $3\frac{9}{12} = \frac{45}{12}$; $5\frac{2}{6} = \frac{30}{6}$. Tell the children that only one of these statements is correct. Ask: *Which one is it? Why are the other two incorrect? What should the correct answers be?*

Differentiation
Less confident learners: Let this group work on the support version of the activity sheet. Plastic fraction sets may be needed if some children still require apparatus to help their understanding.
More confident learners: Challenge these children to add simple mixed numbers involving the fractions $\frac{1}{2}$, $\frac{1}{4}$ and $\frac{3}{4}$ (for example, $2\frac{1}{2} + 3\frac{3}{4}$). Stress the need to add whole numbers first and then the fractions.

Lesson 13 (Apply)

Starter
Refine and rehearse: Write the following numbers on the board: 9, 15, 48, 3, 5, 50, 150, 1, 225, 96, 67, 12, 4, 75, 81. Ask the children to draw a 4 × 2 grid on their whiteboards, choosing a different number from the list above to go in each box. Play 'percentage bingo' by asking questions that have answers from the list. For example: *What is 10% of 150? What is 20% of 20?* The first child to cross out all eight answers on his/her board is the winner.

Main teaching activities
Whole class: Tell the children that in this lesson they will be finding fractions and percentages of whole-number quantities. Remind them how they would calculate $\frac{3}{4}$ of 50: they could divide by 4 to find $\frac{1}{4}$ and then multiply the answer by 3 to get $\frac{3}{4}$ (37.5). Tell them that they can use a calculator. Ask them to calculate $\frac{3}{5}$ of 35 (21).

Remind the children how to calculate percentages of whole numbers, such as 35% of £280. They should divide £280 by 100 and then multiply by 35 (£98).

Group work: Each group will need a mixed set of cards from 'Fraction cards' and 'Percentage cards'. The group should be given a starting value, such as £250, and each child should select a card from the pile of percentage and fraction cards. They should then find the percentage or fraction of the starting value. Others in the group should check the player's calculation.

Review
Ask: *What is 65% of £260? Can you explain the steps in the calculation? Did anyone do the calculation in a different way?* Next ask: *Can you calculate $\frac{5}{8}$ of 96?* Again, ask the children to explain their calculation.

Differentiation
Less confident learners: Limit the cards that this group uses to the easier fractions and percentages.
More confident learners: Give this group more difficult starting values such as £225. Also let them use the full set of fraction and percentage cards.

Lessons 14-15

Preparation
Lessons 14 and 15: Prepare marked sticks as described under 'Equipment' below.

You will need
CD resources
Core, support and extension versions of 'In proportion' and 'Ratio time'.
Equipment
Two sticks: one marked with four equal parts, three white and one coloured, the other marked with eight equal parts, three white and five coloured; table squares for support.

Learning objectives

Starter
● Express one quantity as a percentage of another (eg express £400 as a percentage of £1000); find equivalent percentages, decimals and fractions.

Main teaching activities
2006
● Solve simple problems involving direct proportion by scaling quantities up or down.
1999
● Solve simple problems involving ratio and proportion.

Vocabulary
decimal fraction, decimal place, decimal point, percentage, per cent (%), fraction, proper fraction, improper fraction, mixed number, numerator, denominator, unit fraction, equivalent, cancel

Lesson 14 (Teach)

Starter
Revisit: Revise common fractions as percentages: $1/2$ = 50%, $1/4$ = 25%, $3/4$ = 75%, $1/10$ = 10%, $1/5$ = 20%, $3/10$ = 30%, $4/5$ = 80%. The children should also appreciate that $1/3$ is about 33% and that $2/3$ is about 67%.

Reinforce the relationship between percentages, fractions and decimal numbers. Give one version of a family group and ask the children to provide the other two. For example, if you say 0.36, the children respond 36% and $36/100$.

Main teaching activities
Whole class: Emphasise to the children that proportion is the relationship between a part of something and the whole thing. It compares 'part with whole'. Show the children the stick divided equally into three white parts and one coloured part (see 'Equipment', left). Tell them that we can compare the white parts of the whole stick and say the proportion of white parts is 3 out of 4. Show the children that this can be written as $3/4$ or 0.75 or 75%. Use other examples: *Two parts out of 5 can be written as $2/5$ or 0.4 or 40%.*

Remind the children that, just like fractions, proportional amounts should be cancelled down into their lowest terms even though the amounts remain unchanged. For example, 10 out of 20 = $1/2$, 0.5 or 50%; 6 out of 10 = $3/5$, 0.6 or 60%; and 5 out of 20 = $1/4$, 0.25 or 25%. Talk through some practical problems with the children. For example:
● *An orange drink is made up of 900ml of water and 100ml of orange. What proportion of the drink is water?* (Nine-hundred thousandths of the drink is water, which is $9/10$, 0.9 or 90%.)
● *Strawberry jam is made from 200g of strawberries and 50g of sugar. What proportion of the jam is strawberries?* ($200/250$ of the jam is strawberries, which is $4/5$, 0.8 or 80%.)
Individual work: Ask the children to work individually on the 'In proportion' activity sheet.

Review
Check that the children have a secure understanding of the word 'proportion' as the relationship of part of something with the whole thing. Reinforce the fact that proportions may be the same even though figures used may be different. For example, $12/16$ and $3/4$ are in the same proportion. Ask: *Can you give another pair of numbers that are in the same proportion?*

Differentiation
Less confident learners: This group may need table squares to help with the cancelling down operation on the support version of 'In proportion'. Continue to reinforce the link between proportion, fractions and decimal numbers (eg one out of four = $1/4$ = 0.25 = 25%).
More confident learners: Give this group the extension version of 'In proportion'. Encourage the children to solve proportion problems set in everyday situations. For example, say: *With some times rounded off, what proportion of the day do you spend at school/sleeping/eating?*

▷

BLOCK E

Lesson 15 (Teach, practise and evaluate)

Starter

Reason: Remind children that finding 50% of a number means dividing by 2, 25% means dividing by 4, 10% means dividing by 10 and 20% means dividing by 5. Test these out with questions such as the following: *Find 25% of 60, find 50% of 56, find 20% of 80 and find 10% of 130.*

Also revise finding $3/4$ or 75% of a number by dividing by 4 and then multiplying by 3 (for example, 75% of 48 = 36). Then look at multiples of 10 and 20, such as 30% of 90 = 90 ÷ 10 × 3 = 27 and 80% of 115 = 115 ÷ 5 × 4 = 92.

Main teaching activities

Whole class: Explain that, like proportion, the word 'ratio' is used to compare numbers or quantities. Stress, though, that ratio is the relationship between two or more numbers or quantities and that it compares 'part with part'. Use the coloured stick method again, this time showing eight equal parts made up of three white parts and five coloured parts. Compare the white parts with the coloured parts. We say the ratio of the white to coloured is 3 to 5. Explain that this is usually written 3:5. Point out that, like proportions, ratios are usually simplified to make them easier to work with. For example, 10:2 would be 5:1, 10:30 would be 1:3 and 100:25 would be 4:1. Use some practical examples of ratio questions, such as: *Choc-chip cakes are made from 80g of cake mix and 20g of chocolate. What is the ratio of chocolate to cake mix?* (20:80 is in the ratio 1:4.)

Independent work: Ask the children to work individually on the 'Ratio time' activity sheet. First ratios have to be put into the lowest terms and then amounts have to be put into the correct ratio.

Review

Once the tasks have been checked, revise the last two lessons with more general questions:
● *Explain what the word 'proportion' means.*
● *What does the word 'ratio' mean?*
● *What is the ratio 21:24 in its lowest terms?*
● *Fifteen footballs are in the ratio two white ones for every three yellow ones. How many footballs are white? How many footballs are yellow?*

Ask the children to give feedback about what they have learned in this unit, identifying strengths and areas for improvement.

Differentiation

Less confident learners: Work with this group as they focus on the support version of 'Ratio time'. This reinforces activities started in Unit 1. Ensure that the two ratio numbers are added together to give the length of the strip of squared paper overall.
More confident learners: This group should work on the extension version of 'Ratio time', which gives problems linked to measurement and shape.

Name _____   Date _____

High Street kids

Only three bikes were hired from the Bike Hire shop on High Street on a sunny Sunday in June.

From the clues given below, can you work out the name of the boys who hired the bike at each of the three times and how long they kept each bike? Use the table below to help you sort out the information. Remember to complete as many boxes as you can.

- The city bike went out for 45 minutes.
- Peter went out for a shorter time than the boy who hired the bike at 10.30am.
- The racing bike which was hired at 1.15pm was out longer than Ali's bike, which was not the mountain bike.

	Ali	Peter	Rick		Racing bike	Mountain bike	City bike		30 mins	45 mins	60 mins
10.30am											
1.15pm											
2.00pm											

30 mins							
45 mins							
60 mins							

Racing bike			
Mountain bike			
City bike			

Write your solution in the boxes below.

Name	Departure time	Bike	Duration

Securing number facts, relationships and calculating

BLOCK E

Name _____   Date _____

Favourite snacks

Three friends each enjoy a different sport on a Saturday morning, and they each take a different snack with them. From the clues, can you work out the names of each child, the sport they enjoy and the snack they take with them?

- Jon Smith does not like crisps, nor does he play football.
- Ben's favourite snack is fruit.
- Brown is the rugby ace.
- The first name of Moore is not Sam.

	Brown	Moore	Smith		Biscuits	Fruit	Crisps		Cricket	Football	Rugby
Ben											
Jon											
Sam											

Cricket							
Football							
Rugby							

Biscuit			
Fruit			
Crisps			

Name _____ Date _____

Mark up

Mark the position of these fractions on the number line:

$$\frac{3}{4} \qquad \frac{2}{5} \qquad \frac{7}{20} \qquad \frac{7}{10} \qquad \frac{4}{5} \qquad \frac{1}{2} \qquad \frac{9}{20}$$

What must you do before you can order them? Change to have a common denominator.

Now try these:

$$\frac{8}{12} \qquad \frac{5}{6} \qquad \frac{3}{36} \qquad \frac{1}{2} \qquad \frac{3}{4} \qquad \frac{2}{9} \qquad \frac{5}{18} \qquad \frac{1}{9} \qquad \frac{1}{4}$$

Securing number facts, relationships and calculating

BLOCK E

Securing number facts, relationships and calculating

Lesson	Strands	Starter	Main teaching activities
1. Teach and practise	Use/apply	Tabulate systematically the information in a problem or puzzle; identify and record the steps or calculations needed to solve it, using symbols where appropriate; interpret solutions in the original context and check their accuracy.	Tabulate systematically the information in a problem or puzzle; identify and record the steps or calculations needed to solve it, using symbols where appropriate; interpret solutions in the original context and check their accuracy.
2. Practise	Use/apply	As for Lesson 1	As for Lesson 1
3. Practise	Use/apply	Solve multi-step problems, and problems involving fractions, decimals and percentages; choose and use appropriate calculation strategies at each stage, including calculator use.	Solve multi-step problems, and problems involving fractions, decimals and percentages; choose and use appropriate calculation strategies at each stage, including calculator use.
4. Review	Knowledge	**Use knowledge of place value and multiplication facts to 10 × 10 to derive related multiplication and division facts involving decimals (eg 0.8 × 7, 4.8 ÷ 6).**	**Use knowledge of place value and multiplication facts to 10 × 10 to derive related multiplication and division facts involving decimals (eg 0.8 × 7, 4.8 ÷ 6).**
5. Teach and practise	Knowledge	As for Lesson 4	As for Lesson 4
6. Practise	Knowledge	As for Lesson 4	As for Lesson 4
7 Review	Calculate	**Use efficient written methods to add and subtract integers and decimals, to multiply and divide integers and decimals by a one-digit integer, and to multiply two-digit and three-digit integers by a two-digit integer.**	**Use efficient written methods to add and subtract integers and decimals, to multiply and divide integers and decimals by a one-digit integer, and to multiply two-digit and three-digit integers by a two-digit integer.**
8. Teach and practise	Calculate	As for Lesson 7	As for Lesson 7
9. Apply	Calculate	As for Lesson 7	As for Lesson 7
10. Review and practise	Calculate	Use a calculator to solve problems involving multi-step calculations.	Use a calculator to solve problems involving multi-step calculations.
11. Teach and practise	Counting	**Express one quantity as a percentage of another (eg express £400 as a percentage of £1000); find equivalent percentages, decimals and fractions.**	**Express one quantity as a percentage of another (eg express £400 as a percentage of £1000); find equivalent percentages, decimals and fractions.**
12. Teach and practise	Counting	**Use knowledge of place value and multiplication facts to 10 × 10 to derive related multiplication and division facts involving decimals (eg 0.8 × 7, 4.8 ÷ 6).**	Express a larger whole number as a fraction of a smaller one (eg recognise that 8 slices of a 5-slice pizza represents $^8/_5$ or $1^3/_5$ pizzas); simplify fractions by cancelling common factors; order a set of fractions by converting them to fractions with a common denominator.
13. Practise	Counting	As for Lesson 12	As for Lesson 12
14. Apply	Calculate	Express a larger whole number as a fraction of a smaller one (eg recognise that 8 slices of a 5-slice pizza represents $^8/_5$ or $1^3/_5$ pizzas); simplify fractions by cancelling common factors; order a set of fractions by converting them to fractions with a common denominator.	Relate fractions to multiplication and division (eg 6 ÷ 2 = ½ of 6 = 6 × ½); express a quotient as a fraction or decimal (eg 67 ÷ 5 = 13.4 or $13^2/_5$); find fractions and percentages of whole-number quantities (eg $^5/_8$ of 96, 65% of £260).
15. Apply and evaluate	Counting	As for Lesson 14	Solve simple problems involving direct proportion by scaling quantities up or down.

Unit 3 🔲 3 weeks

Speaking and listening objectives
- Use a range of oral techniques to present persuasive arguments.

Introduction
In this unit of 15 lessons, all of the objectives from the previous two units are revisited. Using and applying mathematics is evident throughout the unit but is more specifically dealt with in the first three lessons. Other lessons reinforce children's knowledge and use of number facts and their ability to use and apply these effectively, and also secure their ability to use efficient methods of calculation. There is a strong emphasis on fractions and percentages, and applying these to problem solving. The relationship between fractions and multiplication and division is further explored. The speaking and listening objective is addressed in a number of lessons.

Use and apply mathematics
- Tabulate systematically the information in a problem or puzzle; identify and record the steps or calculations needed to solve it, using symbols where appropriate; interpret solutions in the original context and check their accuracy.
- Solve multi-step problems, and problems involving fractions, decimals and percentages; choose and use appropriate calculation strategies at each stage, including calculator use.

Lessons 1-3

Preparation
Lesson 2: Prepare an OHT of the 'Complete the grid' activity sheet.

You will need
Photocopiable pages
'Discount store' (page 217), one per child.
CD resources
Support version of 'Flags'; 'Complete the grid'; support, extension and template versions of 'Discount store'. General resource sheets: 'Digit (+ and –) and decimal point cards', a few sets of cards 1-4 for support.
Equipment
Coloured pencils; individual whiteboards and pens.

Learning objectives

Starter
- Tabulate systematically the information in a problem or puzzle; identify and record the steps or calculations needed to solve it, using symbols where appropriate; interpret solutions in the original context and check their accuracy.
- Solve multi-step problems, and problems involving fractions, decimals and percentages; choose and use appropriate calculation strategies at each stage.

Main teaching activities
2006
- Tabulate systematically the information in a problem or puzzle; identify and record the steps or calculations needed to solve it, using symbols where appropriate; interpret solutions in the original context and check their accuracy.
- Solve multi-step problems, and problems involving fractions, decimals and percentages; choose and use appropriate calculation strategies at each stage.
1999
- Identify and use appropriate operations (including combinations of operations) to solve word problems involving numbers and quantities based on 'real life', money or measures (including time), using one or more steps; explain methods and reasoning.
- Choose and use appropriate number operations to solve problems, and appropriate ways of calculating: mental, mental with jottings, written methods, calculator.

Vocabulary
problem, solution, calculator, calculate, calculation, jotting, equation, operation, symbol, inverse, answer, method, strategy, explain, predict, reason, reasoning, pattern, relationship

Securing number facts, relationships and calculating

BLOCK E

SCHOLASTIC

100 MATHS FRAMEWORK LESSONS · YEAR 6   205

Lesson 1 (Teach and practise)

Starter

Rehearse: Show the following simple Sudoku on the board and give the children five minutes to complete it. Then ask them to explain their reasoning to their partner.

Explain to the children that with this Sudoku the numbers 1 to 4 must appear in each row, in each column and in each block of four.

1	4		
			4
	1		
4		2	

Solution:

1	4	3	2
3	2	1	4
2	1	4	3
4	3	2	1

Main teaching activities

Whole class: Tell the children that in this lesson they are going to be carrying out an investigation involving permutations.

Draw the following on the board:

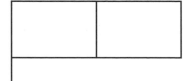

Explain that this is the flag for a new country (the flagpole is on the left) and they may use two colours to colour the flag – for example, red and blue. Ask: *How many permutations are there for the flag?* Children should readily be able to identify two: red/blue and blue/red. Ask them: *What if we can add another colour such as green? How many permutations then?* For this example tell the children that you only want them to consider vertical stripes and use each colour once. The children should work out that there are six alternatives.

Independent work: Tell the children that you now want them to consider a flag with four colours, and then five colours. Explain to them that you particularly want them to think about how they can approach this systematically and to record the steps they have taken to solve the problem.

Review

Ask the children to explain their solutions. Ask: *How did you tabulate the steps that you took? Would you be able to work out how many permutations there would be with 7 or more colours? What if the flag pole was removed and the flags could be reversed; how would this change the number of permutations?*

Differentiation

Less confident learners: It would be helpful to give this group the 'Flags' activity sheet and allow them to use coloured pencils.

More confident learners: Encourage this group to think of other ways the flag could be designed, which would increase the permutations. For example, allow horizontal stripes and ask children to calculate these alternatives.

Lesson 2 (Practise)

Starter

Revisit: Remind the class of the Starter from the previous lesson and show them the following Sudoku to complete:

Unit 3 ▭ 3 weeks

3	1		
			3
	2		
4		2	

Solution:

3	1	4	2
2	4	1	3
1	2	3	4
4	3	2	1

Main teaching activities

Whole class: Show the 'Complete the grid' activity sheet. Explain that in this lesson the children will be working out how to complete the puzzle grid and will be expected to be able to explain their reasoning. Explain that the squares should be filled with the digits 1 to 4 so that each column and row contains one of each number. The position of the numbers is indicated by the < (less than) and > (more than) signs. The double lines tell you that the numbers in the two squares are the same.

Ask the children if they can complete any squares. As they come up, ask them to explain their reasoning. The grid can be completed using the following arguments: We can see that as WC = XD = 3, XC < XD, but XD = 3, so XC must be 2 as XA is 1. So XB must be 4, hence YA is 4. WB = XA = 1, so WA must be 2, then WD is 4, ZA must be 3, so YB = 3, hence ZB = 2, YC =1, so YD = 2, so ZD = 1, then ZC = 4.

Independent/paired work: Give the children activity sheet 'Complete the grid'. Explain that you want them to complete the puzzle and be able to explain how they have worked it out.

Review

Show the 5 × 5 grid and ask the children to complete the grid. They should explain their reasoning as they complete each square. Ask: *How did you decide which squares to complete first?* Allow them to show some of the grids they have designed and ask: *Can you explain how you decided which squares to put the starter numbers in?*

Differentiation

Less confident learners: This group should be encouraged to complete the 4 × 4 puzzle. It may be helpful to give them digit cards to physically move around.
More confident learners: After completing the 5 × 5 grid, suggest that they design a 6 × 6 grid with sufficient clues for their partners to solve.

Lesson 3 (Practise)

Starter

Rehearse: Give the children calculations which can be done mentally, such as: *How much would seven cards at 15p cost?* (£1.05) *How much change would there be from £5 if I bought two books at £2.25 each?* (50p)

Main teaching activities

Tell the children that in this lesson they will be solving problems involving discounts and VAT. Explain that VAT is a tax of 17½ % which is added onto the price of some items. Remind the children of how they found percentages in the earlier units. Introduce the 'Discount store' activity sheet. Tell the children to approximate first and then to check their answers.

Review

Write on the board: £325 less 15%, £340 less 20%. Say: *A bike is in the sale in two shops at these prices. Which is the better deal?* (£325 less 15% = £276.25; £340 less 20% = £272.) Check that the children are able to calculate accurately and that they understand the comparisons. Go through any difficulties they had with the activity sheet.

Differentiation

There are differentiated versions of the activity sheet for more and less confident children.

Lesson 4-9

Preparation
Lesson 6: Prepare the 'Place value questions' activity sheet for display.
Lesson 7: Prepare the 'Column subtraction' activity sheet for display.
Lesson 8: Prepare the 'Multiplication methods' activity sheet for display. Prepare sets of digit cards from the general resource sheet and create some × and ÷ cards.

You will need
Photocopiable pages
'Multiplying and dividing' (page 218), 'Place value questions' (page 219), 'Solve them!' (page 220) and 'Bean growth' (page 221).
CD resources
Core, support, extension and template versions of 'Jake's clever thoughts'; support, extension and template versions of 'Multiplying and dividing', 'Solve them!' and 'Bean growth'; 'Column subtraction' and 'Multiplication methods'. General resource sheet: 'Digit (+ and –) and decimal point cards', a set of positive digits and decimal point card per pair. Interactive resource: 'Number sentence builder'.
Equipment
OHP/interactive whiteboard calculator; a dice marked ×10, ×100, ×1000, ÷10, ÷100, ÷1000; number fans for children.

Learning objectives

Starter
● Use knowledge of place value and multiplication facts to 10 × 10 to derive related multiplication and division facts involving decimals (eg 0.8 × 7, 4.8 ÷ 6).
● Use efficient written methods to add and subtract integers and decimals, to multiply and divide integers and decimals by a one-digit integer, and to multiply two-digit and three-digit integers by a two-digit integer.

Main teaching activities
2006
● Use knowledge of place value and multiplication facts to 10 × 10 to derive related multiplication and division facts involving decimals (eg 0.8 × 7, 4.8 ÷ 6).
● Use efficient written methods to add and subtract integers and decimals, to multiply and divide integers and decimals by a one-digit integer, and to multiply two-digit and three-digit integers by a two-digit integer.
1999
● Use known number facts and place value to consolidate mental multiplication and division.
● Extend written methods to column addition and subtraction of numbers involving decimals. Extend written methods to short multiplication of numbers involving decimals; short division of numbers involving decimals.

Vocabulary
add, subtract, multiply, divide, sum, total, difference, plus, minus, product, quotient, remainder, multiple, common multiple, factor, divisor, divisible by

Lesson 4 (Review)

Starter
Recall: Chant together the 7-times table. Tell the children that, in pairs, they are going to use their knowledge of this table to find the answers to other tables. Ask less confident children to work on the ×70 table (1 × 70, 2 × 70 and so on), more confident children to work on the ×0.7 table and the rest of the class to work on the ×700 table. Ask for a volunteer from each group to give feedback on their results.

Main teaching activities
Whole class: Use the 'Number sentence builder' interactive resource to display the calculations in this lesson. With the class, work out 8 × 40. Ask the children what other number facts they know using these figures. Try to elicit: 320 ÷ 40 = 8; 320 ÷ 8 = 40; 40 × 8 = 320. Tell them to write the answer to 9 × 30 on their whiteboards, plus the associated number facts. If any children find this difficult, remind them to use the known fact 9 × 3 as a starting point. Discuss the relationship between × and ÷. Establish that they are 'inverse operations'. Check the children's understanding by drawing the diagram shown here on the board.

Establish that 7 × 60 = 420. In turn, cover each number and ask the children to give a fact using the numbers left. Repeat until all four facts are established. Extend the task using decimals, for example, 3.6 ÷ 4. Explain to the children that they can use their understanding of the process above to help: 3.6 ÷ 4 can be found by 4 × ? = 3.6. Establish that 4 × 9 = 36, so 4 × 0.9 = 3.6. List associated number facts. Give the children a few problems to practise on their whiteboards, differentiated for each ability group. For example, use 3.75 × 3 for more confident children and use whole numbers only for the less confident group if they are not secure with decimals.

Unit 3 ▭ 3 weeks

Differentiation

Less confident learners: Give these children the support version of 'Jake's clever thoughts', which uses mostly whole numbers.

More confident learners: Give these children the extension version of the activity sheet, which uses a mixture of decimals and simple fractions.

Independent work: Distribute 'Jake's clever thoughts' activity sheet and explain that the children must use the given number facts to solve the related problems on the sheet.

Review

What can the class tell you about multiplication and division? Ensure that the children know the term 'inverse'. Ask them to complete the following: For every multiplication or division fact there are ? others that can be found. Write the following on the board: 75 × 4 = 300. Ask the children to use this information to work out the following: *Four children share £3. How much does each get? What is ¹/₄ of 300? How many 75s in 300?*

Lesson 5 (Teach and practise)

Starter

Revisit and refine: Play 'place value bingo'. Ask the children to draw a 2 × 3 grid on their whiteboards. On the class whiteboard, write six different two-digit numbers. The children choose to multiply or divide each one mentally by 10, 100 or 1000 and write the answer in a space on their grid. Taking each number in turn, roll a dice marked ×10, ×100, ×1000, ÷10, ÷100, ÷1000 to choose an operation, then ask the children to work out the answer. If the answer is on their grid, they can cross it out. Repeat until someone crosses out all of their numbers.

Main teaching activities

Whole class: Write the following place value headings on the board: TTh, Th, H, T, U, . , t, h. Mark 45 on the chart. Ask: *Where will the digits be if you multiply the 45 by 10? What will we need to put in the units column?* Repeat multiplying by 10 twice more, making sure the children understand that the number becomes ten times bigger each time and the need to use a zero as a place holder. Discuss that × 10 × 10 is the same as multiplying by 100. If necessary, put another two-digit number on the board to consolidate. Put 1700 on the chart and divide by 10. Keep dividing by 10 until you reach 1.7. Say: *If you divide by 10, then divide by 10 again, then divide by 10 a third time, this is the same as dividing by which number?* (1000) Discuss the effect with the children, ensuring that they understand that the numbers become ten times smaller each time and that there is no need, when dividing, to use a zero as a place holder for whole numbers as it has no value until decimals are reached. Repeat if necessary.

Ensure that the children understand that when multiplying by 10, 100 and 1000, digits move one, two and three places respectively to the left. When dividing by 10, 100 and 1000, digits move one, two and three places respectively to the right. Reinforce that the decimal point does not move, only the digits.

Divide the class in half. Ask one half to divide 230,000 by 10 six times. Ask the other to divide 230,000 by 100 three times. Make sure they record their answers at each stage. Compare answers and discuss the fact that dividing by 10 six times is the same as dividing by 100 three times.

Independent work: Hand out the 'Multiplying and dividing' activity sheet for children to complete individually.

Review

Key a number into the OHP calculator. Ask the children what the display will show if they multiply or divide by 10, 100 and 1000. Check understanding by asking questions, such as: *What must I do to change 27 into 2700? 761 into 7.61? Why is 36 × 100 the same as 36 × 10 × 10?*

Differentiation

Less confident learners: Give these children the support version of 'Multiplying and dividing', where they divide and multiply only by 10 and 100.

More confident learners: Give these children the extension version of the activity sheet, where they use larger numbers.

Lesson 6 (Practise)

Starter
Revisit: Repeat the Starter for Lesson 5 (playing 'place value bingo').

Main teaching activities
Whole class: Check that children remember what happens when multiplying or dividing by 10, 100 or 1000. Display the 'Place value questions' activity sheet. Discuss and solve the problems. Discuss ways of solving the last problem; elicit that the children could have calculated 53p × 10 = £5.30; £5.30 × 10 = £53; £53 × 10 = £530. Or, if they remembered that 10 × 10 × 10 = 1000, they could have done £0.53 × 1000. Say: *I have £13,000. How many £10 notes would this be? … £1 coins? … 10p pieces? … 1p pieces?*
Individual work: Ask children to complete the 'Solve them!' activity sheet.

Review
Ask the children to work in pairs to invent their own word problems. Invite them to discuss how the problems can be solved, initially with their partners, then share them with the class and discuss as a class.

Differentiation
Less confident learners: Give this group the support version of 'Solve them!' to complete.
More confident learners: Give these children the extension version of 'Solve them!'.

Lesson 7 (Review)

Starter
Revisit: Ask quick-fire questions, such as: 42 + 69, 98 + 37. The children display their answers on number fans. Discuss strategies for adding these pairs. For example: *Add the tens, add the units, then add both answers together.* Or: *Round the most suitable number in the pair to the nearest 10, then adjust. For example: 92 + 49 = 92 + 50 −1 = 142 − 1 = 141.*

Main teaching activities
Whole class: Explain that today the children are going to revisit the subtraction methods they have learned, and look at how these can be applied to decimal numbers. Write 7207 − 3859 on the board. Ask the children to calculate the answer in any way they choose, and then discuss their methods. Remind them that they should approximate first, for example by rounding to 7200 − 3900 = 3300. Display the 'Column subtraction' activity sheet and go through the column methods shown.

Stress that it is important, when doing calculations in columns, that the digits are in the correct columns, so units in line with units and so on. Work through an example using decimal numbers. Write on the board 234.4 − 26.75 and ask for an approximation (eg 235 − 30 = 205). Ask a child to set the calculation out as a column subtraction and to come and explain how the calculation is done. Again, stress the importance of positioning the digits correctly in the column subtraction.

```
    2 3 4 . 4              2 3 4 . 4 0*
  -   2 6 . 7 5          -   2 6 . 7 5
    ───────────            ───────────
    2 0 7 . 6 5            2 0 7 . 6 5
```

Point out that they can add a zero to make the decimal places the same and this will not affect the value of the number as it is after the decimal point. Explain that the subtraction can be done in the same way as for integers, and the decimal point is 'in line' in the answer.
Independent work: Ask the children to complete the 'Bean growth' activity sheet. Remind them to take care when setting out the calculations vertically to ensure the digits are in the correct 'columns'.

Review
Ask the children to give examples of subtractions that they did mentally, mentally with jottings, using informal methods, and using formal written methods. Discuss when the different methods are appropriate.

Differentiation
Less confident learners: Give this group the support version of 'Bean growth', with simpler calculations.
More confident learners: This group should work through the extension version of the activity sheet, with more difficult calculations.

Lesson 8 (Teach and practise)

Starter
Refine and rehearse: Write on the board: 9 × 6 = 54. Ask the children to give examples of related multiplication facts, for example: 9 × 60, 9 × 0.6, 0.9 × 0.6. Discuss the effect of multiplying decimal numbers: 9 × 0.6 = 5.4, 0.9 × 0.6 = 0.54.

Main teaching activities
Whole class: Write 4837 × 8 on the board and ask a child to demonstrate a calculation method for this. Remind the children that first they should approximate, for example 4800 × 10 = 48,000. Revisit the grid method and both expanded and contracted short multiplication, as shown on 'Multiplication methods', which you can display to the class (covering the bottom half).

Then write on the board: 5.39 × 6. Explain that we can easily use similar methods to multiply decimals. Again, ask the children to approximate first (5 × 6 =30) and demonstrate how it is done on the OHP, uncovering the bottom half of 'Multiplication methods'. Stress that it is important that decimal points line up under each other and that the answer is close to the approximation. You may want to point out that if they count the total number of digits to the right of the decimal point in the numbers to be multiplied, there will be the same number of digits after the decimal point in the answer.

Paired work: Working in pairs, the children will need a set of digit cards and a card with a decimal point. A child selects four digit cards and arranges them to make a multiplication sentence, which should also include the decimal point. Both children should work out the answer independently, then agree answers. The second child must then use the same cards to make a different multiplication sentence and predict whether this will give a larger or smaller answer than the previous sentence. Both children work out the answers and compare. If the child predicted correctly, he/she wins that point. They then shuffle the digit cards and repeat the process, taking it in turns to predict whether the second sum will be higher or lower than the first.

Review
Discuss whether predictions were correct. Ask: *How did you decide the order of digits?* Challenge the children to find the highest multiplication total using the digits 1, 2, 3 and 4, multiplying a three-digit number by a one-digit number, first without a decimal point and then with a decimal point, for example: 4 × 321 = 1284, 4 × 32.1 =128.4.

Differentiation
Less confident learners: This group should use digit cards without the decimal point to make their sentences.
More confident learners: Challenge this group to make a multiplication sentence with the highest or lowest total. They should check all possibilities using the digits chosen.

Lesson 9 (Apply)

Starter
Revisit: The children will need number fans to show their answers. Give quick-fire division questions such as:
- *Divide 8.1 by 9.* (0.9)
- *Divide 320 by 40.* (8)
- *What do I have to divide 72 by to get 8?* (9)
- *A box of 24 eggs is divided into 4 cartons. How many are in each?* (6)
- *What is one twentieth of 640?* (32) *Divide 7 into 47.* (6R5)

Main teaching activities
Whole class: Check that all the children understand that multiplication is repeated addition. Say: *I buy four ice lollies at 96p each. How much is that?* Demonstrate the working as 96 + 96 + 96 + 96 = £3.84. Ask the children if they could work it out in a different way. Let them work in pairs on their whiteboards and then share their answers with the rest of the group. Record some of their examples on the board. Hopefully the following examples will emerge, but if not, introduce them to the children.

Securing number facts, relationships and calculating

BLOCK E

▶

$96 \times 4 = (90 \times 4) + (6 \times 4)$
$= 360 + 24$
$= 384$

$96 \times 4 = (96 \times 2) + (96 \times 2)$
$= 192 + 192$
$= 384$

$96 \times 4 = (100 \times 4) - (4 \times 4)$
$= 400 - 16$
$= 384$

Discuss what is happening at each stage of each method. Ask the children to work out the following, using the method of their choice: 65×6 and 59×4 (less confident); 236×7 and 352×9 (average ability); 2389×4 and 76×23 (more confident). Emphasise the importance of setting out each calculation clearly, as shown above. When they have finished, choose one of the questions and work it out together using each method. Check they understand the processes involved.

Independent work: Give the children a range of questions to answer in their exercise books. These could be written on the board or taken from the appropriate class textbook. For most of the class, HTU × U would be appropriate.

Review

Display the following on the board:

$74 \times 8 = (70 \times 8) + (70 \times 4)$ | $24 \times 99 = (24 \times 100) + 24$
$= 560 + 280$ | $= 2400 + 24$
$= 840$ | $= 2424$

Ask the children if they think the calculations are correct. Encourage them to estimate the answers. Invite the children to explain why both sums are wrong, and ask volunteers to correct them.

Differentiation

Less confident learners: This group should use numbers in the range TU × U.
More confident learners: This group should use numbers in the range ThHTU × U and TU × TU.

○

Lessons 10-15

Preparation
Lesson 12: Prepare 'Fraction boxes' activity sheet for display.
Lesson 13: Prepare sets of 'Percentage cards' for each pair of children (differentiate according to ability).

You will need
CD resources
'Can you calculate it?', 'Fraction boxes' and 'Ratio problems'; core, support and extension versions of 'What percentage?'; core, support, extension and template versions of 'How many parts?'. General resource sheet: 'Percentage cards'.
Equipment
OHP/interactive whiteboard calculator; calculators; individual whiteboards and pens.

Learning objectives

Starter

● Express one quantity as a percentage of another (eg express £400 as a percentage of £1000); find equivalent percentages, decimals and fractions.
● Use a calculator to solve problems involving multi-step calculations.
● Use knowledge of place value and multiplication facts to 10×10 to derive related multiplication and division facts involving decimals (eg 0.8×7, $4.8 \div 6$).
● Express a larger whole number as a fraction of a smaller one (eg recognise that 8 slices of a 5-slice pizza represents $^8/_5$ or $1^3/_5$ pizzas); simplify fractions by cancelling common factors; order a set of fractions by converting them to fractions with a common denominator.

Main teaching activities
2006
● Use a calculator to solve problems involving multi-step calculations.
● Express a larger whole number as a fraction of a smaller one (eg recognise that 8 slices of a 5-slice pizza represents $^8/_5$ or $1^3/_5$ pizzas); simplify fractions by cancelling common factors; order a set of fractions by converting them to fractions with a common denominator.
● Express one quantity as a percentage of another (eg express £400 as a percentage of £1000); find equivalent percentages, decimals and fractions.
● Relate fractions to multiplication and division (eg $6 \div 2 = \frac{1}{2}$ of $6 = 6 \times \frac{1}{2}$); express a quotient as a fraction or decimal (eg $67 \div 5 = 13.4$ or $13^2/_5$); find

▶

fractions and percentages of whole-number quantities (eg $^5/_8$ of 96, 65% of £260).

● Solve simple problems involving direct proportion by scaling quantities up or down.

1999

● Develop calculator skills and use a calculator effectively.

● Reduce a fraction to its simplest form by cancelling common factors in the numerator and denominator. Order fractions such as $^2/_3$, $^3/_4$ and $^5/_6$ by converting them to fractions with a common denominator, and position them on a number line.

● Find fractions, including tenths and hundredths, of numbers or quantities (eg $^5/_8$ of 32, $^7/_{10}$ of 40, $^9/_{100}$ of 400cm). Find simple percentages of small whole-number quantities (eg find 10% of £500, then 20%, 40% and 80% by doubling).

Vocabulary

decimal fraction, decimal place, decimal point, percentage, per cent (%), fraction, proper fraction, improper fraction, mixed number, numerator, denominator, unit fraction, equivalent, cancel, proportion, ratio, in every, for every, to every

Lesson 10 (Review and practise)

Starter

Refine and rehearse: Write the following numbers on the board: 1179; 4601; 26,324; 94,002; 126; 434; 970,042; 1,326,472; 9,001,212. Ask the children to read them out loud as you point to them. Point to various digits and ask children their values. Using calculators, ask the children to work in pairs to investigate how to change some of these numbers using just one addition or subtraction operation: change 1179 to 1679; 26,324 to 26,304 and 970,042 to 978,042. Discuss answers and operations used.

Main teaching activities

Whole class: Explain to the children that this lesson is about calculator use. Ask the children when it is appropriate to use a calculator. Elicit responses such as: to check calculations, calculations using big or difficult numbers, two-step calculations, difficult calculations, and so on.

Remind the children that the calculator can often be used for an inverse operation. For example, if we are given the statement 34 × ? = 221, how can we find ? (Divide 221 by 34 to get 6.5.) Ask: *How could we use the calculator to calculate the number of seconds in a week?* Encourage the children to do this without clearing the display at each step. (60 × 60 × 24 × 7 = 604,800.) Check that the children understand that they can compute a series of calculations on the calculator.

Paired work: Tell the children that you want them to work on the activity sheet 'Can you calculate it?' in pairs, discussing how to use the calculator effectively.

Review

Ask the children to demonstrate how they have completed some of the calculations. Ask: *How much would a set of five games cost if each was £17.50 plus 17 ½ % VAT?* Check that the children are using the calculators correctly to calculate the answer. (£102.81) Ask children to demonstrate the steps for the calculations. Did any of them do it in different ways?

Differentiation

Less confident learners: Ask this group to record the keys as they use them so that you can check their understanding. If possible, give adult support to ensure that the children are using the calculator correctly.

More confident learners: Ask these children to devise their own problems using the calculator to swap with their partners to calculate.

Lesson 11 (Teach and practise)

Starter

Revisit : Play 'Match the fraction'. Give the children a starter fraction such as ¾, and asks them to give an equivalent fraction or a decimal equivalent. They should take it in turns to give the starter fraction.

Main teaching activities

Whole class: Explain to the children that you will be looking at the relationship between fractions and decimals. Remind them that they know decimal equivalents for many common fractions. Ask them for the decimal equivalent of some common fractions, such as $1/2$ (0.5), $1/4$ (0.25), $3/4$ (0.75). Similarly, they will know that $3/10$ is equivalent to 0.3, so ask: *What is the decimal equivalent of $4/10$? … $7/10$?* and so on. Point out that $7/10$ is also equivalent to $70/100$ or $700/1000$.

Write 0.265 on the board. Explain that this is the sum of 0.2 + 0.06 + 0.005. Ask: *What is 0.2 as a fraction?* ($2/10$, which is equivalent to $20/100$ or $200/1000$.) *What is 0.06 as a fraction?* ($6/100$, which is equivalent to $60/1000$.) *What is 0.005 as a fraction?* ($5/1000$) *If we look at the decimals' equivalents that are in thousandths, we can then add them together. Hence: 0.2 + 0.06 + 0.005 = $200/1000$ + $60/1000$ + $5/1000$ = $265/1000$.*

Remind the children that to find the percentage equivalent for a decimal it is necessary to multiply by 100, as 'per cent' means parts per hundred. Hence, the percentage equivalent of 0.265 would be 26.5%.

Independent work: Ask the children to work independently on the 'What percentage?' activity sheet. Show the sheet and explain that they should complete the three columns to show the fraction, the decimal and the percentage. Point out that when they have completed the given examples they should add some of their own.

Review

Write the fraction $3/3$ on the board. Tell the children to use their calculators to work out the decimal. Ask: *What is shown in the calculator display?* (0.3333333). Explain that with some fractions such as $1/3$, there will not be an exact decimal equivalent because there would be an infinite number of 3s following the decimal point. We usually write decimals rounded to an agreed number of places, so, for example, to two decimal places $1/3$ would be 0.33. Ask the children: *Can you work out $2/3$ rounded to three decimal places?* (0.667) Point out that in this instance it was necessary to 'round up'. Give some other examples of fractions for the children to convert, such as $3/5$ and $1/6$.

Differentiation

Less confident learners: Give this group the support version of the activity sheet, which uses common simple fractions. Go through the worked example with the children and encourage them to use this as a structure to follow.

More confident learners: The extension version of the activity sheet uses more complex fractions. Children have to think about recurring decimals such as 0.3333. Ask them to think about why there are recurring numbers in decimals.

Lesson 12 (Teach and practise)

Starter

Recall: Play 'Target 100'. Give the children a number such as 19 and ask them to multiply it by another whole number to get as close as possible to 100. (5) Let them show that number on their whiteboards, then ask them to use a decimal number to get even closer (5.263). Repeat with other numbers, such as 37 and 41.

Main teaching activity

Whole class: Remind the children that they can convert 0.265 to a fraction by splitting the decimal into 0.2, 0.06 and 0.005, then converting each digit of the decimal to a fraction ($2/10$, $6/100$ and $5/1000$) and then converting all the fractions to thousandths so that they could be added.

Ask: *What is the sum of $1/4$ and $1/2$?* Most children will readily answer $3/4$. Point out that when adding $1/4$ and $1/2$ they have actually converted the $1/2$ to $2/4$ and then added. Explain that we can convert any fraction to an equivalent fraction by multiplying the numerator and the denominator by the same value: Hence:

$$1 \times 2 = 2$$
$$2 \times 2 = 4$$

This can be applied to any fractions so that you can convert them to fractions with common denominators. Hence the common denominator when adding $1/2$ and $1/4$ is 4 (we convert the $1/2$ to quarters).

Ask the children to try adding together $1/3$ and $1/6$. Invite a child to demonstrate on the board how to convert $1/3$ to $2/6$ and then add this to $1/6$ to get $^3/_6$. Point out that the answer $^3/_6$ is also the equivalent of $^1/_2$.

Independent/paired work: Display the 'Fraction boxes' activity sheet. Tell the children that you want them to select pairs of fractions from boxes A, B or C and, by finding a common denominator, add them together. The children may work with partners and suggest pairs of fractions for their partner to add, and then check each other's work. After they have done this, encourage them to try adding three fractions together.

Review

Ask the children how they would add together $^1/_2$ and $^1/_3$. Explain that in this example both fractions have to be changed to equivalent fractions, which have a common denominator. How did they decide which denominator to use? Encourage a child to demonstrate how they converted both fractions to sixths, and hence had $^3/_6 + {}^2/_6$, giving the answer $^5/_6$. Ask: *How could you calculate $^1/_2 - {}^1/_3$?* Discuss any difficulties that the children encountered.

Lesson 13 (Practise)

Starter

Revisit and refine: Repeat the Starter from Lesson 12 but this time tell the children that they can also choose to give a percentage equivalent. Encourage them to find as many equivalents as they can.

Main teaching activities

Whole class: Ask: *What is 50% of £80? What is 25%?* Remind the children that 'per cent' means per hundred, so 50% is 50 parts out of 100. Ask them to work out 60% of £150, working in pairs and recording their method on whiteboards. Ask them to explain how they calculated their answers and discuss which methods were most effective. Possible methods may be to: find 10% (£15) and multiply this by 6; find 10% and 50% and add the two together; find 10%, double it to find 20%, total the two to give 30% then double; find 1% and multiply by 60.

Discuss the simplest strategies to use; encourage the children to use jottings and mental methods. Ask: *How would you find 59%?* (Suggest taking 1% from 60%.) *How would you find 15%?* (10% plus half of 10%.) Demonstrate finding 48% of 625 using the OHP/interactive whiteboard calculator: input 625, divide by 100 to find 1% (6.25), then multiply by 48 to find 48% (300).

Independent/paired work: Write some amounts on the board, such as £400, £200, £60, £500. The children work in pairs, each pair with a set of cards from the 'Percentage cards' general resource sheet. They should select a percentage card and use it as an operator on each of the amounts on the board. They should do the calculation independently and then compare with their partners. Repeat with another percentage card. Allow the children to check using the calculator calculations they find difficult.

Review

Discuss any difficulties the children may have had in the lesson. Demonstrate how to find percentages using the calculator percentage key, using the example 25% of £625. Enter the amount (625) press × followed by 25 then the % key. Ask the children to find 35% of £840 (£294) and 17½% of £25 (£4.37).

Lesson 14 (Apply)

Starter

Rehearse: Play 'Order them'. The children will need whiteboards and pens. Draw a blank number line on the board, mark 0 at the start and 1 at the end. Write some fractions and decimal values between 0 and 10 on the board and ask the children to write them in order on their whiteboards. For example: $^1/_2$, 0.35, 0.76, $^1/_4$, 0.09, $^1/_{10}$ (0.09, $^1/_{10}$, $^1/_4$, 0.35, $^1/_2$, 0.76). Ask the children to

Differentiation

Less confident learners: Initially limit the children to working with fractions from box A of the 'Fraction boxes' activity sheet; when they are confident with these they may then use the fractions in box B.
More confident learners: Let these children combine fractions from any of the boxes; then encourage them to find the sum of several fractions.

Differentiation

This activity can be differentiated by giving different percentage cards to different ability groups, and by allocating different amounts for the groups to find the percentages.
Less confident learners: Limit the percentage cards to multiples of 10 (10%, 20%, 30%, 40%).
More confident learners: Give more complex amounts to find percentages of, such as £125, £380, £55.

Securing number facts, relationships and calculating

BLOCK E

show the answers on their whiteboards when you say *Show me*. Write the numbers in order on the blank number line for the children to check their own work. Ask the children to suggest other numbers to add to the line, which they also position on their own line.

Main teaching activities
Whole class: The children will need a calculator and individual whiteboards and pens. Tell them that in this lesson they will be looking at using fractions as an operator. They will be familiar with finding simple fractions of amounts, such as $1/2$, $1/3$ and $1/4$. Ask: *What is $3/4$ of 60?* (45) The children should show their answers on their whiteboards. Invite a child to explain how he/she did the calculation. Encourage them to check the calculation using a calculator, pointing out that we enter the amount 60, divide by 4 and then multiply by 3. Ask the children to work out $3/8$ of 40. They may use their calculators and should show their answers on their whiteboards. Again, invite a child to work though this example for the class, ensuring that they understand how to use the calculator appropriately.

Independent work: Introduce the 'How many parts?' activity sheet. Explain to the children that they will be using fractions as operators. They should try to calculate the answers and then check their calculation using their calculators. Encourage them to work independently on this activity.

Review
Ask the children to find $3/10$ of 450. (135) Encourage them to do the calculation mentally. Ask a child to explain how. Give other questions, such as $4/5$ of £3. (£2.40) Ask: *How did you work it out? Is it easier with money?* Try $3/8$ of 200. (75)

Lesson 15 (Apply and evaluate)

Starter
Refine and rehearse: Play 'Order them' (see Lesson 14) but this time select five children to start and ask them to each give a fraction or decimal value for the rest of the class to order. Then allow each child to add another value.

Main teaching activities
Whole class: Tell the children that in this lesson they will be solving problems involving ratios. Work through the following example: *If, in a packet of 30 orange and lemon drops, we know that orange and lemon are in the ratio 3:2, how many sweets of each colour are there?* Ask the children to discuss with their partners how they could solve this problem, then ask for suggestions and discuss their ideas. Tell them that you want them to use what they have been learning about fractions as operators. The question tells us that for every three orange sweets there are two lemon ones. To find the number of orange sweets, we need to calculate how many there are as a fraction of the total (which is $3/5$, or 3 in every 5). We then multiply 30 by $3/5$ to find the number of orange sweets. (18) Similarly, the number of lemon sweets is $2/5$ of 30, which is 12.

Independent/paired work: Children should complete the 'Ratio problems' activity sheet individually and then work together to pose ratio questions for each other.

Review
Give the children an example to work through independently to assess their understanding, such as: *In a class of 36 children there are four boys for every two girls. How many girls are there in the class?* (12) You may choose to use examples that the children have devised. Encourage the children to explain their working out. Say: *Let's discuss ways of checking your answers.*

Ask the children to write evaluations of their learning in this unit, identifying their strengths and areas for improvement.

Differentiation
Less confident learners: Provide this group with the support version of 'How many parts?', which features easier values. Discuss how they should approach each step, ensuring that they know how to find the information they need.
More confident learners: Provide this group with the extension version of the sheet, where the values used in the questions are more complex. Encourage them to devise some questions of their own to test a partner.

Differentiation
Less confident learners: Discuss with the children the stages that they need to go through to solve the problems. If necessary, talk through each problem before they tackle it so that they know exactly what is required. For the second part of the activity, suggest that they use the questions they have just answered as a basis for their own questions by changing the amounts.
More confident learners: Encourage these children to think of more complex ratio problems to pose to each other (eg extending the problem to include costs).

Name _____   Date _____

Discount store

'Pluto Technology' is having a sale, and all items have been reduced.
Work out the sale price of the following items.

Item	Usual price	Reduced by	Sale price
14-inch colour TV	£125.00	20%	
Portable CD player	£99.00	10%	
Mobile phone	£130.00	15%	

'Discount warehouse' boasts that it has the lowest prices anywhere, but their prices do not include VAT, so you must add $17\frac{1}{2}$ % to all the prices.
Work out the full price of the following items.

Item	Usual price	+ VAT	Full price
14-inch colour TV	£72.00	$+17\frac{1}{2}$ %	
Portable CD player	£80.00	$+17\frac{1}{2}$ %	
Mobile phone	£96.00	$+17\frac{1}{2}$ %	

If you bought the three items, what is the least you could pay? _____

The items cost less at one store than the other. If you bought all three items from this store, how much less would you pay than if you bought them at the other store? _____

Name _____ Date _____

Multiplying and dividing

1. Multiply or divide each number in the shapes.

x 100
34   170
601   4311

x 1000
18   9002
361   171

_____

_____

÷ 10
17   839
3206   8

÷ 100
432   16
3   9701

_____

_____

2. Feed each number through the function machine. What comes out each time?

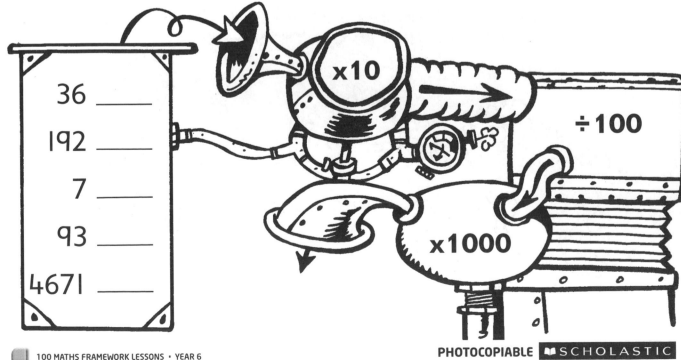

36 _____

192 _____

7 _____

93 _____

4671 _____

x10

÷ 100

x1000

Name _____   Date _____

Place value questions

1. How many times larger is 2600 than 26? _____

2. How many times larger is 26 000 than 26? _____

3. Bars of soap costing 53p each are put into packs of ten.

How much does one pack cost? _____

4. Ten packs of soap are put into a box. How much does a box cost? _____

5. Ten boxes of soap are delivered to the local corner shop.

How much does the shopkeeper pay? _____

Securing number facts, relationships and calculating

BLOCK E

Name _____   Date _____

Solve them!

 Vilmington Netball Association has 1000 members. Each member has been asked to contribute £7.75 towards the cost of new netball courts.

How much money is the Association hoping to raise? _____

 Becksworth Garden Centre produces bedding plants in trays of 75. The local park keeper buys 100 trays.

How many plants will he get? _____

Each tray costs £11.65. How much does he spend on plants? _____

 **Raffle tickets are 10p each.**

How many were sold if a club raised £81.70? _____

 **Jenny earns £5.40 an hour as a school cleaner.**

What does she earn for 100 hours work? _____

 There are 100 lamp posts down one side of a street. The lamp posts are 5.65m apart.

How far is it from the first one to the last?

(Watch this – there is a catch!) _____

 A factory uses 896cm of wire per box of paper clips. There are 100 paper clips in each box.

How much wire is used for each clip? _____

 A shopkeeper buys packets of sweets in boxes of 100. Each box costs £87.00. He sells the packets of sweets for 95p each.

How much profit does he make

a) per packet? _____   b) per box? _____

 Cans of beans are packed in boxes of 100. There are 10 boxes packed in a crate.

How many cans of beans are there in a crate? _____

Each box costs £36.00. How much does one can of beans cost? _____

Securing number facts, relationships and calculating

BLOCK E

Name _____   Date _____

Bean growth

Children in Class 8 have been growing beans.

Each child has measured his or her plant in centimetres. Their results are shown below.

	Ben	**Rashid**	**Ali**	**Chris**
Tuesday	0.35	0.9	0.4	0.25
Wednesday	1.4	1.35	1.02	0.98
Thursday	2.03	2.09	1.99	3.25
Friday	4.68	4.31	3.98	5.06
Monday	8.76	10.06	4.20	11.28

Complete the following table to show how much each plant grew each day.

	Ben	**Rashid**	**Ali**	**Chris**
Tues – Wed				
Wed – Thurs				
Thurs – Fri				
Fri – Mon				
Total growth Tues – Monday				

How much was the total growth for each day?

Tues – Wed _____

Wed – Thurs _____

Thurs – Fri _____

Fri – Mon _____

📖 SCHOLASTIC PHOTOCOPIABLE

Securing number facts, relationships and calculating

BLOCK E

Comments

Year 6	✓	Comments
Use knowledge of place value and multiplication facts to 10 × 10 to derive related multiplication and division facts involving decimals (eg 0.8 × 7, 4.8 ÷ 6).		
Express one quantity as a percentage of another (eg express £400 as a percentage of £1000); find equivalent percentages, decimals and fractions.		
Use efficient written methods to add and subtract integers and decimals, to multiply and divide integers and decimals by a one-digit integer, and to multiply two-digit and three-digit integers by a two-digit integer.		
Solve problems by collecting, selecting, processing, presenting and interpreting data, using ICT where appropriate; draw conclusions and identify further questions to ask.		
Select and use standard metric units of measure and convert between units using decimals to two places (eg change 2.75 litres to 2750 ml, or vice versa).		
Visualise and draw on grids of different types where a shape will be after reflection, after translations, or after rotation through 90° or 180° about its centre or one of its vertices.		

100 MATHS FRAMEWORK LESSONS • YEAR 6

Teacher name _____   Class name _____

End of year objectives
Year 6

	Use knowledge of place value and multiplication facts to 10 × 10 to derive related multiplication and division facts involving decimals (eg 0.8 × 7, 4.8 ÷ 6).	Express one quantity as a percentage of another (eg express £400 as a percentage of £1000); find equivalent percentages, decimals and fractions.	Use efficient written methods to add and subtract integers and decimals, to multiply and divide integers and decimals by a one-digit integer, and to multiply two-digit and three-digit integers by a two-digit integer.	Solve problems by collecting, selecting, processing, presenting and interpreting data, using ICT where appropriate; draw conclusions and identify further questions to ask.	Select and use standard metric units of measure and convert between units using decimals to two places (eg change 2.75 litres to 2750 ml, or vice versa).	Visualise and draw on grids of different types where a shape will be after reflection, after translations, or after rotation through 90° or 180° about its centre or one of its vertices.

Consolidation level 4, start level 5

CLASS